World Yearbook of Education 2011

How do curriculum, conceptions of knowledge and the schooling experiences of young people engage the great issues of this tumultuous time? Curriculum is always influenced by the events that shape our world, but when testing and benchmarking preoccupy us, we can forget the world that is both the foundation and the object of curriculum.

This edited volume brings together international contributors to analyse and reflect on the way the events of the last decade have influenced the curriculum in their countries. As they address nationalism in the face of economic globalization, the international financial crisis, immigration and the culture of diaspora, they ask how national loyalties are balanced with international relationships and interests. They ask how the rights of women, and of ethnic and racial groups are represented. They ask what has changed about history and civics post 9/11, and they ask how countries that have experienced profound political and economic changes have addressed them in curriculum.

These interactions and changes are a subject of particular interest for an international yearbook in that they are almost always permeated by global movements and influenced by multinational bodies and practices. And as these essays show, in curriculum, global and international issues are explicitly or implicitly also about local and national interests and about how citizens engage their rights and responsibilities.

This volume brings together a new approach to perspectives on curriculum today and a new collection of insights into the changes from different parts of the world which discuss:

- How is the world represented in curriculum?
- How do responses to world events shape the stories we tell students about who they are and can be?

This book will be of great benefit to educational researchers and policy-makers, as well as undergraduate and postgraduate students.

Lyn Yates is Foundation Professor of Curriculum and also Pro Vice-Chancellor (Research) at the University of Melbourne, Australia.

Madeleine Grumet is Professor of Education and Communication Studies at the University of North Carolina at Chapel Hill, North Carolina, USA.

World Yearbook of Education Series

Series editors: Terri Seddon, Jenny Ozga, Gita Steiner-Khamsi and Agnes van Zantén

World Yearbook of Education 2011

Curriculum in Today's World:
Configuring Knowledge, Identities,
Work and Politics

Edited by
Lyn Yates and Madeleine Grumet

LONDON AND NEW YORK

First edition published 2011
by Routledge
2 Park Square, Milton Park, Abingdon, Oxon OX14 4RN

Simultaneously published in the USA and Canada
by Routledge
270 Madison Avenue, New York, NY 10016

Routledge is an imprint of the Taylor & Francis Group, an informa business

© 2011 selection and editorial material, Lyn Yates and Madeleine Grumet;
individual chapters, the contributors

The right of the editors to be identified as the authors of the editorial
material and of the authors for their individual chapters, has been asserted
in accordance with sections 77 and 78 of the Copyright, Designs and
Patents Act 1988.

Typeset in Minion by
HWA Text and Data Management, London
Printed and bound in Great Britain by
CPI Antony Rowe, Chippenham, Wiltshire

British Library Cataloguing in Publication Data
A catalogue record for this book is available from the British Library

Library of Congress Cataloging-in-Publication Data
A catalog record has been requested for this book

ISBN13: 978-0-415-57582-9 (hbk)
ISBN13: 978-0-203-83049-9 (ebk)

Contents

Illustrations

Figure

Tables

Contributors

Ann-Marie Bathmaker is Professor of Education at the University of the West of England, Bristol, UK. Her research focuses on vocational and post-compulsory education, and new forms of higher education. She is particularly interested in constructions of teaching and learning in changing policy and socio-economic contexts, and the implications for social justice, equity and human agency. Her recent research includes a study of widening participation in new forms of higher education (the FurtherHigher Project), an evaluation of Work-Related Learning in English schools, and a longitudinal project exploring the construction of professional identities in English further education. She is currently working on a project which investigates working-class and middle-class participation in higher education at the two universities of Bristol in the UK, and a study of the construction of knowledge in English General Vocational Education.

Madeleine Grumet is Professor of Education and Communication Studies at the University of North Carolina, where she has served as Dean of the School of Education. Prior to her appointment at Carolina, she served as Dean of the School of Education at Brooklyn College, City University of New York. A curriculum theorist, specializing on arts and humanities curriculum, Professor Grumet has published many essays that interpret curriculum and teaching through the lenses of feminism, psychoanalysis and the arts. She is the author of *Bitter Milk: Women and teaching*, a study of gender and the relationship of teaching and curriculum to experiences of reproduction.

Catherine Mason Hammer is a middle school social studies and language arts teacher at New Kent Middle School in New Kent County, Virginia. She recently completed her M.A.Ed in curriculum and instruction with a focus on secondary social studies education at the College of William & Mary. Previously she worked as a research assistant and program coordinator at the Center for Strategic and International Studies in Washington, DC.

Diana Hess is Professor of Curriculum and Instruction at the University of Wisconsin-Madison in Madison, WI. Her research focuses on democratic education, social studies, and the use of controversy in the curriculum. Her

2009 book, *Controversy in the Classroom: The democratic power of discussion*, won the 2009 Exemplary Research Award from the National Council for the Social Studies.

Ursula Hoadley is Senior Lecturer at the University of Cape Town, South Africa. Her research and teaching foci are curriculum, teachers' work and the sociological study of pedagogy. In particular she is concerned with the foundational years of primary schooling, and with social class and the differential social and academic outcomes engendered through educational processes. She has also conducted a number of comparative studies of national curricula, and has engaged in policy processes related to the construction of the national curriculum in South Africa. She has authored numerous journal articles, book chapters and a book, *Curriculum* (with Jonathan Jansen, Oxford University Press, 2009).

Berit Karseth is Professor at the Department of Education at the University of Oslo, Norway. Her main research interests are curriculum policy and issues related to professionalism and knowledge development. Professor Karseth is for the time being president of the Nordic Educational Research Association. Her most recent publications in English include: *Qualifications Frameworks for the European Higher Education Area: A new instrumentalism or 'Much Ado about Nothing'?* (Learning and Teaching, 2008); 'Building Professionalism in a Knowledge Society: Examining discourses of knowledge in four professional associations', (co-editor Monika Nerland, *Journal of Education and Work*, 2007); and 'Curriculum Restructuring in Higher Education: A new pedagogic regime?' (*Revista Española de Educación Comparada*, 2006).

Elizabeth Macedo is Curriculum Professor at State University of Rio de Janeiro (UERJ), Brazil. Her current research focuses on curricular policies of Brazil, viewing them as enunciations, and concentrates specifically on struggles between a universal knowledge and the demands of the difference in the curricula. She is also studying Brazilian curricular thought of recent decades. She is the author and editor of books published in Brazil. She is Chair of the Division of Curriculum of the National Association of Research of Brazil and Treasurer of the International Association for the Advancement of Curriculum Studies (IAACS).

Eyal Naveh is Professor of History at Tel Aviv University and at the Kibbutzim College of Education and a senior fellow at the Israel Democracy Institute. He teaches US history at the history department and the law school. He has also taught Israeli history in Israel and abroad. Professor Naveh received his PhD from UC Berkeley, USA. His major research fields are history education and US intellectual and cultural history. Beside his academic publications he has written seven textbooks for the Israeli public school system. His last three books are *Reinhold Niebuhr and Non Utopian Liberalism* (Sussex Academic Press, 2002), *Histories: Toward a dialogue with the Israeli past* (Babel Publications, 2002), and *United States – an Ongoing Democracy* (Open University Press, 2007). He is the coordinator and adviser of the Israeli–Palestinian two narratives history teaching project.

William F. Pinar Before moving to the University of British Columbia in 2005, where he holds a Canada Research Chair in curriculum studies, William F. Pinar taught curriculum theory at Louisiana State University, where he served as the St. Bernard Parish Alumni Endowed Professor. He has also served as the Frank Talbott Professor at the University of Virginia and the A. Lindsay O'Connor Professor of American Institutions at Colgate University. Pinar is the author, most recently, of *The Worldliness of a Cosmopolitan Education* (Routledge, 2009) and the editor of *Curriculum Studies in South Africa* (Palgrave Macmillan, 2010).

Tariq Rahman PhD is Tenured Distinguished National Professor of Sociolinguistic History at the National Institute of Pakistan Studies, Quaid-i-Azam University, Islamabad. Since June 2007 he is also Director of NIPS. He is a highly published scholar with over 90 articles in scholarly journals; 9 books; 4 encyclopaedia articles; 22 contributions to books and several book reviews. His most famous book, *Language and Politics in Pakistan*, published by Oxford (Pakistan) in 1996, remains in print and has recently (2007) been published by Orient Longman in India. His history of language-learning among the Muslims of South Asia, *Language, Ideology and Power* (OUP, 2002), remains a landmark in the field. His latest book, *Denizens of Alien Worlds* (OUP, 2004), connects the medium of instruction with world view, poverty and politics in Pakistan. He now intends to write a social history of Urdu. Dr Rahman has been a guest professor in Denmark and Spain. He has been a Fulbright research scholar (1995–96) at UT Austin. He was also the first incumbent of the Pakistan Chair at UC Berkeley (2004–05). He has lectured or contributed conference papers in the UK – where he obtained his MA and PhD – as well as the USA, Germany, France, China, Korea, India and Nepal. He also contributes columns and book reviews to the English language press in Pakistan.

Anatoli Rapoport is Assistant Professor of Curriculum and Instruction at Purdue University College of Education. Before he received his PhD in Social Studies Education, he worked as a classroom teacher and school administrator for almost 20 years. His research interests include comparative aspects of education, influence of culture and ideology on education, and global and international perspectives in citizenship education. He has published in *The Social Studies, International Journal of Social Education, Journal of Social Studies Research, International Education, Intercultural Education, Teachers and Teaching: Theory and Practice, Educational Forum, Contemporary Issues in Comparative Education*, and *World Studies in Education*. He is the author of two books: *Fields Unknown* and *Civic Education in Contemporary Global Society* (with A. Borshevsky).

Kirsten Sivesind is Associate Professor in Education in the Department of Teacher Education and School Research, University of Oslo. She researches on education governance, curriculum policies, general didactics and philosophy of comparative history. She currently participates in the coordination team for 'Foundational texts', a research group within Cultrans, at the University of Oslo. Her publications in English include 'Reformulating Reform: Curriculum history revisited' (Dissertation for the Degree Dr. Philos., 2008); 'Norway' (co-author Tobias Werler, *The Education Systems of Europe*, Springer, 2007); and 'Curriculum Theory and Research in Norway' (co-authors Bjørg Brandtzæg Gundem and Berit Karseth, *International Handbook of Curriculum Research*, LEA, 2003).

Jeremy Stoddard is Assistant Professor of Curriculum & Instruction in the School of Education at the College of William & Mary. His research focuses on critical and socio-cultural analyses of curriculum, pedagogy, and media in social studies and democratic education. In particular, he examines the construction of ideologies and nature of intellectual work in teacher pedagogy with different types of instructional texts, including textbooks, historical evidence, film, and other digital media.

Miantao Sun is Chief Professor of Shenyang Normal University and Director of the Research Institute of Educational Administration of Shenyang Normal University. His research interest mainly focuses on philosophy of educational administration, educational policy and educational administration.

Jason Tan is Associate Professor in Policy and Leadership Studies at the National Institute of Education, Singapore. He has a keen interest in comparative and international education.

Peter Taubman is Professor of Education in the School of Education at Brooklyn College, where he teaches graduate courses in education and English. He is also a co-founder of the Bushwick School for Social Justice, in Brooklyn, New York. He has written extensively on teacher identity, classroom teaching, psychoanalysis and the problems with audit culture. His most recent book, *Teaching by Numbers: Deconstructing the discourse of standards and accountability in education,* published by Routledge Press, received the 2010 Outstanding Book Award from AERA's Division B, the 2010 Critics Choice Book Award from the American Educational Studies Association, and the O.L. Davis, Jr Outstanding Book Award from AATC. His most recent book, *Disavowed Knowledge: Psychoanalysis, teaching and education,* will be published by Routledge.

Georgina Tsolidis was a secondary school teacher and educational consultant and policy analyst before taking up academic positions at Monash and Ballarat Universities. She has an on-going interest in social justice issues. She has researched extensively in schools and has a particular interest in cultural difference and ethnicity.

Lyn Yates is Foundation Professor of Curriculum at the University of Melbourne, Australia, where she is also Pro Vice-Chancellor (Research). She is a past president of the Australian Association for Research in Education. Her publications include *What Does Good Education Look Like? Situating a field and its practices* (Open University Press, 2004), *Making Modern Lives: Subjectivity schooling and social change* (with Julie McLeod, SUNY Press, 2006) and *The Education of Girls: Policy, research and the question of gender* (ACER Press, 1993). Her research interests are in knowledge, inequalities, identities and changing forms of education policy and practice. She recently (with Michael Young) edited a special issue of the *European Journal of Education* (45 (1) 2010) on 'Knowledge, globalisation and curriculum' and is preparing for 2011 publication a book on *Australia's Curriculum Dilemmas: State perspectives and changing times* (Melbourne University Publishing).

Michael Young is Emeritus Professor of Education at the Institute of Education, University of London and holds the post of Visiting or Honorary Professor at the Universities of Bath (UK), Witwatersrand, and Pretoria (South Africa) and Capital Normal University (Beijing). His most recent book is *Bringing Knowledge Back In* (Routledge, 2008). His research interests focus on the sociology of knowledge in school, vocational and professional curricula. He is currently leading a research project funded by the British Academy on 'Educational Futures: lessons from the sociology of knowledge' with Professor Johan Muller (University of Cape Town).

Jiang Yu is an academic in the Research Institute of Educational Administration, Shenyang Normal University.

Series Editors' Introduction

The World Yearbook of Education 2011 takes up the question of curriculum and its relationship to 'the world'. Addressing this theme, the volume editors, Lyn Yates and Madeleine Grumet, remind us, that 'the world' is not a simple entity. What counts as 'the world' is never still. It shifts over time and space, according to standpoint and the means of making it knowable. 'The world' is also 'our horizon' that defines 'what is, has been and what is possible' for us in our local lives. Yet it is 'this world' in all its ambiguity that sits at the heart of curriculum, the instrument that prepares young people for the world and their lives within it.

Working through four key themes, the volume offers a perspective on curriculum that teases out its relationships with the world. What emerges is an understanding of curriculum that fixes the fluidity of this world-in-the-making as publicly agreed messages for those who learn at particular points in time and space. These curricular moments capture the sense of what matters to adults who, through their involvement in official decision making processes, define and authorize curricula that are conveyed to the young. But as the chapters show, these intergenerational communications, the way they are fixed and their implications in forming personhood, are always contested. Curriculum is a consequence of struggles to fix knowledge, identities, work and politics that make the world.

The chapters grapple with the relationship between curriculum and what sometimes seems to be an emerging world. Ten years on from 9/11, the idea of the world is in flux. Vulnerability, hope and pragmatic efforts to sustain economies, even build a world without violence, motivate curriculum making. Yet together these chapters reveal the persistent anchoring of curriculum in nations, regardless of 'one-world' global policy steering or the complexities of local relations, cultures and conflicts. Curriculum is formed in local places that are lived and negotiated as part of a nation. This national frame lived through everyday experience further complicates the relationship between curriculum and the world. So the struggles that fix curriculum confront the dilemmas of contemporary personhood, how to be part of one world, local worlds and nations, that pursue international competitive advantage as well as national belonging.

The strength of this volume lies in the way it establishes a platform for rethinking curriculum in the world that is simultaneously global, local and national. In this powerful contribution, Lyn Yates and Madeleine Grumet take us beyond the one-world imaginaries of knowledge economies and millennium goals. They remind us that, as in the past, curriculum is the locus not just for our hopes and fears, but also for 'the contradictions and tensions of our history, our institutions and our politics'. They surface an agenda for curriculum making, research and politics that is about making the future and the contribution that knowing the world educationally can make to that collective project.

The World Yearbook of Education 2011 is a powerful contribution to the Routledge World Yearbook of Education series. Since 2005, these volumes have taken up the challenge of identifying, grasping and understanding the implications of globalizing education. The past six volumes have problematised these issues. *WYB 2005* opened up the question of globalization and nationalism. Volumes from 2006 to 2008 tackled emerging effect at the interface between education and the worlds of knowledge, work and politics. *WYB 2009* took these questions back to a consideration of childhood and *WYB 2010* surfaced the complexities of global–regional–national relations that are sedimented and mythologized in a notion like 'the Arab World'.

Now, *WYB 2011* takes us back to core questions of schooling, the curriculum. As series editors, we are grateful that scholars of such standing as Lyn Yates and Madeleine Grumet took on the work of preparing this volume. Editing a *World Yearbook of Education* is never easy, given the intellectual demands of the intellectual agenda that the series pursues and the time frames that must be negotiated alongside busy lives. Yet this volume helps us, collectively as education researchers in the world, to move towards more fruitful analysis and public knowledge about education and its contribution to the world.

Terri Seddon, Jenny Ozga, Gita Steiner-Khamsi and Agnès van Zanten
Melbourne, Oxford, New York and Paris, 2010

Acknowledgements

The chapter 'Conceptualising Curriculum Knowledge Within and Beyond the National Context' by Berit Karseth and Kirsten Sivesind was originally published in the *European Journal of Education*, 45, 1, 2010: 103–120. The editors thank John Wiley and Sons for the permission to reproduce this work.

Lyn Yates would like to acknowledge funding support from the Australian Research Council for the project 'School knowledge, working knowledge and the knowing subject' from which this publication project in part was generated.

The editors would like to express their appreciation for editorial assistance by Kate O'Connor which greatly facilitated their work of producing this volume.

Introduction

1 Curriculum in Today's World: Configuring Knowledge, Identities, Work and Politics

Lyn Yates and Madeleine Grumet

The collapse of the Cold War and rise of new forms of war, the digitization of information, globalization of production and the challenges to cultural hegemony produced by migration and the identity politics of the 1970s, have all contributed to the sense that we do not know this world. And yet, the *world,* however vague or intuited, is our horizon, the limit, at any instance, of what is, has been, and what is possible for the figure of our local lives. The world is the object that curriculum points to as we introduce each generation to the shared histories, practices and possibilities that shape personhood. The school curriculum is the program nations establish to prepare young people for the world. It points to the world and engages in the formation of personhood. At times of important political change, curriculum becomes a key site for attention and reworking.

Curriculum's story of the world has always been influenced by politics. Sometimes, especially in proposals to change what is taught as national history, or in the curriculum changes that follow major political events such as the ending of apartheid in South Africa, the political direction of curriculum is explicit. But often its politics and sources and motives are obscure, indirect. There is the real and reasonable space and time that it takes to make any sense of events, reflected not just in topics, in what is said, but in the ways disciplines of human and cultural inquiry develop over time. Then there is the overt concern of schooling with young people's cognitive development, and the sorting and coding that frames the institutional forms in which curriculum must be offered, and scholarship reformulated into courses of instruction for students along the continuum of K–12 schooling through university and graduate studies. And for each of these cohorts there are deliberative councils which may involve diverse political constituencies to decide not only what enters the curriculum but also how it is taught and how it is to be known.

Curricula that appear not to be directly political, may directly bear that origin. For example, we can point to college level courses instituted in the United States in response to its participation in wars on the European continent. The renowned Western Civilization course established in 1919 at Columbia University was derived from its predecessor, a War Aims course initiated in 1918 to introduce prospective soldiers to the European countries and traditions they were about to defend. And as the United States readied to fight Germany, it turned from its model of free election of subject choice to the British model of requirements. This

Columbia course, bringing together the departments of economics, government, philosophy and history, was paralleled by a multidisciplinary course at Stanford called Problems in Citizenship as well as one at Dartmouth. We do not know whether the original lectures of these courses acknowledged their national concerns and defensive motives. It is hard to tell whether the suspicion of historian John Higham, reported in Carnochan (1993: 69), that these courses were motivated by the war-time anxiety about this nation's immigrants and their ties to their countries of origin, was operating, although that concern would provide a genealogy for the xenophobia that pervades Western civilization curriculum, enduring decades after the threat of war in Europe had passed.

Post 9/11, the *New York Times* of Saturday, 24 November 2001 records a similar moment, in a report entitled 'Defending civilization: how our universities are failing America and what can be done about it'. The report was issued by the American Council of Trustees and Alumni, a conservative group that the *Times* identified as devoted to curbing liberal tendencies in academia. The report proceeds to excoriate American colleges for anti-American bias and to advocate for more courses on American history and Western civilization.

Language studies proliferate as various regions of the world become significant to national interests; so as the Japanese economy boomed, so in many of their trading partners did Asian Studies and Japanese language study, and more recently studies of China and its languages. Today, in the United States, studies of the Middle East, Afghanistan and Pakistan and their languages are becoming more prominent in the curricula of higher education.

In contrast, the curricula of K–12 education, requiring some collective and more extensive consensus, change more slowly. Traditionally, this curriculum looks back; it selects from the nation's history and culture, topics and types of formal learning that are considered to be particularly foundational to that generational formation. In some countries national curricula have been highly prescribed and uniform; elsewhere, as in the USA and Canada, they are determined by states or provinces and by textbook publishers, and by federal funding initiatives and testing formats. At times of important political change, curriculum often becomes a key site for attention and reworking.

As we write, in the USA a new program for the school curriculum in Texas is under consideration, one that will affect other states due to Texas' large share of the textbook market. If passed, students will learn more about the virtues of free enterprise, biblical values and the Confederacy's cause, and less about slavery and civil rights. Other changes will water down criticism of Senator Joe McCarthy's anti-communist witch-hunt in the 1950s and portray the UN's funding for international humanitarian relief and environmental initiatives as threats to individual freedom and US sovereignty. In Australia, a country that has not had a strong tradition of 'civics' in its school curriculum, a new national curriculum is being constructed, and developing foundations for 'citizenship' is seen as one of the priorities for this. The story of what account schooling should be giving young Australians of who 'we' are has been the subject of intense and bitter public debate over the past decade, with different visions of Australian history and identity as a nation central to that debate (Macintyre and Clark 2003). The priority to be given to celebration of Australia's democratic traditions compared with recognition of ills done to the Aboriginal population, the degree of emphasis to be given to the 'Anzac' tradition (soldiers dying to defend freedom on foreign soil in Europe and Asia in the world wars), the extent to which the story of Australia is to be linked primarily to the traditions of England and Ireland rather than those of its indigenous population or of the home countries of its large numbers of immigrants from other parts of the world, are all part of those debates. At the same time, economic and political imperatives are cited as justifications for a greater turning towards Asia in what is taught; for teaching Asian languages, rather than European ones, as the foreign languages of priority.

In other parts of the world too, political changes produce new agendas for curriculum (Osler and Starkey 2005). With the formation of the EU for example, legal definitions of citizenship and of citizen entitlements, rights and protections have been reworked. In the face of 'temporary' workers, and refugees, being a citizen is not co-terminous with being a resident of a country. And being a member of the EU confers rights to mount legal challenges, to move, and to work that originate from outside national frameworks. In the EU context, curriculum research and curriculum development projects are now initiated both from within member countries and also as cross-country EU projects.

The world is never still; nevertheless in the last fifty years we have witnessed profound changes: collapse of colonial powers and their domination; dissolution of the Soviet Union; globalization of production, rapid dissemination of culture and information through communication on the world wide web; the development of international terrorism; all leading to new nations, new alliances, new enemies, new conditions for work and citizenship that influence curriculum today.

It is interesting to speculate whether these changes in international politics and national specificity have stimulated the imposition of an audit culture on schooling. The rising prominence of comparisons, benchmarking and borrowings between countries; and the impact of agendas and publications of influential meta-national agencies such as OECD and the World Bank is evident in many national discussions and policies (Silova and Steiner-Khamsi 2008; Robertson and Dale 2009; Rizvi and Lingard 2010). International comparisons of education achievement have been reported, at least since the 1950s, but in the 1990s and in the current decade, particularly under the aegis of the OECD, they have taken on a much more systemized agenda. Through its publication of league tables of national performance on mathematics, literacy and science in its *PISA* reports (the Programme for International Student Assessment) and in its dissemination of a wide array of education 'indicators' in its *Education at a Glance* reports, the OECD incites national attention, both public and political, to a 'global' perspective on national systems of schooling. This perspective is one where the function of schooling is seen through the lens of economics and where the content of schooling (its curriculum) is visible only in the form of quantitative measures and graphs (Hopmann, Brinek and Retzl 2009). In its PISA and DeSeCo projects, the OECD promotes a view that what matters is not what is learnt about the world, but what competencies and orientations (such as motivation to be a 'life-long learner') are being produced in learners, as if these are essentially culture-neutral and context-free. The assessment programs themselves are not tied to what schools have taught in particular countries, but to what problem-solving abilities and 'competencies' are agreed to be the desired outcomes of mathematics or literacy or science.

These influential benchmarking projects, while explicitly outcomes oriented and not claiming to comment on curriculum, have been a key impetus and source of evidence in many curriculum policy discussions. For one thing, national systems are required to account for and be benchmarked against other national systems, and this challenges former national specificities of curriculum approach and aims, such as the cultural orientation to curriculum as the formation of the whole person in the European *Didaktik* tradition (Hopmann, Brinek and Retzl 2009). Gauthier and Le Gouvello (2010) argue that the OECD activities are producing a radical challenge to the French system, one which would replace the construction of curriculum as a tacit and historical cultural given with new forms of explicit policy-making, more attuned to global instrumental agendas. And Karseth and Sivesind begin their discussion in this volume by considering whether it matters if Norwegian students no longer study one of their great playwrights, Henrik Ibsen. They ask 'Can a national culture be described through examples like Ibsen's plays, and will they embody values that are relevant for a global context? Is there a public legitimacy for the cultivation of national cultures as an overall purpose of the curriculum and how does this match ideas of qualifying students for life?' (Karseth and Sivesind, this volume: 58).

The strong assessment emphasis of the benchmarking activities also casts its own particular orientation to curriculum making (Grumet 2006; 2007; Taubman 2009). As Karseth and Sivesind argue, 'organisations such as OECD advocate a new political technology where formalised curriculum-making is ignored or even contested in favour of assessment and accountability systems' (Karseth and Sivesind, this volume: 59).

A different form of meta-national pressure on curriculum is visited on developing countries, through the work of NGOs such as the World Bank (Silova and Steiner-Khamsi 2008), or though inter-country commitments such as the Millennium Development Goals of the United Nations (Yates 2006). The Millennium Development Goals, for example, include equal education participation for girls and women in all countries. The projects and accounting associated with these goals decline to make specific the curriculum content expected of such education. Like the economic agendas of OECD, the focus here too is on measurable indicators of inputs and outputs as the key agenda for schooling, rather than the substance of what is taught. Nevertheless, in the field of academic curriculum inquiry, these new agreements to have targets for schooling (and other aspects of social and economic life) that apply globally have contributed to some broader discussion about cultural difference, and human rights and capabilities in relation to curriculum, across countries as well as within them (Walker and Unterhalter 2007; Unterhalter 2009).

In many countries today, curriculum policies and politicians speak of a new global economically competitive world that curriculum must address – and must be benchmarked against. But they speak too of anxieties about citizenship, about alienated youth, about the need for different kinds of skills in the world of the twenty-first century. Inevitably curriculum reveals the concerns, anxieties, of the adults who shape it.

And so in putting together chapters for the *World Yearbook of Education 2011*, we are eager to know how curriculum scholars in countries across the globe understand what is going on in their schools. How do curriculum, conceptions of knowledge, conceptions of the rights and responsibilities of citizens, and the school experience of young people engage the great issues of this tumultuous time? Our focus in the volume is not, primarily, a political science of curriculum, a story of how power is being exercised, or who is getting to decide between countries or within countries the form and content of the curriculum that has come to be developed. Rather it focuses on the 'what' of curriculum today: what is being put in place in different parts of the world, and how curriculum scholars understand this.

'Curriculum' is of course an ambiguous term. It encompasses different kinds of focus, including policy statements at the overarching level; curriculum guidelines and frameworks; textbooks; the enacted curriculum of what teachers do and what happens in classrooms; unintended and hidden curriculum relating to school practices and environment; and the issue of what young people themselves receive and perceive as curriculum. Curriculum inquiry may be conceptually tied to what is done in schools; or broadened to refer to other pre- and post-school education institutions; or it may be set free from both of those locations and used to refer to practices outside formal institutions and intentions, or used metaphorically to talk of the curriculum of public spaces, or monuments. A single volume cannot encompass all kinds of curriculum study and all kinds of curriculum questions.

In this volume we have restricted our focus specifically to the curriculum of schooling because it is in schooling that young people undergo a compulsory and institutionalized introduction to the world. Curriculum here is the publicly sanctioned or agreed version of what young people are to learn and who they are to become, additional to, and not reducible to, either their formation in their family setting or the socialization or acculturation of simply being in their culture. And we have restricted our focus to particular kinds of questions about curriculum, and to particular themes within that: its 'configuring' of identities, knowledge, work and politics. We have invited the contributors to choose the way in which they ground their discussions, and the evidence they look to in order to represent curriculum. In some cases, the story is of national policies; in other cases it is of the textbooks in use and the values and stories they pick out; in other cases again, it is of the structuring implicit in a particular new set of school practices or assessment arrangements. But the issues they address in each case relate to the configuring and reconfiguring of curriculum today, and the issues of nation and global context, of political change, of new identity and cognitive demands this world has now generated.

We realize that even in an era of intense nationalism when the interests and aims of various countries appear discrete and particular there are always systems of exchange, of identification and differentiation that link apparently distinct national interests to each other. However, in this last decade, as economy and population flows have affected countries and curriculum across the world, it is newly interesting to explore the relation of curriculum to the world from multiple national perspectives. In developing an agenda for the *World Yearbook of Education 2011*, we attempted to anticipate the retrospective that in 20 or 30 years will study how we made curricular sense of our times, and so we asked contributors to consider the following questions:

- What kind of world is being represented in curriculum?
- What are the ways of knowing this world that curriculum extends to students? and
- What is being produced from those ways of doing curriculum?

We had originally intended to title this volume 'Curriculum in vulnerable times'. *Vulnerable* is a term most evidently associated in the USA with the post-9/11 world – signalling a changed awareness of that country's relationship to the world. Of course many other countries suffer ongoing conflict, Pakistan, Iran, and Israel for example, and directly experience vulnerability; but the post-9/11 period has produced a widespread experience across most countries of sharpened concerns about terrorism and weapons and international relationships. For curriculum, that raises questions about the story that is told in each place about the nation and its relation to other parts of the world; and about the sense of its citizens, their diversity, religion, values and relationships it tries to build. Sometimes this story may be told explicitly, through history or civics subjects; sometimes it may be reflected in the arrangements of language policies, or policies on diversity and representation, or in the ways literature is taught.

Vulnerable is also a term that might be associated with other types of uncertainties that are now prominently part of a global rhetoric of concern: in particular the global financial crisis; and issues of environment and climate change (Bowers 1993). Many countries introduce their new curriculum reports and guidelines of recent times with extensive reference to the new vocational skills that will be needed for both individuals and that nation to flourish in the twenty-first century. They speak to a sense of economic vulnerability in the future, and address a role for curriculum to form a new kind of person. Here curriculum serves political purposes in configuring where responsibilities lie for future economic well-being. And in national settings as diverse as China, England, Singapore, South Africa, we can see the anxieties and interests in renewed attention to configuring how foundations for the new economy should be built. Curriculum scholars have had considerable interest in the ways this task for curriculum intersects other stories of nation, culture and identity.

And *vulnerable,* or at least uncertain, might also be applied to the issue of knowledge itself in these times. Sources of knowledge production are both proliferating (especially via the internet) and also evidently (for education) being steered in new ways by global bodies such as the World Bank and the OECD. While calls for the basics and resurrection of a canon are common in many places, universities themselves are busily re-arranging disciplines and interdisciplinary endeavors to develop new kinds of thinking seen as needed for the big problems of the day. These developments raise new challenges about what selections of knowledge and what forms of knowledge are appropriate and foundational in the school curriculum.

The postmodern critique of knowledge that has characterized much intellectual work of recent decades challenged the generalizations of the academic disciplines, their reliance on rationalism and commitment to Enlightenment ideals of progress. It has been subject to much public criticism for being preoccupied with forms and languages and with the ways these distort and reduce the complexity of experience. But in relation to school curriculum, much of this challenging of traditional subject content came in the first instance not from abstract intellectual theory but from scholars concerned with inequalities and difference of students in school – especially of gender and race and the problem that only some perspectives in a national culture were being given the imprimatur of truth in the school curriculum, while others were marginalized (Grumet 1988; Yates 2009). But in curriculum studies preoccupations with postmodernism and with the microdynamics of classrooms have also distracted curriculum scholars from thinking about what the schools are saying to students about their worlds and about their places in it.

In this volume we are interested in both what schools are saying to students and how they are saying it. Post-structuralist approaches to language are evident in chapters that examine how, for instance, conceptions of national identity or of multiculturalism are constructed. Other chapters examine politics and policy implementations and their effects, such as the attempts to re-work approaches to knowledge and learning in the wake of political change in South Africa that brought such new hopes for the relationship between the mass of learners and what curriculum might offer. And a number of writers draw on sociological and epistemological perspectives to analyze and criticize the way in which new vocational agendas are undermining more fundamental and traditional roles of the school curriculum.

The questions about curriculum which chapters in this volume address are both local and global, interpreted specifically by nations and states, yet framed by the world we share. The chapters are organized in four main parts, to emphasize four themes, but these are very much inter-connected themes, and represent interconnected elements and effects of the curricula being discussed. The first part takes up the theme of curriculum and national/global identities: what story is curriculum telling today in different parts of the world about who *we* are? The second part is concerned with curriculum and the economy, with how work and the economy (national and global) are being positioned as a story to young people in schools today, and what kinds of reworking of curriculum is underway to accompany this story. In the third part, writers consider curriculum and knowledge, and what configuring or reconfiguring of epistemologies is evident in the curriculum developments today. And in the fourth part we take some examples of curriculum's response to politics and vulnerabilities, to focus on what kinds of story are constructed in relation to particular political concerns.

Admittedly, these are not innocent questions. Despite the important changes in the ways we think about the world since the end of the Cold War, the development of global economies, 9/11 and the threat of international terrorism, in many nations curriculum hides or compensates for these upheavals by turning away from the world to a hypnotic fascination with an audit culture, high-stakes testing, and benchmarking (Grumet 2006; 2007; Taubman 2009). Peter Taubman's chapter in this volume discusses at more length this 'life under audit', and its emptying out of affective relationships in the curriculum context of the USA. The international comparative data is ostensibly concerned with competencies and capabilities in such areas as 'problem-solving' or 'communication', but the substance of which identities are being formed, and how this enters into how young people in different parts of the world learn to understand others, is left out of these influential political agendas. Recent attempts to return depth to curriculum call for a new disciplinarity, asking the academic disciplines to anchor curriculum in substance (Muller 2000). But that too does not of itself resolve the substantive selections that are necessarily made, as is apparent from the ongoing debates over the construction of Australia's first national curriculum, and its proposed selections to represent a systematic development in history or science or English.

So, we were interested in this volume in how curriculum scholars across the globe understand the mediating of the world that is taking place in their school curricula today, and particularly the story that is being constructed of national/global identities. How does curriculum address nationalism in the face of economic globalization, the development of the European Common Market, the international financial crisis, immigration and the culture of diaspora? How are the rights of women, of ethnic and racial groups presented? How does Russia tell the story of Russia after the collapse of the Soviet Union? How does Israel represent citizenship? How does Singapore do this – a physically tiny country built on a gathering of different ethnic groups with different religious and historical allegiances, and now with a strong global agenda and commitment to education as its key economic foundation? What has changed about history and civics in countries such as Australia, South Africa and the USA post-9/11 and after the end of apartheid? How do language policies reflect a stance on the national/transnational agendas?

In this volume we include a study by Anatoli Rapoport of Russian textbooks and their changing treatment of key elements of Russian history as national boundaries and political agendas change; and a study by Tariq Rahman of the textbooks used in different kinds of schools in Pakistan, and how they portray the history and identity of that nation, including more particularly how they portray who is 'Other', who is a potential enemy. In the USA, Jeremy Stoddard, Diana Hess and Catherine Mason Hammer trace the changing textbook treatments of September 11 near to the event and subsequently, and the kind of portrayal of the nation this embodies. Contributions from Israel by Eyal Naveh and from Australia by Georgina Tsolidis explore some ways the curriculum configures difference (and anxieties) within its citizenry. Elizabeth Macedo considers the effects of deploying the abstraction of diversity across Brazil's curriculum guidelines. William Pinar examines the tacit presence of the United States as a figure against which Canadian identity is asserted, questioning how this diversion distracts the Canadian curriculum from addressing the complexity of its own national issues.

Throughout the volume, contributors from Europe, Africa, South America, North America, the Middle East, Australia and Asia write about their curriculum today and address its constructions of national and global identities through these questions:

- How in each case is the curriculum pointing to the world and (re-)doing 'who *we* are'?
- What stories is it telling its future citizens about how they relate to each other and to people in other parts of the world?
- How does a country's relationship to other entities, national, transnational, or global, influence its curriculum?
- What recognitions and denial of difference and what values are part of the agenda?

Themes of nation and global change, of values and difference, of politics and who is other, are often overt in those parts of curriculum that tell the story of history, or civics, or make selections of texts and languages for study. But they are found too in a second kind of re-structuring that is the subject of many of the chapters in this volume: how curriculum today is construing its relationship to the economy, including what it sees as the knowledge and skill foundations of the future, and what is being represented as the work of schools and school students in this configuring. One enduring concern of curriculum scholarship and research has been with inequality, and the different kinds of successes and futures set up in schools for children of different class, race and gender. As the assumed relation between schooling and economy takes on new global forms, curriculum scholars study the ways in which old or new forms of inequality are being recreated or are rebuilt in new ways. In South Africa for example, Ursula Hoadley considers how the post-apartheid curriculum has been structured to transform a previously segregated one and with what effects. Anne-Marie Bathmaker takes up the most recent vocational agendas of curriculum in the UK, to consider how these change or continue the history of social class-based hierarchies of learning. Equally of interest is the orientation of emerging economies, such as China, to the global and to the potential to be 'modern' in their take-up of science. How does curriculum address changes in production related to new technologies, dispersed industries and work forces as it projects work futures for young people and adjusts credentials accordingly? Here Miantao Sun and Jiang Yu trace the reworking of curriculum as China moved from a prioritization of political commitment and manual labor in the period of the Cultural Revolution, to its current powerful engagement with the global economy and the knowledge-base of that engagement. Jason Tan discusses Singapore's efforts to develop a strong positioning for itself in a global knowledge-based economy, and identifies tensions in this development with its equally strong values and citizenship agenda.

Beyond shared rhetorics of forming 'flexible life-long learners', what are countries actually marking out as important in the structures of their schooling? What concept of vocation is at work, and does this reflect or not reflect difference between different national economies? How are national qualifications frameworks structuring the relationship between curriculum and the future economy? Michael Young's chapter argues that notwithstanding ubiquitous references to a new 'knowledge economy', the agendas of contemporary curriculum reform in the UK and elsewhere represent an emptying out of knowledge. And from a different location and starting point, Peter Taubman's chapter similarly focuses on what is being emptied out of the curriculum in the USA in its new competitive concern with audit and standards.

The very question that this volume poses, 'how do countries around the world configure curriculum in relation to changes in politics, demographics, economy?' rests on an assumption of nation, and, it follows, of curriculum constructed by different countries to project and fulfil their national identities. This assumption extends one of the taken-for-granted assumptions about the curriculum's function of socialization: curriculum of public education, certified by the 'state' is expected to prepare children to participate in its customs, laws and culture. Whether globalization is understood to point to transnational processes of production, trade, and investment, or to porous national boundaries and increased flow of peoples around the globe, it is understood to have challenged, if not diminished, the clarity of national identities. Furthermore, as conflicts such as the Cold War, and the alliances that it shaped, have been somewhat resolved, and as international terrorism deploys conflicts that move across alliances and national and religious identities, the specificity of national interests and concerns also appears diluted. Our recognition of these changes may suggest a less fluid past, a time when France was France, and did not have to worry about MacDonalds, or when China's economy was not significant to Iran's ambitions. But of course even before post-structuralism instructed us to be suspicious about simple stories and generalizations, we have recourse to the history of nations which attests to their heterogeneity: dispersed among tribes and clans; saturated with colonial economics and governance; colluding in the alliances and the exchange of arms. And as we read the chapters from our contributors we recognize that the nations that provide the locus of their work, their culture, indeed their lives, continue to be contested projects, as do the curricula that represent their aims.

The etymology of *nation* recognizes the instability of this concept. Although derived from natus or nativity and signifying the place of one's birth, and then associated with a common race or stock, the idea that geography is destiny is a myth that accompanies this term. It is interesting to note this fourteenth-century usage:

> The term derives from **Latin** *natio* and originally described the colleagues in a **college** or students, above all at the **University of Paris**, who were all born within a *pays*, spoke the same language and expected to be ruled by their own familiar law. In 1383 and 1384, while studying theology at Paris, **Jean Gerson** was twice elected procurator for the French *nation (i.e. the French-born Francophone students at the University)*. The Paris division of students *into nations* was adopted at the **University of Prague**, where from its opening in 1349 the **studium generale** was divided among Bohemian, Bavarian, Saxon and various Polish *nations*.
>
> (http://www.spiritus-temporis.com/nation/etymology.html)

Designating groups of university students as nations and recognizing the necessity for the university to address their diversity, suggests the tension that exists between curriculum and a nation's identity and world view: a tension expressed in current accountability systems, in attempts to grasp and rationalize globalization, in programs to articulate a nation's history and culture with the diversity of its citizens, in projects to educate students to new ways of working with new technologies. As we read the contributions of colleagues to this volume it becomes clear that the relationship between nation and curriculum is reciprocal: nations construct curriculum and curriculum constructs nations.

References

Bowers, C.A. (1993) *Education, Cultural Myths, and the Ecological Crisis: Toward Deep Changes*, Albany, NY: State University of New York Press.

Carnochan, W.B. (1993) *The Battleground of the Curriculum*, Stanford, CA: Stanford University Press.

Gauthier, R.-F. and Le Gouvello, M. (2010) 'The French curricular exception and the troubles of education and internationalization: will it be enough to "rearrange the deckchairs"?' *European Journal of Education*, 45, 1: 77–92.

Grumet, M. (1988) *Bitter Milk: Women and Teaching*, Amherst, MA: University of Massachusetts Press.

Grumet, M. (2006) 'Where does the world go, when schooling is about schooling?', *Journal of Curriculum Theorizing*, 22, 3: 47–54.

Grumet, M. (2007) 'The beast in the matrix' in B. Stern (ed.) *Curriculum and Teaching Dialogues*, 9, 1&2: 235–246.

Hopmann, S., Brinek and G. Retzl, M. (eds) (2009) *PISA zufolge PISA. PISA According to PISA*, Vienna: LIT-Verlag.

Macintyre, S. and Clark, A. (2003) *The History Wars*, Carlton: Melbourne University Press.

Muller, J. (2000) *Reclaiming Knowledge: Social Theory, Curriculum and Education Policy*, London: RoutledgeFalmer.

Osler, A. and Starkey, H. (2005) *Changing Citizenship: Democracy and Inclusion in Education*, Maidenhead: Open University Press.

Rizvi, F. and Lingard, B. (2010) *Globalizing Education Policy*, London: Routledge.

Robertson, S.L. and Dale, I.R. (2009) 'The World Bank, the IMF and the possibilities of critical education', in M. Apple, W. Au and L. Gandin (eds) *International Handbook of Critical Education*, New York: Routledge.

Silova, I. and Steiner-Khamsi, G., (eds) (2008) *How NGOs React. Globalization and Education Reform in the Caucasus, Central Asia and Mongolia*, Bloomfield, CT: Kumarian Press.

Taubman, P. (2009) *Teaching by Numbers*, New York: Routledge.

Unterhalter, E., (2009) 'Social justice, development theory and the question of education', in R. Cowen and A. Kazamias (eds) *International Handbook of Comparative Education*, Dordrecht: Springer.

Walker, M. and Unterhalter, E. (2007) 'The capability approach: its potential for work in education', in M. Walker and E. Unterhalter (eds) *Amartya Sen's Capability Approach and Social Justice in Education*, London/New York: Palgrave.

Yates, L. (2006) 'Does curriculum matter? Revisiting women's access and rights to education in the context of UN Millennium Targets', *Theory and Research in Education*, 4, 1: 85–99.

Yates, L. (2009) From curriculum to pedagogy and back again, Pedagogy, Culture and Society, 17, 1: 17–28.

Part I

Curriculum and National/Global Identities

2   Dressing the National Imaginary

Making Space for the Veiled Student in Curriculum Policy

Georgina Tsolidis

Introduction

One of the fundamental purposes of schooling is to establish within subsequent generations a familiarity with the stories we tell about ourselves and it is left to national curriculum policy to regulate this process. In 'liquid times' (Bauman 2000) the crafting of such stories becomes increasingly vexed. Rather than being connected and contained within the nation, ethnicity, culture and language are disestablished. Further to this, the nation as a bounded entity cannot be taken for granted. Instead borders are permeable and the histories, languages and cultures of those within the nation blend and blur with each other and those in other nations. In such a context, sure-footed histories of places and peoples become destabilized. In this process, globalization makes difference familiar and simultaneously feeds xenophobia.

It is left to curriculum to select stories that reflect nations as bounded entities and simultaneously prepare students for globalized times – a responsibility fraught with contradiction. Such contradictions can be particularly pronounced in countries such as Australia, where nation building has relied on immigration. In such countries, curriculum policy can be burdened with multiple responsibilities: assimilating minorities, providing them with opportunities to maintain distinct cultural identities, and promoting understanding of cultural difference within the general population.

In this chapter, the role of curriculum is explored with reference to the Australian national imaginary. The aim is to reflect on the role curriculum plays in inscribing a sense of Australianness and how this intersects with the experiences of minority students identified with Islam. Currently, Islam is constructed as the epitome of otherness and the communities identified with this religion are backgrounded by the destruction of the Twin Towers in New York and the train bombings in London and Barcelona. Islamophobia is having an impact on communities in Australia as elsewhere. In this climate visible markers of Islam are under attack, including Muslim women who choose to wear a hijab.

In many countries, including France, Denmark, Holland and Australia, the sartorial choices of Muslim school girls have become a conduit for public debate about Islam and its place within the national imaginary. Whether schools allow students to wear the hijab has come to represent how a society views itself – its stance on multiculturalism, religious tolerance and particular forms of democracy and egalitarianism. In France for example, whether school girls are allowed to wear the hijab has been linked to the French Revolution and the establishment of a secular state. This debate illustrates the important role anticipated for schooling as a process that works towards social cohesion. Debates about Muslim students' sartorial choices are echoed by more subtle and complex initiatives enacted through curriculum policies intended to frame particular narratives of nationhood and belonging.

Educating Towards a National Imaginary

In his elaboration of the social processes that create cohesion, Castoriadis (1997) makes the argument that social institutions (language, values, norms) work to shape our understandings of ourselves as individuals, as well as our sense of social unity. He argues that individuals and society are constituted through a web of meanings that animate the social institutions of a given society. This web of meanings or magma is a signification of the social imaginary. This is at once social, because it is shared by a collective or a 'we', and imaginary because different people constitute it in different ways, at different times. Castoriadis argues that the normative role of pedagogy is a contradictory one. One aim is to develop the learner's capacity for independent learning and reflexivity. The goal is to teach the capacity to learn and anything else that may be taught along the way should be incidental to this aim. Paradoxically, the other pedagogical aim is to induct the individual into existing institutional practices such as language, family and values. This is instruction in conformity. However he contends that institutions are fabrications of a collective imaginary and as such are how the collectivity represents itself. Nonetheless, once conjured, these institutions take on the sense of being pre-given, fixed and self-perpetuating. Rather than maintain their power through coercion they are powerful because individuals participate in their fabrication and pedagogy is instrumental to this process. Pedagogy has the paradoxical task of producing autonomous subjects, who nonetheless internalize existing institutions. For Castoriadis the capacity for independent thinking and reflection is the way of addressing this paradox and the similar paradox of politics, which he names the impossibility of politics, that is, democracy's dependence on democratic individuals and vice versa. It is the task of pedagogy to protect democracy by creating independent and reflexive thinkers who can function internal to its institutions.

In globalized times, independent and reflexive thinkers need to function within localized institutions but also at a level that transcends the national. The world is becoming smaller with borders that are increasingly permeable. A pedagogy that protects democracy must instill in students a sense of the world rather than the nation and a sense of social justice that accounts for inequalities as these operate within and between localized communities, nations and countries. Attitudes towards cultural difference become a cornerstone of such democratic literacy. The movement of people is foundational to globalization and demands an elaboration of the labyrinthine relations between capital, the search for resources and the purchase of labour that expels some people from their homelands while allowing others to engage in a privileged cosmopolitanism. Democratic literacy needs to engage students in explorations of such processes that are framed by more than liberal notions of tolerance. These are see-sawing processes whereby the drop into poverty experienced by some is in direct response to the upward mobility of others. Contemporary debates about learning and teaching related to cultural difference have as their backdrop events occurring at a global level. Giroux for example, draws on the work of Castoriadis and illustrates the need for independent thinking by pointing to the dominant discourses that seek to explain US interventions in the Middle East in relation to weapons of mass destruction and the need for these to be critically assessed rather than understood unquestioningly as a truth (Giroux 2004).

The capacity to understand and evaluate dominant discourses remains central to how we live our lives locally and globally. This understanding frames the examination of curriculum policy undertaken in this chapter. Curriculum policy is a dominant discourse that shapes the stories students hear about the social institutions that at some level, govern their lives. These policies frame the imagined 'we' or the collective imaginary of nation. As Yates and Grumet argue in the Introduction to this volume, through the selection of socially valued knowledge, curriculum policy instructs about the past and in so doing lays bare the future directions we are rewarding as educationalists. It is instructive to explore such policy and examine its potential to develop independent thinking or democratic literacy in students whose collective imaginary is not restricted to nation. Because either they or their forebears were born elsewhere, through travel, through cultural globalization or through our networked society, students' lives are no longer contained within the nation state. The aim is to explore how curriculum engages with this reality. Particular attention will be given to cultural difference and how this is accounted for within curriculum policy. At extreme ends of a spectrum, curriculum can integrate cultural difference as a positive element of the national narrative or it can attempt to reclaim an imagined past buoyed by the fiction of cultural purity.

A National Narrative

Since colonization, white settlement in Australia has been linked with Britain. It wasn't until intense immigration after World War Two that the traditional demographic shifted. A massive influx of immigrants from southern Europe – Italy, Greece and the former Yugoslavia – challenged the conception of Australia as a British outpost in the Asia-Pacific region. However, the resistance to immigrants who were 'non-white' and non-Christian remained. The so-called white Australia policy was formally abandoned in the early 1970s and the arrival of 'boat people' from Vietnam in the 1980s challenged accepted beliefs that many held about suitable immigration. Immigration has continued to broaden with people now coming from an increasingly diverse range of countries.

Close to half (45 per cent) of Australia's population was either born overseas or have at least one parent born outside Australia. People enter from more than 200 nations, making Australia one of the most ethnically diverse nations in the world. According to the 2006 census, four-fifths of Australia's overseas-born population lived in capital cities, reinforcing overall patterns of residence. Most overseas-born Australians come from the UK and New Zealand. However the population reflects various periods of immigration including that from Europe after World War Two. Consequently Italian and Greek remain commonly spoken languages. More recently immigration from the Middle East (mostly Lebanon) and Asian countries has contributed to increased diversity, including religious, particularly Hinduism and Islam. The age structure of the population reflects immigration patterns with for example, the Italian and Greek communities being two of the most rapidly ageing while the Sudanese community is the youngest (ABS 2009).

Schooling and Social Cohesion

The influx of immigrants in the period after World War Two was considered by many to pose a threat to the Australian way of life. This was a way of life characterized fundamentally as British which it was hoped, would be reinforced through British immigrants who were encouraged to immigrate through incentives. Despite these incentives the desired intake of British immigrants did not eventuate. The number of non-British immigrants accepted was a product of an ambitious immigration programme considered necessary for national security and industrialization. Nonetheless, these 'new Australians' created disquiet because of their 'foreignness' and this triggered a range of policies, including ones geared towards assimilation. A key aim of the settlement policies during this period was to placate xenophobia and assure the population that their existing way of life would continue. However by the late 1970s it was evident that assimilation was not likely to be straightforward. Minorities were becoming dissatisfied with the lack of employment opportunities and the prospects for their children given the education they were receiving. This dissatisfaction was beginning to take voice through an ethnic rights movement (Zangalis 2009).

The 'sink or swim' approach to the acquisition of English by the children of immigrants was not working. Students were left to learn English as if by osmosis and simultaneously remain abreast of other subjects. Faced with classes where significant numbers of students were non-English speakers, teachers began to agitate through their unions for smaller class sizes and specialist language support to assist these students. This was most evident in areas where immigrants settled in large numbers, which were primarily working class areas. Schools in these suburbs were already experimenting with non-traditional curriculum and challenging approaches to teaching and assessment that served a reproductive function. By the late 1970s government policy shifted from assimilation to integration. Teachers had been instrumental in provoking a new approach whereby students would be given support to learn English towards social integration. This was achieved through dedicated Commonwealth Government funding for the teaching of English as a Second Language by specially trained teachers. Curriculum policies were developed that reflected a broader shift away from assimilation, to integration and by the 1980s, the introduction of multiculturalism (Tsolidis 2001).

Multicultural curriculum developed at the state and national level through a range of committees that included representatives from key ethnic minority organizations (Tsolidis 2008). This move reinforced a view of multiculturalism that stressed liaison between schools and minority communities, mother tongue maintenance, bilingual education and multicultural perspectives across all curriculum areas. The aim was to provide minority students with an opportunity to retain their cultures, acquire those skills necessary to function fully in Australian society and where possible to support bilingual learning approaches. Curricula that would encourage all students to acquire a second language and understand the importance of cultural difference within Australian society was also developed (Ministry for Education 1986). Much of this work was framed under the rubric of inclusive curriculum – the idea that schooling should value the cultures and perspectives students brought with them to the classroom and that this would be done in meaningful ways. Their existing knowledge and experience would be a basis for assessment and for further learning (Ministry for Education 1985). School communities would be charged with the responsibility of mediating broad curriculum guidelines against local needs and expectations. In the area of language learning for example, all students would be introduced to a second language but the choice of which one would be decided locally (Tsolidis 1997). Multicultural curriculum policy has been critiqued as Janus-faced: encouraging diversity on issues of little significance while firmly maintaining structures that reward dominant knowledges (Hage 1998). Perhaps its benefits are more variegated than this. Regardless of this debate, it did have some symbolic and strategic worth as a policy framework that allowed moves away from assimilation. This worth is becoming more evident subsequently with the so-called culture wars and the precipitation of more strident political posturing about 'stranger danger'.

Values Education

In 2005 the Commonwealth Government published the *National Framework for Values Education in Australian Schools*. It set out the values that should be taught to all students. This Government was associated with unequivocal support for the so-called War on Terror, the aggressive discouragement of asylum seekers through a range of controversial initiatives, including the excision of national territories to allow the processing of these people to occur 'off shore', and the introduction of a citizenship test that promulgated a very narrow and historically situated view of Australian identity. In this context, the move towards a national values curriculum was met with some skepticism (Tsolidis 2010).

In themselves the values seem unremarkable and with the possible exception of one, are not recognizable as peculiarly Australian. The nine values include compassion, freedom, honesty, integrity, respect, responsibility, tolerance and doing your best. The list also includes 'fair go', a term which is possibly identifiable as particularly Australian, even if what it describes may not be so. 'Fair go' is explained in the document as, 'Pursue and protect the common good where all people are treated fairly for a just society'. The policy introduces these nine values with the following statement:

These shared values such as respect and 'fair go' are part of Australia's common democratic way of life, which includes equality, freedom and the rule of law. They reflect our commitment to a multicultural and environmentally sustainable society where all are entitled to justice.

(Australia, DEST 2005)

This statement introduces a representation of Australianness that centres fairness and egalitarianism, a core component of the self-narrative, along with opportunity and tolerance. Importantly these are linked to multiculturalism, environmental sustainability and justice. It is instructive to note in this context that the Prime Minister at the time and key members of his government understood multiculturalism in ways that reinforced the view that immigrants and their children needed to adopt dominant Australian values. This will be discussed further in a subsequent section of the chapter.

Curriculum – Setting a National Agenda

The education of Australian school students is divided between Government and non-Government schools, with the latter comprising systemic Catholic schools, and what are known as Independent schools. Within each of these sectors there is great variation. Within the non-Government sector there are elite Catholic and Independent schools as well as parochial Catholic schools, often under-resourced. The Independent sector also contains schools associated with less mainstream ethno-religious communities, including Islamic, Jewish and Greek Orthodox schools as well as schools associated with particular pedagogies including for example, Steiner schools.

In broad terms the detail of curriculum policy has been left to State and Territory authorities to determine. It has been anticipated that non-Government schools would work within loosely framed parameters that would provide all students access to core elements of the curriculum and thus enable them to sit exams to determine eligibility to higher and further education. Recently however, there has been a move towards establishing a national curriculum. This has been a complex process driven by the national government. The National Curriculum is aimed at providing a framework that allows all Australian students (K–12) to study in the same broad areas while giving teachers some flexibility of interpretation. A number of subjects have been developed under the stewardship of expert committees. The draft curriculum frameworks have been circulated for community comment. Currently, there is consultation on the mathematics, English, history and science frameworks. The National Curriculum project is being spearheaded by Professor Barry McGaw who describes it as follows:

The curriculum will provide important professional opportunities for teachers and freedom for schools to determine precisely how it's implemented, but it quite deliberately sets out what we are calling learning entitlements for students. It says these are the skills students should have the chance to develop; this is the knowledge they should have the opportunity to acquire. In addition to the capabilities, we've identified several dimensions that we think also can be integrated into the subject area, built in across the curriculum. One of these is the Indigenous dimension, another is an Asia dimension, and a third is a sustainability dimension.

(McGaw cited in ACARA 2010)

It is evident from this statement that curriculum is being developed to conjure a particular national narrative, one sensitive to indigeneity, Asianess and sustainability. This curriculum could have been shaped as readily in response to a host of alternative dimensions. Not surprisingly the public consultation is triggering debate about this storyline and its emphases. With the release of the National Curriculum for consultation, some are arguing that such perspectives are missing in what appears to them to be a narrow view of what students should be learning (Tudball 2010). The political nature of the selection of knowledge is most evident in relation to history given its pivotal role in shaping the national imaginary. This role was made more evident by the public debate around the so-called history wars.

The history wars involved leading academics and politicians, including the then Prime Minister John Howard, in debates about the colonial settlement of Australia, its impact on the indigenous population and contemporary understandings and representations of these events. Core differences on these issues have bled into debates about the way Australianness is understood more broadly. The history wars were in essence a battle over the representation of Australian identity. For conservatives, including the former Prime Minister, a 'black armband' view of history is one that places undue emphasis on negative rather than celebratory aspects of the national narrative. This position was exemplified by his steadfast refusal to apologize to Indigenous Australians for past injustices. In 2009 Prime Minister Rudd declared the history wars over. He called for a truce to bridge the polarization that had occurred. He argued that while interpretations could vary, a core storyline was needed, one that presented agreed-upon events chronologically (Mark 2009).

Professor Stuart Macintyre, a key protagonist in the history wars, was given the responsibility for developing the history component of the National Curriculum. In 2004, Macintyre published the second edition of the book he co-authored with Anna Clarke entitled *The History Wars*. In it they make the following statement:

Increasingly, however, historians, teachers and commentators of varying political persuasions have employed the child as a symbol of the future. This isn't simply a debate over contrasting historical approaches, or contested historical terms. It is also a struggle over common ground. Education is a national concern – it is everyone's business. Pedagogical as well as political beliefs about what students should know frame the debate over school history. In this way, the discourse of standards, of education rigour and historical core knowledge has become the salient language of history education. And it is this rhetoric – of the future of the past, the child projected onto the nation – that has given the education arena of the History Wars such urgency.

(Macintyre and Clarke 2004: 172–3)

Whether the debate is framed around history, values or civics and citizenship education, one of the aims of curriculum policy is to induct students into a way of being Australian. This is evident in Macintyre's comments quoted above – the debate about history is one that involves everyone because it is about what children, who are our future, should know about our past. This is a statement about the importance of a collective view of who we are and where we have come from. It is this shaping of a collective view that sits at the centre of this debate. The history wars attest to how this process is complicated vis-a-vis indigenous perspectives and our ability to tell a coherent and uncontested narrative about colonization. Issues of perspective are also likely to arise with reference to migration and its place in our national imaginary.

The notion of the child projected onto the nation is a salient one for the examination being undertaken in this chapter. We need to consider which children are being projected onto the Australian nation and in turn, which Australia is being projected to our students through curriculum. These issues will be explored with reference to the contribution curriculum makes towards social cohesion. The context for this will be Islamophobia and how it is influencing curriculum policy related to Muslim students. In other words, is the Muslim child being projected on to the Australian nation? And is the curriculum being projected onto Australia one that teaches democratic literacy that enables all students to comprehend and contest dominant discourses about the nation and what is constituted currently as a threat to its wellbeing?

Threatening Social Cohesion

In 2005 a series of violent clashes began in Cronulla, a seaside suburb near Sydney. These became a focal point for debates about the place of cultural diversity within Australia. The riots occurred over several days and those who participated were represented as either 'Australian' or 'of Middle Eastern appearance'. Implicitly or explicitly the Cronulla riots focused attention on immigration. How those 'of Middle Eastern appearance' behaved, became a retrospective means of determining the suitability of some groups to settle here in the first place. The Cronulla riots have become a 'pivotal moment' in the Australian social imaginary – a prompt for reconsidering meanings that are ascribed to Australianness through a range of public discourses. The Deputy Prime Minister of the day made a series of public statements linking the riots to immigration and the suitability of Muslims to settle in Australia. He argued that 'confused, mushy, misguided multiculturalism' was to blame for a soft approach that enabled 'second-generation immigrants' to develop values that were not compatible with those accepted in Australia (Gordon and Topsfield 2006). Such immigrants needed to adopt Australian values, he argued, or be repatriated. Thus Muslim youths, regardless of being born in Australia, were not part of the collective 'we' but instead vulnerable to repatriation, reinforcing their status as perpetual 'other'.

The Cronulla riots have been significant in the representation of those described as Middle Eastern, commonly understood to be Muslim also. Whilst the Arabic-speaking and Muslim communities have had long histories in Australia, the 2005 riots have come to represent 'the problem' with a community that is understood as having a way of life and a belief system that challenges Australian values. The 'problem' with Muslims and Arabs has been exacerbated by a political backdrop that emphasizes the so-called war on terror. In this setting the problem is with Muslims and Arabs and it is a problem caused by 'their culture'. Yet despite the sure-footedness that surrounds the problem and its cause, 'their culture' remains amorphous, positioned variously against religious, ethnic, national and political criteria.

Because of such factors, Muslim women who choose to wear a burqua or hijab become ready targets for those who understand Islam as threatening in some way. Gender relations are fundamental to the ways in which ethnicity, culture and nation are imagined. In the case of women, their role in demarking ethnicity is complex. Whilst their bodies can become the conduits for 'authenticity' through the policing of their sexuality and their role as bearers and nurturers of children, it would be a mistake to construct them as simply acted upon by men within their communities. The wearing of the burqua, for example, has been debated by feminists, some of whom see its adoption as agentic. Duits and van Zoonen (2006) comment on the Dutch situation and argue that the wearing of a headscarf by Dutch school girls, particularly in a climate fuelled by Islamaphobia, is as much a political as a religious act. However, unlike choices by boys to wear clothing with overt political messages, these girls' choices are construed as cultural or religious, thus denying them political agency. Duits and van Zoonen also compare Muslim girls' sartorial choices with those of girls who adopt the hyper-sexualized dress promulgated through popular culture. In both cases they argue, it is left to teenage girls to defend their choices as their choices, rather than choices forced onto them by others. The headscarf is one extreme of a spectrum of sexuality that culminates at the other end with porno-chic, it is left to all girls to negotiate their place within this minefield of sexual double standards in response to the specificities of their own cultural locations.

Schooling and Sartorial Choice

Women's sartorial choices are more significant in the context of institutions, particularly schools, which through their practices provide strong messages of inclusion and exclusion. In Australia the choice made by Muslim students to wear a headscarf has met with resistance. Its (non)place and by implication, that of the students who choose the veil, became a political cudgel in debates about Australianness.

> It [the headscarf] has become the icon, the symbol of the clash of cultures, and it runs much deeper than a piece of cloth. The fact of the matter is we've got people in our country who are advocating – and I'm talking about extremist Islamist leaders – the overturning of our laws which guarantee freedom. I have no concerns about people who wear a cross or people who wear a skull-cap because I haven't heard any leaders of those communities stand up and say the very fabric of our society should be overturned.
>
> (AAP 2005)

These comments were made by Bronwyn Bishop, a Senator in the Australian national government. She began a short-lived campaign to disallow the wearing of hijabs in Government schools, following on from the French move in that direction at the time. The campaign received little support, including from within the Senator's conservative party and fizzled. Nonetheless, Bishop's comments are instructive. Women's dress is seen as symbolic of a deeper malaise that threatens the core of what is understood to be Australian culture. Iconic status is attributed to the hijab in a war about how we see ourselves as a community. Bishop's sentiments are clearly echoed by others, given that Muslim women have consistently reported being spat on and verbally abused, and having their hijabs torn off, particularly at times when anti-Islamic feeling has been at the fore (Poynting and Noble 2004).

While the move to ban headscarves was unsuccessful, some schools have found alternative ways of actively discouraging this form of dress, made evident in the following newspaper excerpt.

> The Islamic Council of Victoria is urging the inquiry to support a 'fundamental right' to freedom of religious observance as it applies to dress. Council executive committee member Sherene Hassan told the inquiry one Victorian student was told that she would not be admitted to school if she wore a hijab. 'That individual was so keen to attend that school she decided not to wear her headscarf', she said. In another case, a student wore a hijab in a class photograph but it was airbrushed so it would not stand out, she said. 'You can imagine that was quite demoralising for the individual,' Ms Hassan said.
>
> (Metlikovec 2007)

Muslim women who choose to wear the hijab and burqa, become the most visible marker in a politics of panic. Their choice can be read as a willful act of defiance in times when Islamophobia is rife and dress becomes a symbol of a culture towards which there is marked antipathy (Alvi *et al.* 2003; Martino and Rezai-Rashti 2008). It is noteworthy that this battle over the hijab has occurred in the context of Government schooling. Public education becomes a battleground over the constitution of aspects of Australianness taken to be fundamental. Australia has a strong history of state schooling, established as free, secular and compulsory. Increasing pressure through teacher organizations and ethnic communities in the 1970s resulted in strong government support for multicultural education in the 1980s. While the constitution of multicultural education has shifted in emphasis with various governments, there have been consistent attempts to include various cultural, linguistic and religious perspectives within Government schools. The scrutiny of Muslim girls' sartorial choices sits uncomfortably with this ethos.

The Cronulla riots signalled a possible threat to social cohesion, and because of this, multiculturalism became implicated in the 'soul searching' about Australian values. It was understood as both cause and solution. For some, there was pride in the success of Australian multiculturalism, and the violence, which was marked as 'ethnic', was abhorred for violating the belief that ours is a truly tolerant society. For others, the violence was understood as the product of 'mushy, misguided, multiculturalism' (Gordon and Topsfield 2006), which has emphasized unbridled relativism and thus failed to draw a line in the sand between what is and what is not tolerated in Australia. In both cases, tolerance is assumed to be a core Australian value, either to be showcased through the exercise of more tolerance, or protected by coming down hard on those who do not share it as a fundamental belief.

The Muslim woman can create discomfort through her sartorial choices because as individuals and as a society the figure of the veiled woman forces us to confront what lies behind our feelings of disquiet at her presence. In order for Australian identity to remain comprehensible as Australian, there needs to be a sense of ownership and a right to grant entry on prescribed terms. This is a way of defining and protecting what is assumed as shared and doing so in relation to a 'they' constituted as a moral threat because they do not share the same set of values. This process is relatively simple once the 'they' is externalized as outside the 'we'. However, in relation to the strangers within the 'we' the process is more complicated. The 'stranger within' is involved enough to be familiar, yet separate enough to be judged a threat. This stranger has been understood within sociology as simultaneously vulnerable and iconoclastic (Bauman 2004). The 'stranger within' has enough insider information to be part of the 'we', yet does not share foundational assumptions and in this way unsettles the status quo by asking the hitherto unaskable questions. Opinions need to be developed about students in schools who wear headscarves. Like the school photograph that was air-brushed it would be easier if we could make her veil and the issues it represents disappear from sight. Hers is an active choice to adopt the stance of the stranger and as such, insists on our self-evaluation. At a time when global Islamophobia is promulgated, her choices because they are stark, cast her as Other in dramatic and visible ways.

Conclusion

Curriculum policy serves to narrate a nation by providing subsequent generations with a story line about who we were, are and want to be. The aim here has been to consider how various curriculum policy frameworks related to cultural difference nuance this story line differently. This has been situated beside a more detailed consideration of Muslim students in the context of contemporary Islamophobia and its impact on students who wish to name their difference through dress. The argument is made that the child that is projected onto the nation is not Muslim and as a result the nation that is projected onto students is not inclusive of cultural difference. Further to this, the projection of national identity as narrow ill-prepares students for a world where national boundaries are increasingly irrelevant and forms of cosmopolitanism are in high demand. Following Castoriadis and Giroux, an argument has been put forward that democratic literacy requires a capacity to look critically at dominant discourses, including those that constitute a national imaginary.

The Australian national imaginary is often reiterated with reference to egalitarianism and a 'fair go'. This is illustrated by the inclusion of 'fair go' in the national values curriculum. A desire to be fair is of course interpreted variously and this is very evident in the public discourses that surround the place of Muslims in the national imaginary. The place of such communities came into prominence with a series of violent clashes on the beaches and in the suburbs of Sydney and the public discourses these elicited. Gangs of youths were identified as either Australian or of 'Middle Eastern appearance' in media reports which created a sense that these youths had been fighting over what it means to be Australian and who could lay claim to the label and associated life-style. Gender relations have been a critical and recurring theme in the Sydney unrest and events leading up to it. The way young men of 'Middle Eastern appearance' have treated 'our girls' was signalled as one of the provocations for the eruption of violence (ABC 2006). The clashes have involved icons of Australianness – beaches, flags, life savers – and in turn, these have been used to explain the un-Australian nature of the clashes. There is talk of the clashes having been provoked by neo-Nazis who fuelled and exacerbated a mild discontent with free alcohol and pamphleteering (Hannan and Baker 2005). Clearly these events have struck a chord and the debates that surround them dramatically crystallize the competing discourses about Australianness, how multiculturalism has been implicated within these discourses and the place of gender within various understandings and enactments of belonging. The events have been a catalyst for much media debate about Australian values and culture (Shanahan 2006; Topsfield and Rood 2006; ABC 2006). This has been an unsettling experience in a country that has represented itself as a land of immigrants and an exemplar of multiculturalism.

In the current climate, given the so-called war on terror and the associated culture wars, Islamophobia is markedly virulent. It is not surprising, then, that Australians associated with the Middle East or Islam have become increasingly vulnerable. The murky boundaries between ethnicity, religion and politics were evident through these clashes, with people seemingly randomly enmeshed by virtue of their complexion or clothing – for example an Indian café owner because of his turban. In this context, 'Middle Eastern appearance' becomes a euphemism for those who are identified as threatening the Australian way of life and like the school girl's hijab in the photograph, air-brushed out of sight and mind.

References

AAP (2005) 'Bishop defends headscarf comments', *The Age*, 29 August 2005. Online. Available HTTP: <http://fddp.theage.com.au/news/national/bishop-defends-headscarf-comments/2005/08/29/1125167579957.html> (accessed 28 July 2010).

ABC (2006) 'Riot and revenge', *Four Corners*, 13 March 2006 (Reporter: Liz Jackson).

ABS (Australian Bureau of Statistics) (2009) '2070.0 – A Picture of the Nation: the Statistician's Report on the 2006 Census'. Online. Available HTTP: <http://www.abs.gov.au/ausstats/abs@.nsf/mf/2070.0?OpenDocument> (accessed 27 July 2010).

ACARA (Australian Curriculum Assessment and Reporting Authority) (2010), 'Development and Consultation Overview: K-10 Draft Curriculum' ACARA video. Online. Available HTTP: <http://www.australiancurriculum.edu.au/Home/Transcript> (accessed 1 August 2010).

Alvi, S., Hoodfar, H., and McDonough, S. (eds) (2003) *The Muslim Veil in North America: Issues and debates*, Toronto: Women's Press.

Australia, DEST (Department of Education, Science and Training, Australian Government)- (2005) *National Framework for Values Education in Australian Schools*, Canberra: Commonwealth of Australia.

Bauman, Z. (2000) *Liquid Modernity*, Cambridge: Polity Press; Malden, MA: Blackwell.

Bauman, Z. (2004) *Identity*, Cambridge: Polity.

Castoriadis, C. (1997) *World in Fragments: Writings on politics, society, psychoanalysis, and the imagination*, Stanford, CA: Stanford University Press.

Duits, L. and van Zoonen, L. (2006) 'Headscarves and porno-chic: disciplining girls' bodies in the European multicultural society', *European Journal of Women's Studies*, 13: 103–117.

Giroux, H. (2004) 'Cultural studies and the politics of public pedagogy: making the political more pedagogical', *Parallax*, 10, 2: 73–89.

Gordon, J. and Topsfield, J. (2006) 'Our values or go home: Costello', *The Age*, 24 February 2006. Online. Available HTTP: <http://www.theage.com.au/news/national/our-values-or-go-home-costello/2006/02/23/1140670207642.html (accessed on 27 July 2010).

Hage, G. (1998) *White Nation: Fantasies of White supremacy in a multicultural society*, Sydney: Pluto Press/Comerford and Miller.

Hannan, E. and Baker, R. (2005) 'Nationalists boast of their role on the beach', *The Age*, 13 December 2005. Online. Available HTTP: <http://www.theage.com.au/articles/2005/12/12/1134236003135.html?page=2> (accessed 21 August 2007

Macintyre, S. and Clarke, A. (2004) *The History Wars*, Carlton: Melbourne University Press.

Mark, D. (2009) 'Rudd calls for end to "history wars"', ABC News. Online. Available HTTP: <http://www.abc.net.au/news/stories/2009/08/27/2669177.htm> (accessed 6 June 2010).

Martino, W. and Rezai-Rashti, G. (2008) 'The politics of veiling, gender and the Muslim subject: on the limits and possibilities of anti-racist education in the aftermath of September 11', *Discourse: Studies in the Cultural Politics of Education*, 29, 3: 417–431.

Metlikovec, J. (2007) 'Muslim girl's headscarf airbrushed', *Herald Sun*, 5 June 2007. Online. Available HTTP: <http://www.news.com.au/heraldsun/story/0,21985,21848974-2862,00.html> (accessed 21 August 2007).

Ministry of Education (1985) *Ministerial Paper Number Six*, Victoria Ministry of Education, Victoria.

Ministry of Education (1986) *Education in, and for, a Multicultural Victoria*, Policy Guidelines for School Communities, Ministry of Education, Victoria.

Poynting, S. and Noble, G. (2004) *Living with Racism: The experience and reporting by Arab and Muslim Australians of discrimination, abuse and violence since 11 September 2001*, Report to the Human Rights and Equal Opportunity Commission, April. Online. Available HTTP: <http://www.humanrights.gov.au/racial_discrimination/isma/research/index.html> (accessed 6 August 2010).

Shanahan, A. (2006) 'Citizenship cane', *Weekend Australian*, 18 November 2006. Online: Available HTTP: <http://www.theaustralian.news.com.au/story/0,20867,20774740-28737,00.html> (accessed 27 July 2010).

Topsfield, J. and Rood, D. (2006) 'History in the making as pupils face national test', *The Age*, 18 August 2006.

Tsolidis, G. (1997) 'Responding to the pupils' culture and language', in J. Sachs and L. Logan (eds) *Meeting the Challenge of Primary Schooling*, London: Routledge.

Tsolidis, G. (2001) *Schooling, Diaspora and Gender*, Buckingham: Open University Press.

Tsolidis, G. (2008) 'Australian multicultural education – revisiting and resuscitating', in G. Wang (ed) *The Education of Diverse Populations: A global perspective*, Dordrecht: Springer.

Tsolidis, G. (2010) 'Simpson, his donkey and the rest of us – Public pedagogies of the value of belonging', *Educational Philosophy and Theory*, 42, 4: 448–461.

Tudball, L. (2010) 'Curriculum's narrow focus leaves students bereft of big ideas', *The Age*, 2 March 2010. Online. Available HTTP: <http://www.theage.com.au/opinion/politics/curriculums-narrow-focus-leaves-students-bereft-of-big-ideas-20100301-pdi2.html> (accessed 1 August 2010).

Zangalis, G. (2009) *Migrant Workers and Ethnic Communities: Their struggles for social justice and cultural rights: the role of Greek-Australians*, Melbourne: The Social Sciences.

3   Nationalism, Anti-Americanism, Canadian Identity

William F. Pinar

Introduction

> Yet there is much to be said for approaching the question of Canada's identity from the outside.
>
> (Jill Conway 1974: 71)

'If anything offers the possibility for community and commonality in this era of multiplicity and difference,' Cynthia Chambers (1999: 147) suggests, 'it is the land that we share.' 'Deeply ingrained in Canada's national psyche,' (White 2007: 11) 'the land,' as Chambers is keenly aware, is complicated by Canadian history, specifically the nation's status as a colony displacing indigenous peoples: the First Nations, Métis, and Inuit. Displacement characterizes the genesis of all three nations comprising North America.[1] Indeed, one of the 'worst' consequences of European colonization, Conway (1974: 72) judges, is psychic. As Fanon (1967) knew, colonial cultures are not only political and historical facts, they are also psychic facts, among them (Conway underlines) the consequences of severance from the originary culture. Such separation constitutes, she suggests, a psychic loss that deprives colonial (and colonized) peoples not only of 'creativity on their own terms' but also of identity itself, about which they are left 'confused' and 'uncertain' (Conway 1974: 72). John Ralston Saul (2005: 32) believes Canada remains 'emotionally and existentially hampered by its colonial insecurity'.

By emphasizing its differences with its southern neighbor – Canadian peacekeeping vs. American militarism, Canadian multiculturalism-as-mosaic vs. the American melting pot – does the depiction of Canada in the Canadian curriculum also convey nationalism by implying a national exceptionalism? If so, is national pride built at the expense of factual accuracy? While not mistaken, for instance, the 'mosaic/melting pot' distinction is, Kymlicka suggests, overdrawn. He points out that while the US does not endorse multiculturalism at the federal level, lower levels of government, such as states or cities, often do. 'If we look at state-level policies regarding the education curriculum, for example, or city-level policies regarding policing or hospitals,' Kymlicka (2003: 371) points out, 'we shall find that they are often indistinguishable from the way provinces and cities in Canada deal with issues of immigrant ethnocultural diversity.' Lipset (1990: 218) believes that 'particularistic demands by minorities have led to increased institutionalization of multiculturalism on both sides of the border'. Within Canada, he reports, 'a backlash against the mosaic concept is occurring' (Lipset 1990: 187) and immigrant groups often doubt the sincerity of Canada's commitment to multiculturalism, which they deride as rhetorical (Kymlicka 2003: 377). While its multiculturalism may not be distinct from that of the United States and other Western democracies, Canada is the only country to have constitutionalized its commitment in section 27 of the Canadian Constitution (Kymlicka 2003: 375).

If, like Americans, Canadians also emphasize their differences from others (especially differences from Americans), does the Canadian identity threaten to become overdetermined by what it is not? By embracing negation, does Canadian identity vitiate self-critical encounter? By rereading two representations of Canadian identity separated by almost 30 years,[2] I provide fragmentary answers to these key curricular questions. The first publication communicates a studied ambivalence over nationalism; the second embraces such ambivalence and its consequent uncertainty over national identity as evidence of nationalistic exceptionality. To the extent these two moments in Canadian curriculum studies reflect, however indirectly, the provincially differentiated curriculum across Canada, it appears that an anti-American Canadian nationalism – symbolized by an identity structured by negation – has intensified.

1974

> Canada has not escaped some of the excesses of nationalism.
> (Geoffrey Milburn and John Herbert 1974: 4)

In 1974 the Ontario Institute for Studies in Education (OISE) published a collection of essays entitled *National Consciousness and the Curriculum: The Canadian Case*. In their introduction, Milburn and Herbert (1974: 5) cite two developments during the preceding decade that have 'significantly' altered Canadian public opinion regarding issues of Canadian culture. The first is a greater awareness of what they call the Canadian habit of 'dependency'; the second is a 'greater appreciation of the uniqueness of the Canadian experience' (1974: 5). That the second follows from the first is evident in the Milburn and Herbert (1974: 6) assertion that US 'domination' of Canada has been 'much more extensive' than British or French; it pervades 'every aspect' of Canadian life. That view – that Canada is dominated by the United States – becomes the ground against which the figure of mid-twentieth-century Canadian nationalism emerges.

Canadian fears regarding domination by the United States did not start in the 1960s. George Tomkins (1974: 18) reminds us that 'concern [in Canada] about American books reached a peak in 1847 when it found that half of the books used in the schools came from the United States'. Indeed, 'concern' escalated on occasion to 'repulsion' (1974: 18; see also Tomkins 1981: 159, 162). But, Tomkins (1981: 162) concludes, 'it would be a mistake to assume that the cultural content of Canadian curricula was American dominated, at least before 1960'. If not, then why was Canadian fear sometimes so pronounced? American strong-arming of the Canadian government during the Cuban missile crisis may provide one answer, although George Grant (2005 [1965]: 12) suggests that the majority of Canadians approved. Indeed, the event evidently helped bring down the Diefenbacker government.

This animating element of (English-speaking) Canadian nationalism is evident in Milburn and Herbert's (1974: 6) assertion that 'separation' from the American 'colossus' is what drives those seeking a Canadian 'identity'. So conceived, Canadian identity is less a reflection of internal features but, rather, a tactic to create distance through difference from the 'colossus'. Milburn and Herbert were not alone in acknowledging this status. Canadian political scientist Peter Regenstreif (1974: 54) proclaimed: 'Canada was founded first and foremost as an essentially defensive reaction – primarily against the United States.' What are the consequences of constructing an identity as 'defensive reaction'? How might it show up in the Canadian school curriculum?

'The ascription of "influence," whether in historical or other terms,' Tomkins (1981: 157) notes, 'is notoriously difficult and carries with it the further danger of violating the research canon that correlation is not to be equated with causation.' If 'influence' is difficult to assess, can 'domination' be any easier? Milburn and Herbert reference no data. Is proximity (see Tomkins 1981: 163) equivalent to threat? In this 1974 publication, not one example is given of the American 'domination' of Canada. Given significant policy differences – including over taxation, gay marriage, the US invasion of Iraq (Resnick 2005: 85) – such 'domination' would appear not to be political. While there may well be 'hazards of sleeping with an elephant' (Potter 2005: xxxviii), the threat may come more from inside, than outside, Canada. In his analysis of George Grant's *Lament for a Nation*, Andrew Potter (2005: lxiii) argues that Grant demonstrated the 'most important fault-line' in Canadian federal politics is not between the political left and right or between the French and the English, but 'between those who favor an independent Canada and those who desire every closer continental integration'. Grant (2005 [1965]) himself suggested that the 'central problem for nationalism in English-speaking Canada has always been: in what ways and for what reasons do we have the power and the desire to maintain some independence of the American Empire?'

Internally Canadian identity bifurcates into French and British, that duality fractured further by the presence of the First Nations (see Gunew 2004: 5; Renaud 1974: 37; Haig-Brown 2008: 13), other indigenous peoples, and the arrival of new immigrants. As Philip Resnick (2005: 17) suggests, 'Canada is made up of three founding peoples, not two.' Canadian identity is, then, not 'single' (Milburn and Herbert 1974: 7; see Chambers 2003: 245), as the country is a 'multination state' (Kymlicka 2003: 382). In addition to multiculturalism, regionalism predominates (see Tomkins 1974: 16; Chambers 2003: 221; Hodgetts 1968: 84), at least presumably, despite Tomkins (1974: 23) complaint that in the curriculum the 'great regional and cultural diversity' of Canada has been 'ignored'. Has alterity – as Nature or culture or region or the 'American colossus' – functioned as a series of constitutive exteriors, resulting in the designation of 'survival' as the central and ongoing national thematic (Chambers 1999: 141; 2003: 245)?

While a main threat to survival, the Canadian climate has been viewed favorably, as during the 1890s, when Canadian nationalist George Parkin embraced the 'northernness' of the country, an attitude evident in the Canadian national anthem 'the true north strong and free'. Due to its northern climate, Parkin was confident that Canada would have no 'Negro problem' nor would it 'attract the vagrant population of Italy and other countries of Southern Europe'. Indeed, climate was claimed as a 'fundamental political and social advantage which the Dominion enjoys over the United States' (quoted passages in Tomkins 1974: 19). This valorization of 'the North' was not left in the past; Conway (1974: 78) comments that besides anti-Americanism, Canada's most powerful mythology is the 'mystique' of the North, with its associated celebration of 'wilderness' as a 'source of power' (O'Brian and White 2007: 4).

The conflation of physical with political and cultural survival is evident in Milburn and Herbert's (1974: 7) observation that school textbooks in Quebec have 'preached' the doctrine of '*survivance*'. In Quebec, this 'siege mentality' (Resnick 2005: 13) has meant an ongoing struggle for cultural survival, but the resistance (the so-called 'Quiet Revolution') it expressed was focused more on Anglophone Canada than it was on the United States. Indeed, Quebec nationalism included an 'openness' to – on occasion an 'admiration' of – the United States (Vickers 1994: 361). With their nationalism structured by anti-Americanism, Anglophone Canadians were 'unprepared for a Quebec nationalism which was not based on a similar set of rejections' (Vickers 1994: 360). Indeed, efforts to construct a pan-Canadian identity, Kymlicka (see 2003: 377) concludes, have failed amongst the Québécois.

Survival is prominent in Margaret Atwood's controversial (see Dean 1994: 158–159) thematic guide to Canadian literature for schools, entitled *Survival* (see Tomkins 1986: 269). In Atwood's analysis of North American literature, Lipset (1990: 60) notes, she suggests that the symbol for the United States is 'the Frontier', connoting 'a place that is *new*, where the old order can be discarded'. The central image for Canada, Atwood concludes, is 'Survival, *la survivance*, hanging on, staying alive' (Lipset 1990: 60). For Tomkins (1981: 158), the term has 'clear negative connotations' in that 'survival' implies resistance to 'hostile' or 'alien forces'. Those include Nature (Lipset 1990: 21) and the United States. Vickers (1994: 353) acknowledges that for many the survival of Canada depends on accenting differences from the United States.

Late twentieth-century Canadian curriculum reform followed Hodgetts' (1968) landmark *What Culture? What Heritage?* As Tomkins (1974: 23) notes, this widely read report on the state of civic education concluded that Canadian history was taught in narrow, even pedantic, ways that failed to ignite student interest. Never mind, as Resnick (2005: 21) asserts, that 'Canadian history is pretty dull stuff ... when compared to that of countries like the United States or France with revolution in their blood'. Hodgetts found that (in Tomkins' words) 'many pupils expressed an active dislike for Canadian studies, and more than a few indicated a preference for American history, about which they often claimed to be more knowledgeable' (Tomkins 1986: 328). (Hodgetts [see 1968: 99] blamed the dullness of Canadian history not only on Canadian schoolteachers, but on their university professors as well.) Hodgetts' study marked the 'the birth of the formal Canadian Studies movement' (Tomkins 1986: 327), institutionalized in March 1970 by the establishment of the Canada Studies Foundation, dedicated to improving the quality of Canadian studies at the elementary and secondary school levels.

At universities, in contrast, Canadian Studies never became important (see Lorimer and Goldie 1994: 3), perhaps because the study of 'things Canadian' was imprinted with its founders' nationalism that has 'seriously constrained' subsequent generations of scholars in theorizing Canadian experience 'as we actually live it' (Vickers 1994: 353). In her early 1990s assessment, Jill Vickers (1994: 357) judged Canadian Studies to be a 'largely incoherent' field held together only by the legacies of its founding fathers' nationalism and anti-Americanism.

The implication that Canada is defined as much by its differences from the United States as it is by its own internal distinctiveness (see Vickers 1994: 353) also surfaces in a reflection Tomkins (1981: 165) makes regarding the 'Americanization' of the Canadian curriculum. On this occasion he dates 'Americanization' to the mid-1950s, when, he reports, it displaced the old 'imperial curriculum' in Anglophone Canada. His point is that Americanization provoked the 'demand for more Canadian content' (Tomkins 1981: 165). The associated public school curriculum development project, Tomkins (1974: 24) emphasizes, was 'in no sense' like the US curriculum reform (see Pinar 2004: 68). In contrast, Canada-centered curriculum reform was to be 'teacher-based': indeed, Tomkins (1974: 26) reassured his readers that 'from the beginning, the "top-down" or "teacher-proof" approach to curriculum reform that has characterized so much of the American efforts of the 1960s has been rejected'. Once again Canadian distinctiveness is defined as difference from the United States.

'Canadian national consciousness' – summarizing what Regenstreif (1974: 55) sees as 'evidence of intensifying Canadian nationalism' – was reflected, in part, by a 'growing number' of Canadian teachers becoming concerned about the teaching of Canadian Studies in the nation's schools (Milburn and Herbert 1974: 8; Tomkins 1974: 18). Teachers may not have been only 'reproducing' dominant ideology (as reproduction theorists have simplistically and obsessively insisted; Pinar 2009), they may have also been recoiling from foreign influences (from Europe as well as from the United States) that Tomkins (1981: 159) suggests followed the 1960s replacement of church with state control. Richler (1974: 106) acknowledges '1970' as dating 'a new sense of self-awareness in Canada', when 'the spirit of nationalism was rampaging over the land'. Canadian nationalism, he acknowledges, has 'its murky underside, anti-Americanism', which he judges as 'sometimes justified' (1974: 106). Starting from the American Revolution, anti-Americanism appears to ebb periodically, but as refracted through the 1974 collection, it appears as a constant but animating force and not only in the Canadian Studies movement.

While the 1974 OISE publication never confronts how anti-Americanism affects Canada's capacity for self-critique and self-understanding, it does problematize nationalism by scrutinizing historical, political, cultural (including gendered) elements. One wonders how contributors to that OISE publication would judge another publication that appears almost 30 years later, wherein such problematization is nowhere in evidence, wherein Canada nationalism is, simply, asserted. To that publication I turn next.

2001

> While Canadians can't seem to agree on what they are, they have no trouble at all agreeing on what they're not.
>
> (Dennis Sumara, Brent Davis, and Linda Laidlaw 2001: 147)

The source for the distinctions Sumara, Davis, and Laidlaw (2001: 145) draw between Canada and the United States turns out to be academic meetings; they report finding themselves 'taken aback' by the 'virulent' exchanges they have witnessed at US meetings. The modest size of this data set was not discouraging. To account for the differences they noticed between Canadian and US conferences, Sumara, Davis, and Laidlaw (2001: 145) point to how Canadian cultural myths are expressed in Canadian curriculum. Disclaiming any essentializing or reifying intentions, they do not posit a 'quintessential' Canadian identity (2001: 146). Historically Great Britain was the marker of the 'quintessential' identity of Anglophone Canada; in Québec nationalists accented French language and culture as the 'quintessential markers' of identity (Resnick 2005: 33).

While theory is not 'determined' by its national setting, it is, presumably, 'dependent' (2001: 146), and Sumara, Davis, and Laidlaw (2001: 45) propose the idea of 'ecological postmodernism' to depict this dependency. Such a phrase points to the ways 'humans' tend to 'adapt' to new situations and 'reinterpret' the past (2001: 147). Apparently associated with a Deweyan (Dewey 1920: 183) conception of reconstruction (see Pinar 2010: 304–306), more so than with postmodern celebrations of difference, uncertainty, and unintelligibility (Lather 2007: 76), this conception turns out to be not only not American but, indeed, anti-American. Sumara, Davis, and Laidlaw (2001: 147) assert that Canadians are 'not overbearing … totalizing … monolithic … unified … static': Canadians are 'not Americans'. In contrast to America's 'inward-looking nationalism' and 'outward-looking imperialism', Sumara, Davis, and Laidlaw (2001: 147) continue, Canada is characterized by 'peace-keeping, not policing'.

Although American influences were, we are told, 'ever-present' in the classroom and on school library shelves (2001: 157), evidently they never took hold, as the two countries are presented as opposites. Canada was constructed not through violent revolution and the genocide of indigenous peoples but through 'conflict, co-operation, and conciliation' (2001: 153). Because the Canadian nation was formed by 'stitching together' various cultural differences, curriculum studies scholars in Canada appreciate that 'meanings' and 'identities' are not 'discovered', nor can they be 'fully represented' (2001: 150).

Unlike Americans, Sumara, Davis and Laidlaw (2001: 154) continue, Canadians are circumspect in the representation of identity. We are told, for example, that in contrast to the monolithic American identity, Canadian identity is 'not unified' but 'shifts' (2001: 154–155). Consequently, curriculum studies in Canada can be characterized as a form of 'ecological postmodernism' (2001: 150), a phrase that declines any dissociation between the biological and the phenomenological. Rejecting grand narratives (2001: 157), the Canadian 'sensibility' (2001: 158) expresses 'deep commitments' to the layering of history, the inability of language to represent experience, and the complexity of translation. Sumara, Davis, and Laidlaw (2001: 159) remind us that understanding curriculum is 'always rooted' in the local, a point emphasized in US curriculum studies as well (Pinar 1991). Among the four 'challenges' Cynthia Chambers (2006a: 30) sets for Canadian curriculum theorists is to 'write from this place' and 'write in a language of our own', devising 'interpretive tools that arise from and are fit for this place'. That implies, as Chambers (2006b: 6, 13) reminds, attention to 'borders', but not only what lies beyond them, but what they divide within.

Conclusion

> [T]his [current] wave of Canadian nationalism is greater than at any time since the 1960s.
>
> (Cynthia Chambers 2006b: 7)

This juxtaposition of 'then and now' (Pinar 2007) reveals one of those 'shifts' that Sumara, Davis and Laidlaw reference. In the 1974 collection, there is a strong self-consciousness of nationalism's problematic character, its dissonance with Canadian cosmopolitan ideals, prominently among them the embrace of difference (Chambers 2003: 238). Nationalism, Herbert and Milburn (1974: 143) concluded, is a 'fuzzy, unclear, and sometimes dangerous concept'. Despite this distrust of nationalism, there was 'sympathy' for the construction of a Canadian 'identity', provided that identity is one face of a coin, the other side of which is 'world community' (1974: 144). For Herbert and Milburn, the 'thirst' for Canadian identity and the 'desire' for 'international understanding' (based on 'equality' and 'interdependence') must be balanced (1974: 144). In these concepts – 'thirst' and 'desire' – are foreshadowed Tomkins' (1986: 440) acknowledgement of the 'psychic significance' of curriculum questions. That psychic significance becomes, for Herbert and Milburn, focused on self-knowledge, on using national consciousness as a 'liberating force' (Herbert and Milburn 1974: 147). In this conception, the national becomes the portal to the international.

In the 2001 comments, Canadian nationalism seems no longer problematic, no longer a provocation to self-knowledge or a portal to internationalism. 'Self-doubt' – what Resnick (2005: 89) suggests is the 'dominant motif in Canadian political culture' – is nowhere in evidence. Rather than Canadian identity defined by internal difference – the originary Indigenous and Francophone populations juxtaposed with British and subsequent immigrants, especially from East and South Asia – it is defined summarily by what Canadians are not: Americans. Such identity-by-negation recalls Regenstreif's (1974: 54) characterization of Canada as a 'defensive reaction'. 'Instead of liberty, individualism, achievement, and optimism,' he told the OISE conference, 'Canada institutionalized authority, order, ascription, and a certain pessimism' (1974: 54). Given the substitution of self-accolades for self-knowledge in the 2001 statement, perhaps Conway's (1974: 78) observation holds true then and now: 'The anti-American myth operates to divert the critical gaze firmly to the south, leaving startling unanimity in a society that protests with correctness that in other respects it is not conformist.'

While no text updates Tomkins' canonical curriculum history, there are clues to the transition between the two historical moments (as these are refracted through these two publications). One such clue comes in George Richardson's study of the Province of Alberta's *Program of Studies*. Discussing the transition from the 1981 to the 1991 programs, Richardson (2002: 78) counts four 'seismic shocks to Canada's national identity', among them a receding significance of British influence, growing concern over 'the exact nature of Canada's relationship with the United States', the 'emergence of French Canadian nationalism', as well as 'the rapidly changing demographic composition of the nation'. Richardson observes no 'them–us' characteristic of modern nationalism, but, rather, a national identity that was 'ambiguous and uneasy'. These adjectives do not apply to Sumara, Davis, and Laidlaw's 2001 statement, wherein the binary 'them–us' structures Canadian identity.

After chronicling a series of issues on which Canadians assume they have a better record than the United States (including the livability of cities and the environmental policies of the provinces/states), Kymlicka (2003: 365) finds 'striking' how quickly Canadians 'overlook any such embarrassing facts that contradict their preferred self-image'. That 'Canadians differ profoundly from Americans' (Resnick 2005: 84) need not be summarized by stereotypes; they contradict Canadian claims for appreciating diversity. In his claim that Canadians resemble Europeans more than they do Americans, Resnick (2005: 84) may underestimate the growing significance of the other continents – especially Asia – to Canadian society (both in terms of immigrants and economically and politically), but in historical terms[3] his point stands.

'A new model of nationalism for the twenty-first century,' Resnick (2005: 47) proposes, 'may yet turn out to be a version of "nationalism lite"'. Reminiscent of Hodgetts' (1968: 76) 'low-key patriotism', this playful phrase performs what it depicts, a nationalism that does not take itself entirely seriously. It is also serious, however, as Resnick specifies that 'such nationalism seeks to be open to other cultures and nations, to a level of political and economic integration beyond the nation-state, to a global/cosmopolitan dimension of identity'. Such nationalism would then seem to be an internationalism as well. Is this the version of nationalism that registers across the Canadian curriculum now?

Despite resemblances with the United States, Canada is in no danger of disappearing. In his *Lament for a Nation* (1965), George Grant predicted that Canada would become totally immersed in the political realities of continental economic integration, a prediction many were certain would be confirmed with the implementation of Free Trade. In Vickers' (1994: 33) judgment, that fear was contradicted by the ongoing 'vitality' of both French- and English-Canadian cultures, as well as the 'dynamic movements' of immigrant cultures and the 'revival' of the cultures and languages of the First Nations. Lipset (1990: 221) points to high, not popular, culture, finding that:

> the vitality of the creative arts north of the border is striking. The country is producing world-class novelists, playwrights, dancers, painters, and other artists in numbers never before witnessed. Canadian complaints about being ignored by American reviewers no longer hold; they now pay considerable attention to the Canadian cultural scene.

American attention may not always be welcomed, especially if it becomes aggravated with envy, of Canadian oil reserves for instance. But sensible skepticism – wariness of sleeping with an 'unruly elephant' (O'Brian 2007: 27) – can deteriorate into paranoia unless linked to facts. Recall Grant's (2005 [1965]: 35) invocation of Canadian 'self-restraint' as prerequisite to the 'good life' (in contrast, he thought, to the American 'emancipation of the passions'). That restraint might well extend to expansive, if reductive, summaries of national difference.

Pride in country is an entirely appropriate state of mind, especially when it does not mask internal problems but prompts efforts to solve them. Grant's embrace of Canadian nationalism, he always insisted, was not 'anti-American', but 'simply a lack of Americanism' (2005 [1965]: 34). Such patriotism – certainly I have expressed my own (Pinar 2009: 45–55) – is what Saul (2005: 245) characterizes as 'the positive form of nationalism', e.g. 'self-confidence and openness and to a concept of the public good'. In contrast is 'negative nationalism', fueled by fear and anger and a desperate conviction that one nation's rights exist by comparison with those of another nation' (2005: 245). Such bifurcation obliterates the particularity patriotism aspires to preserve.

Would not the point of both US and Canadian curriculum be to study differences *and* similarities between the two nations, to 'dwell in tensionality in the realm of the between, in the tensionality of differences' (Aoki 2005 [1987]: 354)? As that great Canadian curriculum theorist sagely observed, the very concept of 'identity' risks 'reducing our life reality to an abstracted totality of its own, pretending to wholeness' (2005 [1987]: 354). That pretence obscures the tensioned lived landscape of difference *and* similarity, that 'common ground' (Chambers 2008: 125) that is Canada.

Acknowledgement

I thank Professor Terry Carson for his helpful comments on the first draft of this chapter and for his recommendation of Lipset's *Continental Divide*. My thanks as well to Professors Nicholas Ng A-Fook and Teresa Strong-Wilson. Appreciative acknowledgement does not imply agreement with my analysis. This abbreviated version follows the editors' recommendations.

Notes

1   Genocide is the more accurate term for the fate of the First Nations: in what is now the United States the population fell from 5 million to 250,000 by the late nineteenth century (Saul 2005: 29). Lipset (1990: 176) acknowledges that 'the record is clear that the native peoples have been better able to survive in Canada than in the United States' (see also Ng-A-Fook 2007). Carr and Lund (2007: 1) take a harsher view, alleging that 'Canada has long been a welcome home to the KKK and numerous other hate groups'; they juxtapose 'slavery' with the 'colonialism [sic] of First Nations and other peoples'. The 1876 Indian Act, restated in 1920 by Duncan Campbell Scott, Superintendent of Indian Affairs, was 'to continue until there is not a single Indian in Canada that has not been absorbed into the body politic and there is no Indian question and no Indian Department' (Chambers 2006b: 6). Forced assimilation was to be accomplished, in part, by removing 'aboriginal children from their families and communities and [sending them] to church-run residential schools to remove their native languages and cultures' (Carson 2005: 7).

2   While I use years as subheadings, I realize that these two publications are by no means representative of Canadian curriculum studies – or the Canadian school curriculum – during those years. They do, however, provide glimpses of how specific Canadian curriculum studies scholars reconstructed nationalism 'then' and 'now.' The inflated role 'there' (the US) plays in the construction of 'here' (Canada) seems to have only intensified during the roughly thirty-year period between the two publications. Before the forefronting of the American 'colossus', it had been Great Britain and the Commonwealth that constituted the 'there' that blurred the singularity of the 'here' (see Chambers 1999: 139). Cavell (1994: 76–77) reminds that Canadian culture is often depicted as a function of place, alternately defined as 'landscape', 'geography', 'archipelago', or 'North' (a 'Canadian analogy to the idea of West' in the United States; O'Brian and White 2007: 3). This assumption (one shared by Cynthia Chambers, see 2006b: 5), Cavell points out, follows from Northrop Frye's 'Conclusion' to the first edition of *A Literary History of Canada*, wherein he suggests that the question of Canadian identity is not so much 'Who am I?' as 'Where is here?' (quoted in 1994: 77). Cavell complains that Frye's conception of 'place' is abstract, devoid of the social.

3   Terry Carson (2010) points out that the recurring question of Canada's identification with the United States and with Europe remains an open one, personified today (March 2010) in the persons of Prime Minister Stephen Harper (representing the economic and political continentalism George Grant worried would dissolve Canadian national distinctiveness and, eventually, sovereignty) and Liberal leader Michael Ignatieff (representing Canada's European association). As Hodgetts (1968: 120) pointed out, the study of Canadian history remains key to appreciating these issues. While I endorse its strengthening in the schools (and in Canadian curriculum studies), 'history is,' Resnick (2005: 37) notes, 'no more unifying force in Canada'. He cites a 2001 survey of history teachers in secondary schools in English Canada and Quebec that found 'a striking difference in what each held to be important' (2005: 38; see Hodgetts 1968: 71, 76, 80–81, 112 n. 7). While history may be no force for national political unification, it would (more modestly) advance Canadian curriculum studies as it would make less likely the substitution of simplistic stereotypes for complex facts.

References

Aoki, T. (2005 [1987]) 'Revisiting the notions of leadership and identity', in W.F. Pinar and R.L. Irwin (eds) *Curriculum in a New Key: The Collected Works of Ted T. Aoki*, Mahwah, NJ: Lawrence Erlbaum.

Carr, P.R. and Lund, D.E. (2007) 'Introduction: Scanning whiteness', in P.R. Carr and D.E. Lund (eds), *The Great White North? Exploring Whiteness, Privilege and Identity in Education*, Rotterdam/Boston/Tapei: Sense Publishers.

Carson, T. (2005) 'Beyond instrumentalism: The significance of teacher identity in educational change', *Journal of the Canadian Association for Curriculum Studies*, 3, 2: 1–8.

Carson, T. (2010). Personal communication.

Cavell, R.A. (1994) 'Theorizing Canadian space: Postcolonial articulations', in T. Goldie, C. Lambert and R. Lorimer (eds), *Canada: Theoretical Discourse*, Montreal: Association for Canadian Studies.

Chambers, C. (1999) 'A topography for Canadian curriculum theory', *Canadian Journal of Education*, 24, 2: 137–150.

Chambers, C. (2003). '"As Canadian as possible under the circumstances": A view of contemporary curriculum discourses in Canada', in W.F. Pinar (ed.) *International Handbook of Curriculum Research*, Mahwah, NJ: Lawrence Erlbaum.

Chambers, C. (2006a) '"The land is the best teacher I ever had": Places as pedagogy for precarious times', *JCT: Journal of Curriculum Theorizing*, 22, 3: 27–37.

Chambers, C. (2006b) 'Chambers' "Where do I belong?": Canadian curriculum as passport home', *Journal of the American Association for the Advancement of Curriculum Studies*, 2. Online. Available HTTP: <http://www.uwstout.edu/soe/jaaacs/vol2/chambers.htm>.

Chambers, C. (2008) 'Where are we? Finding common ground in a curriculum of place', *Journal of the Canadian Association for Curriculum Studies*, 6, 2: 113–128.

Conway, J. (1974) 'Culture and national identity', in G. Milburn and J. Herbert (eds) *National Consciousness and the Curriculum: The Canadian Case*, Toronto: Ontario Institute for Studies in Education, Department of Curriculum.

Dean, M. (1994) 'Canadian "vulgar nationalism" in the postmodern age', in T. Goldie, C. Lambert and R. Lorimer (eds), *Canada: Theoretical Discourse*, Montreal: Association for Canadian Studies.

Dewey, J. (1920) *Reconstruction in Philosophy*, New York: Henry Holt and Company.

Fanon, F. (1967) *Black Skin, White Masks*, trans. C.L. Markmann, New York: Grove Weidenfeld; originally published as *Peau Noire, Masques Blancs* (1952), Paris: Editions du Seuil.

Grant, G. (2005 [1965]) *Lament for a Nation*, 40th anniversary edition, Montreal and Kingston: McGill-Queen's University Press.

Gunew, S. (2004) *Haunted nations: The Colonial Dimensions of Multiculturalisms*, London: Routledge.

Haig-Brown, C. (2008), 'Taking indigenous thought seriously: A rant on globalization with some cautionary notes', *Journal of the Canadian Association for Curriculum Studies*, 6, 2: 8–24.

Herbert, J. and Milburn, G. (1974) 'Nationalism and the curriculum', in G. Milburn and J. Herbert (eds) *National Consciousness and the Curriculum: The Canadian Case*, Toronto: Ontario Institute for Studies in Education, Department of Curriculum.

Hodgetts, A.B. (1968) *What Culture? What Heritage? A Study of Civic Education in Canada*, Toronto: Ontario Institute for Studies in Education.

Kymlicka, W. (2003) 'Being Canadian', *Government and Opposition*, 38, 3: 357–385.

Lather, P. (2007) *Getting Lost: Feminist Efforts Toward A Double(d) Science*, Albany, NY: State University of New York Press.

Lipset, S.M. (1990) *Continental Divide: The Values and Institutions of the United States and Canada*, New York: Routledge.

Lorimer, R. and Goldie, T. (1994) 'Introduction', in T. Goldie, C. Lambert and R. Lorimer (eds) *Canada: Theoretical Discourse*, Montreal: Association for Canadian Studies.

Milburn, G. and Herbert, J. (eds) (1974) *National Consciousness and the Curriculum: The Canadian Case*, Toronto: Ontario Institute for Studies in Education, Department of Curriculum.

Ng-A-Fook, N. (2007) *An Indigenous Curriculum of Place: The United Houma Nation's Contentious Relationship with Louisiana's Educational Institutions*, New York: Peter Lang.

O'Brian, J. (2007), 'Wild art history', in J. O'Brian and P. White (eds.) *Beyond Wilderness: The Group of Seven, Canadian Identity, and Contemporary Art*, Montreal and Kingston: McGill-Queen's University Press.

O'Brian, J. and White, P. (2007) 'Introduction', in J. O'Brian and P. White (eds.) *Beyond Wilderness: The Group of Seven, Canadian Identity, and Contemporary Art*, Montreal and Kingston: McGill-Queen's University Press.

Pinar, W.F. (1991) 'Curriculum as social psychoanalysis: On the significance of place', in J. Kincheloe and W. Pinar (eds) *Curriculum as Social Psychoanalysis: Essays on the Significance of Place*, Albany, NY: State University of New York Press.

Pinar, W.F. (2007) 'Curriculum leadership then and now', in W. Smale and K. Young (eds) *Approaches to Educational Leadership*, Calgary: Detselig.

Pinar, W.F. (2009) 'The unaddressed "I" of ideology critique', *Power and Education*, 1, 2: 189–200. Online. Available HTTP: <www.wwwords.co.uk/POWER>

Pinar, W.F. (2010) 'The eight-year study', *Curriculum Inquiry* 40, 2: 295–316.

Potter, A. (2005) Introduction to the 40th anniversary edition of G.P. Grant's *Lament for a Nation*, Montreal and Kingston: McGill-Queen's University Press.

Regenstreif, P. (1974) 'Some social and political obstacles to Canadian national consciousness', in G. Milburn and J. Herbert (eds) *National Consciousness and the Curriculum: The Canadian Case*, Toronto: Ontario Institute for Studies in Education, Department of Curriculum.

Renaud, A. (1974) 'Indians in white culture curricula and society', in G. Milburn and J. Herbert (eds) *National Consciousness and the Curriculum: The Canadian Case*, Toronto: Ontario Institute for Studies in Education, Department of Curriculum.

Resnick, P. (2005) *The European Roots of Canadian Identity*, Peterborough, Ontario: Broadview Press.

Richardson, G.H. (2002) *The Death of the Good Canadian: Teachers, National Identities, and the Social Studies Curriculum*, New York: Peter Lang.

Richler, M. (1974) 'Nationalism and literature in Canada', in G. Milburn and J. Herbert (eds) *National Consciousness and the Curriculum: The Canadian Case*, Toronto: Ontario Institute for Studies in Education, Department of Curriculum.

Saul, J.R. (2005) *The Collapse of Globalism: And the Reinvention of the World*, Toronto: Viking Canada.

Sumara, D., Davis, B., and Laidlaw, L. (2001) 'Canadian identity and curriculum theory: An ecological, postmodern perspective', *Canadian Journal of Education*, 26, 2: 144–163.

Tomkins, G. (1974) 'National consciousness, the curriculum, and Canadian Studies', in G. Milburn and J. Herbert (eds) *National Consciousness and the Curriculum: The Canadian Case*, Toronto: Ontario Institute for Studies in Education, Department of Curriculum.

Tomkins, G. (1981) 'Foreign influences on curriculum and curriculum policy making in Canada: Some impressions in historical and contemporary perspective', *Curriculum Inquiry*, 11, 2: 157–166.

Tomkins, G. (1986) *A Common Countenance: Stability and Change in the Canadian Curriculum*, Scarborough, Ontario, Canada: Prentice-Hall; reissued (2008) by Pacific Educational Press.

Vickers, J. (1994) 'Liberating theory in Canadian Studies', in T. Goldie, C. Lambert and R. Lorimer (eds), *Canada: Theoretical Discourse*, Montreal: Association for Canadian Studies.

White, P. (2007) 'Out of the woods', in J. O'Brian and P. White (eds) *Beyond Wilderness: The Group of Seven, Canadian Identity, and Contemporary Art*, Montreal and Kingston: McGill-Queen's University Press.

4   Curriculum Policies in Brazil

The Citizenship Discourse

Elizabeth Macedo

The 1980s in Brazil brought sweeping albeit gradual changes in the public sphere with the end of the 15-year military dictatorship. In 1982, state governors were directly elected, followed in 1986 by legislators who were to draw up a new constitution and in 1990 the first elected president since 1960. The democratic governments marked this transition from dictatorship to democracy by initiating projects for the social sphere: in the area of education, state and municipal governments produced new curricular proposals for their school systems, in order to intervene more strongly (and presumably in a new direction) in the pedagogical work developed in schools under their administration. The discussions that followed the Constitution promulgated in 1988, aimed at the elaboration of the National Education Guidelines and Acts Foundation, providing a complex system of shared responsibilities. The elementary school (first nine years of schooling) was kept within the competence of municipalities; while high school (three years after elementary school) was under the responsibility of the states; nevertheless, the tendency to legislate nationally on education was sustained. States and municipalities were left with the obligation to keep their schools networks, for which they can establish curriculum guidelines, but like all private schools, they must follow national law on national education in what it defines as compulsory. In addition to undergoing a comprehensive national legislation, state and municipal systems are still dependent on decentralization, held by the Ministry of Education, referring to resources that enable substantial parts of its educational programs.

The National Education Guidelines and Foundation Act, promulgated in 1995, proposed some curriculum principles and national guidelines to be developed in the years that followed. In order to develop those guidelines, in 1996 the federal government began to prepare National Curricular Standards (NCS) for elementary education, published in 1998. Although specialists and teaching networks were consulted during the preparation of the NCS, the haste and the individualized manner of the consultations led to a major movement against the NCS. As a result of that movement, the National Education Council[1] declared that the NCS would not be compulsory and could not be considered a criterion for any national evaluation procedure. Following that, the Council itself proposed national curricular guidelines in very generic terms. Consequently, the curricular policy documents in effect in Brazil are the compulsory national curricular guidelines, the non-compulsory national curricular standards and a good number of state and municipal curricular guides, which are compulsory in the public systems of those states and municipalities. Although the NCS are not compulsory, states and municipalities have implemented them. In addition to the formal curriculum, the intervention involved measuring the performance of students; teacher training, especially continued training; and the evaluation of textbooks. That series of actions was possible because the Ministry of Education, MEC (federal government), controls a large part of the funds that maintain public elementary education, even though the municipalities have constitutional responsibility for that level of teaching.

Most of the curricular documents circulating in Brazil mention citizenship training as a principle that justifies schooling. Citizenship had become a magic signifier for the return to democracy – the Federal Constitution itself was called a Citizen Constitution – then assumed by the educational policies. As a magic signifier, citizenship has expressed a series of demands – for freedom, for participation, for reducing social inequalities – articulating different groups of society. In the case of the educational policies, the articulation involved such varied pedagogic discourses as progressivism, Freireanism and various Marxist positions. It also echoed the struggle of minority groups for recognition, as well as general yearning for social promotion and insertion in the consumer market. Briefly, to train for citizenship has no literal meaning and, perhaps because of that, it is such a powerful articulating support for educational policies.

The focus of this text is to understand how the articulation of meanings takes place that makes citizenship this powerful expression of recent Brazilian curricular policies. More specifically, I am interested to see how in that articulation preferential meanings emerged for the citizenship it was intended to shape and the implications of those meanings for a curriculum centered on *difference*. By difference, I am not considering the demands of minority groups incorporated in the curriculum, something equivalent to US identity politics. Though we may say that in Brazil such demands have recently begun to be manifested and are clearly expressed in the NCS cross topics, cultural plurality and sexual orientation, my interest has been to analyze the place of the difference as such. In contrast, I understand that a curriculum focused on the difference must transcend the mere sharing of selected repertoires of meanings in different cultures. This distinction is coded in the term, *différance*, implying the possibility of meaning-making processes of hybridization; constructed in the present to rewrite repertoires of shared meanings. It is informed by Derrida's concept of *différance*, here described by Lois Shawver: 'the hidden way of seeing things that is deferred out of awareness by our distraction by the imagery that captures our attention' (2010). Thus, a curriculum centered on the *différance* must make room for new creations, different from what is already known, deconstructing the setting mechanisms that prevent the proliferation of *différance*.

Even if it were possible to work with the idea that the group of curricular actions in Brazil form a single policy – as an instituting moment, always partial and incomplete – it would be a very extensive exercise. To that end, I have opted to focus my analysis on the policy developed at a national level and, more specifically, on that referring more directly to the curriculum. I work, basically, with national curricular documents, and consider that their analysis can lead us to understand the processes by which some meanings are being fixed and others excluded from the curricular dynamics. Although my analysis is focused on curriculum documents in its conclusions, I will make some comments on possible impacts of preferential meanings they seek to build on the identity of the individuals directly involved in schooling.

Curricular Policy as an Instituting Moment

Although today we live in a globalized world, immersed in a culture that is becoming homogenous, I want to point out the possibilities of escape, the *différance* always present in the signification process. I see, therefore, the curriculum as a practice of attributing meanings that involve new and old significants that inhabit the interval between a certain 'original meaning', historically constructed, and that which is being constructed uninterruptedly. These are meanings that occupy an ambivalent region between the shared, familiar meanings and those that are projected in the new enunciation, which Bhabha (2003) has called a third space of enunciation.

Based on that concept of curriculum, curriculum policy could be considered a process whereby some preferential meanings are fixed, defining provisional positionalities in very specific historical and cultural formations (Hall 2003); it is referred to here as signifiXation, a process which, in short, intends to restrict the possibilities of saying differently.

It is in that sense that I am using the discourse theory of Laclau and Mouffe (2004) to see curriculum policy as the movement of hegemonic articulation in the direction of the signifiXation of some meanings that intend to address the subjects to which they are destined. The discourse theory as proposed by Laclau and Mouffe resorts to the notion of a nodal point as a signifier capable of generating the unity of a discursive formation of some kind without this referring to any foundation. A perfect signifiXation would be that established around a nodal point that could articulate all the demands, a totally empty signifier[2] capable of representing the totality. However, as the difference constitutes the system and cannot be eliminated, the dimension of social antagonism is ineradicable. The more a signifier is emptied of meanings, the more easily it can assume the function of representing the totality which is incommensurable to it, although it can never cease to be a particularity. As the structure is not formed as an objective order, the symbolic is always interrupted by the Real and makes the future dimension – the subject – indispensable. Therefore, there is no possibility of a signifiXation in the displaced structure, but of partial and contingent signifiXations. The production of particular discourses, of signifiXations is, therefore, a decision-making process that Laclau (1998) defines as the 'leap from the experience of undecidability to a creative act' (p.112) or as 'the moment of the subject'[3] (p.112).

In the case of recent national curriculum policies in Brazil, I maintain that citizenship (or training for citizenship) has worked as one of the nodal points around which the documents are written where it takes on a metaphorical dimension capable of condensing different meanings, which occurs through the partial suppression of any claim of literal contents. For example, various groups

– from liberals to Marxists and also market related perspectives – would sustain citizenship training as an important curriculum goal, articulating their demands for freedom and economic and cultural equality. Curriculum policy, in that perspective, is formed in the unceasing struggle among the different subjects to fulfill the sense of citizenship.[4] This is a fulfillment that will never be complete because of the ambivalence of the actual process of giving meaning to citizenship. That means that the process of fulfillment of what is understood by citizenship is also a process of emptying of its literal contents that would permit that all the different subjects feel represented. In that dual movement of fulfilling/emptying lies the ambivalence of the power to fix the meaning of citizenship. To each of the groups, it offers only partial recognition that makes the political struggle for the power of signifying incessant.

Although discursive closings may be impossible and the political struggle ineradicable, there are discursive strategies that permit a more effective and lasting hegemony. Myths are examples in which the particularity of a signifier that seeks to represent the totality is blended in such a way with it that its particular nature is almost obliterated. The nation – and its citizen correlate – is one of the particulars universalized by the self-denominated modernity. It imposes itself as a way of political organization of the world to the point of assuming, in Brazil, a metaphorical nature that allows us to use expressions like 'indigenous nations' or 'Zulu nation'. To the extent, however, that particularity goes on being a particularity, the metonymical process that would erase it calls for constant political action that has been more or less coercive throughout the centuries.

The elimination of the particular or its subordination to global identities has been challenged in our time. The invented nature of traditions like the nation (Bauman 2005) – and the mechanisms of coercion, obliteration or persuasion that sustain them (Harding 2000; Willinsky 1998) – have been denounced. The differences no longer erupt as something marginal, because there are no standards that push them out of the center. With that, the particularity of signifiers like nation and citizenship, among others, becomes more obvious, and the negotiation necessary for them to be able to represent the totality (that is, for their hegemonization) becomes more visible. In that negotiation, however, the meanings shared as universally undeniable by the subjects throughout the centuries – the old hegemonies – are in a prominent place, but their meanings are re-created: a re-creation that always occurred, but which becomes clearer at the moment when the old hegemonies weaken.

In the case of curricular policies defined in Brazil, going beyond the way in which signifiers like nation and citizenship are fulfilled inside documents, the actual defense of a national curriculum would also serve as an example of the weakening of modern hegemonies. This is a debate that intensified in the 1930s, directly related to the construction of a national identity, a Brazilianness sustained by the myth of the three races.[5] With the intensification of industrialization, the national curriculum was also a lever for economic development contributing toward training the worker to work in an expanding industrial market.[6] Although the meaning of national might articulate different positions, the Western idea of nation imposed on the 1889 republic had challenged it to constitute a uniform country in national terms. In addition to the national symbols that were valorized – language, the history and geography of Brazil, and moral and civic education – the reforms of the 1930s were concerned about creating a national teaching system and eliminating the foreign presence, such as immigrants whose children attended schools taught in their native languages.

In the 1990s, when the NCS were presented with the intention of becoming national teaching standards,[7] the erosion of the idea of nation stirred up the discussion of the national definition of curricula. What was evident, among other aspects, was that although called national, their references transcended any national project, being included in the logic of the neoliberal global market. The creation of the NCS, unlike what happened in the 1930s, answered, among other demands, the need to establish a training standard that would allow the equivalence of diplomas within the scope of the Mercosur,[8] as well as the insertion of Brazilian workers in a more globalized and demanding labor market: 'The worker's profile has been changing, and soon the survival in the labor market (in the world) will depend on the acquisition of new skills' (Brazil Secretaria de Educação Fundamental 1998a: 138).

But fifteen years after the publication of the NCS, a period in which a series of actions made them viable, although not compulsory, as national references, it is possible to perceive the superficiality of the argument that neoliberal globalization would destroy national identities. In Brazil the projection of a national identity under the focus given to training the citizen was not relinquished: the preferential identity defined in the different documents forming the policy, is the citizen, countless times described as Brazilian. I will now analyze the curricular documents to understand how citizenship is a powerful nodal point that stops the emergence of other possible meanings. I am concerned, especially, that the strength of that preferential addressing works to the effect of erasing the *différance*.

Who is the Citizen?

Citizenship arises in recent national curricular policies of Brazil in practically all the documents, articulating demands made for schooling by various groups. In the curricula of all the subjects, citizenship is mentioned, as well as in documents dealing with topics such as cultural plurality, environment, and sexuality among others. The actual NCS justifies its need by problematizing citizenship in the world and Brazilian contexts. In the curricular standards in action,[9] the first activity proposed to teachers in all the specific modules is a discussion on how the learning process of their subject can contribute toward educating the citizen (Brazil, Ministério da Educação, Secretaria de Educação Fundamental 1999). Even the directions for evaluating textbooks define a category called citizenship and ethics in which the books are expected, among other requirements, to teach respect and appreciation of popular knowledge, the presence of topics like workers' rights, the discussion of current topics involving ethnic-racial, gender and religious diversity (Brazil, Ministério da Educação, Secretaria de Educação Básica 2007). The large number of references to citizenship throughout the documents imparts form, in the different policy texts, to the first objective listed for elementary school teaching:

> To understand citizenship as social and political participation, as well as the exercise of political, civil and social rights and duties, taking, in everyday life, attitudes of solidarity, cooperation and repudiation of injustices, respecting the other and demanding for oneself the same respect.
>
> (Brazil, Secretaria de Educação Fundamental 1998a: 55)

The choice of citizenship as the 'spinal column of school education' (Brazil, Secretaria de Educação Fundamental 1998b: 23) has received few criticisms, although there are a large number of studies that oppose the national curricular policies. Reading the documents as a whole enables us to perceive the variability of the demands articulated under the heading of citizenship. The struggle for citizenship through the school is the condensation of a series of unattended demands presented by the most diverse groups. It articulates demands for freedom, equality of social opportunities, racial democracy, rights of ethnic and cultural minorities, and sexual freedom, diluting them in the hybrid demand for citizenship, but at the same time guaranteeing them greater power of negotiation.

It is important not to reify the articulation of demands from different groups around a fluctuating signifier like citizenship. The actual demands being articulated need to be viewed as signifiXations produced by articulation processes. In other words, the meanings of freedom or of equality of social opportunities are also fluctuating, so that we cannot see the unsatisfied demands as material reality. On the other hand, it is necessary to understand those demands as fixed meanings in other hegemonic struggles. It is in that sense that I will enumerate demands articulated in the documents as if they 'simply existed', but without essentializing them.

When analyzing the policy in question, I consider that the citizenship signifier is being filled in by fragments of discourses that express positions of groups that are formed as a group (and as subjects) as from the moment in which they take an attitude to the points under dispute. The multiple qualifications for the word *citizenship* reveal the fluctuation of their meanings: national, Brazilian, active, full, for all, pluricultural, practical and effective. Those meanings point to a first line of analysis. I am not talking about just any citizenship, but of a national citizenship, a republican right, assured legally by the Constitution and by Brazil's participation in international forums, for example, for defending human rights. It is because of the constitutional text that Brazil is presented as a democratic legal state, defined as 'a kind of sociability that penetrates all the social spaces' (Brazil, Secretaria de Educação Fundamental 1998b: 20), whose principles are 'sovereignty, citizenship, the dignity of the human person, the social values of work and of free enterprise and political pluralism' (1998b: 19). In that sense, citizenship is initially defined by its formal aspects, encompassing political and civil rights, and assuming liberal patterns. In Brazil the political doctrine of liberalism has come up against resistance from large social and educational sectors. It is argued that liberalism is incapable of fostering the social justice it proclaims, thus deepening the inequalities that sustain capitalism. Except for sectors more to the right of the political spectrum, the market is seen as incapable of arbitrating social conflict. It has become necessary, therefore, as a way of legitimating the actual reform with the larger sectors of the country, to expand the meanings of citizenship beyond the rights defended in the area of liberalism. To that end the republican right, assured by the Constitution, is reiterated at the same time as a deficit of citizenship is denounced either because of the country's blatant social and economic inequalities, or because of the disrespect for cultural plurality or for human rights. As this involves increasing the legitimacy of the reform discourse, the connections between the project of formal citizenship and the production of inequalities are attenuated.

Considering the visible connection between the central idea of citizenship in the documents and the concept of nation[10] – it is, after all, a national citizenship – it is interesting to observe how the exclusion on which it is based is masked in the concept. After all, the construction of the national called for the creation of a structure which, as Bauman (2005) reminds us, ranks collective rights above individual interests. It demanded, therefore, for that task, mechanisms of coercion and persuasion that might justify it, which was guaranteed by the invention of the national identity, and its requirements of exclusivity. The illusion of belonging, via birth and participation in an imagined community (Anderson 1983), was only possible because the state, and society, its corollary, took on the task of certifying it. The national citizen is, therefore, constituted by an invisible symbolic power that unifies all society.

To create the illusion of being fully constituted, however, the symbolic systems need an external enemy that stabilizes them, that stops the fluctuation of meanings that prevents their complete constitution. That real or imaginary enemy, as Zizek (1990) points out, permits imagining a national essence to be stolen by it. Enemy nations (and wars) played that role of enemy, although also inside national frontiers enemies were created accused of stealing the national 'Thing' as a way of our 'hiding the fact that we never had what was said was stolen from us' (Zizek 1990: 57).

A national citizenship can only, therefore, be considered in a situation in which the feelings of nation are emptied, so that those enemies (or many of them) may participate in the fantasy of Brazilianness. That emptying has been facilitated by the multiple criticisms that the idea of nation has been suffering as much because of the post-colonial phenomenon as of globalization and of the dissemination of market principles (Bhabha 2003; Chaterjee 2000; Hall 2003). In the case of the policy analyzed, enemies are not incorporated by destroying the idea of nation, but by articulating their demands to the national project. In the documents analyzed the articulation of enemies to the national project is based on a widely disclosed fantasy in which the nation is described as a country in which 'ethnic, regional and cultural diversity continues to play a crucial role'[11] (Brazil, Secretaria de Educação Fundamental 1998a: 16): a singular country 'due to its special historical constitution in the cultural field', which 'represents, in the world scenario, a hope for overcoming frontiers and building a relationship of trust in humanity' (Brazil, Secretaria de Educação Fundamental 1998c: 121). This fantasy is so entrenched that it appears even in the constitutional definition of the country as a 'fraternal, pluralist society without prejudices, founded on social harmony' (Brazil, Congresso Brasileiro 1988). In the documents analyzed, that fantasy of society is referred to as 'Brazilian sociocultural heritage', an expression used countless times in all the documents and whose valorization is one of the objectives of elementary school education (Brazil, Secretaria de Educação Fundamental 1998a: 55).

Diversity in the Brazilian cultural heritage does not appear as a recent phenomenon, nor is it described as depending on migrations originating from globalization or from criticisms of the concept of national. It is, rather, characteristic of a nation with a violent history of slavery and open to immigration. It is also peculiar to a society with major regional inequalities that provoke internal diasporas. Without deeper historical analyses of these phenomena, with the partial exception of the African diaspora which is emphasized in the transversal topic 'Cultural Plurality', Brazil is being presented as a plural country, in such a remote way that it is as if it were its vocation:

> Cohabiting today on national territory are around 206 indigenous ethnic groups … together with an immense population formed by the descendents of African people and a numerous group of immigrants and descendents of peoples from various continents, with different cultural and religious traditions. The difficulty of classifying the groups that came to Brazil and formed its population is indicative of the diversity, whether of the continental, or regional, national, religious, cultural, linguistic or racial/ethnic profile … Diversity marks Brazilian social life.
>
> (Brazil, Secretaria de Educação Fundamental 1998c: 24, 25)

Although still talking about migrations and that diversity involving migrant ethnic groups, as well as indigenous peoples, the idea of migration is lost in a distant past, as 'Brazilian sociocultural heritage'. In that sense, the national identity has as a 'fundamental trait' the 'affirmation of diversity' (Brazil, Secretaria de Educação Fundamental 1998c: 121). The insertion of the demands of diversity in the idea of nation depends, however, on erasing part of its literal content, which facilitates the articulations so as to enable the nation to continue resting on a homogeneity that includes diversity as another side of it. With that I do not want to say that the insertion of the demands of diversity have not altered the meanings of national, which have to be negotiated with its enemies. I am just saying that as a way of facilitating the balance of positions that sustains the hegemony of the nation as an articulating nucleus of the policies, those demands need to be divested of their radicality, radicality being understood as the possibility of existing as a legitimate other.

With diversity shared and inscribed in a kind of national past, the commitment to citizenship becomes a commitment to the diversity which justifies, also, the proposition of a national curricular policy.

> It is important that there should be parameters on the basis of which the country's educational system is organized, in order to guarantee that, beyond the cultural, regional, ethnic, religious and political diversities that permeate a multiple and complex society, the democratic principles that define citizenship are also guaranteed.
>
> (Brazil, Secretaria de Educação Fundamental 1998a: 50)

When justifying the national curriculum policy, as well as when defining it, the meanings of pluricultural national citizenship slide again, to the effect of signifiXating citizenship as something that recognizes national diversity, but which needs to guarantee something that goes beyond that diversity. In the first versions of the documents, one of the expressions of that 'goes beyond' was insertion in a global work market which called for high standards of performance and which made citizenship viable based on consumption. That sense was erased from subsequent versions,[12] expressing the difficulty of hegemonizing it. On different fronts, the scholars' criticisms of a (post-)modernized social efficiency[13] were very strong, to the point that the few references to globalization were made in the context of affirmation of the place and of the national:

> In a world marked by a process of cultural worldization and economic globalization, international political forums take on growing importance. Nonetheless ... the pursuit of a society integrated into the environment in which the nearest 'other' is found, in the closest community and in the nation itself, arises as a need for attaining the integration of humanity as a whole.
>
> (Brazil, Secretaria de Educação Fundamental 1998a: 16)

There is another 'beyond' that gains prominence in the different meanings assumed by pluricultural national citizenship in Brazil, mentioned in the above quotations and in many other passages of the documents. The Ministry of Education's standards allude to that 'beyond' to defend the need for 'national references that can say what are the "common points" that characterize the educative phenomenon in all Brazilian regions' (Brazil, Secretaria de Educação Fundamental 1998a: 49). Accordingly, pluricultural national citizenship incorporates and valorizes the country's cultural diversity at the same time as it establishes a common horizon for everyone, as a way of guaranteeing 'the democratic principles that define citizenship'. This movement is understandable in a country with profound economic and social inequalities that end up producing very specific articulations between demands for recognition of cultural and racial particularities and for economic and social equality.

> One must consider the principle of equity, that is, that there are differences (ethnic, cultural, regional, gender, age group, religious etc.) and inequalities (socioeconomic) that need to be taken into account for equality to be really attained.
>
> (Brazil, Secretaria de Educação Fundamental 1998b: 21)

When translating that plural national citizenship which seeks equality in terms of a pedagogic discourse, new articulations are established that expand the fluctuations of the meanings of that citizenship. Also in this case, there are very effective shared historical meanings in the signifXation processes. The role of the school in training that citizenship explains even more clearly its connections with a goal of equality going beyond diversity, 'guaranteeing the access of citizens to the whole of public assets, among which are included that of socially relevant knowledge'[14] (Brazil, Secretaria de Educação Fundamental 1998a: 50).

By these means, the role of the school in producing the plural national citizen – he/she who masters socially accumulated knowledge – reintroduces the enemy which symbolically closes the idea of plural national citizen. If non-citizenship, as a social problem, lies in all the documents in the form of rhetoric of absence, at that moment, it becomes more explicit when localized in the subject who does not master that knowledge. Unlike plural citizenship, which is national, non-citizenship is the property of the subjects. As such, its principal reference is not stories of segregation and prejudice, but the non-mastery of basic knowledge required for the full exercise of plural national citizenship. Therefore, besides the enemy being an individual, what characterizes him as such is something that is outside him and which can be acquired, provided there is a quality educative intervention. That horizon without enemies, an illusion of total inclusion, transforms plural and inclusive national citizenship into an excellent articulating nucleus of the discourse of the reform, permitting stabilization of the hegemonic articulations that are at the base of the curricular policies. Like every powerful closing, it excludes other meanings producing certainties that naturalize the exclusions.

About Exclusions

I wanted throughout this chapter to understand how curricular texts were being constituted as discursive closings that mobilize intentionalities and propose preferential forms of readings. Certainly there is no text without closings; every text creates symbolic places in which it intends to put its readers. In the case of texts that intend to intervene, such as political texts, it is still more crucial to create those places, even if that intention requires them also to make contact with those they hope to persuade. Even if there are other constraints, the curricula can only intervene if they are read and if they convince the reader of the adequacy of the addressings they propose. I am using the term addressings to indicate the way the text addresses its readers so they perceive themselves to be the intended readers of the text and so that they also position themselves as open to the message of the text. The effectiveness of address as an instrument of intervention depends, therefore, on its waiving its intention of absolute control. It is a paradox with which curricular policies need to live. Clearly, total saturation would not even be possible, because as political texts they are constructed by many hands in the midst of negotiations and agreements.

The texts of recent national curricular policies in Brazil project the citizen as a preferential identity and construct around it an aura of positivity as a way of making intervention more effective. When mobilizing different meanings, the documents present citizenship as a desire of all society, in which there are no exclusions, except those that may be overcome with the actual intervention. With that, citizenship becomes a very powerful projected identity, contributing toward erasing the difference as the actual deferment of meanings that is in the basis of the discursive. Textual formations articulated around metaphorical signifiers like citizenship try to hinder the proliferation of meanings specific to the *différance*.

At this point it is important to recognize that the strong role that policies give school training in citizenship is experienced also by the uneducated in a country where, for example, the illiteracy rate of people over 15 years was 13.6 per cent (MEC/INEP n.d.) in the last census in 2000. To what degree does making the schooling essential for participation in civic life deprive the uneducated subjects of their claim to national citizenship?

Testimonials in which underemployed adults attribute their economic situation to their uneducated condition show that the connections between education and more effective participation in national life are very strong. The importance that uneducated parents give to school as a way for their children to have access to the world of formal work confirms such connections. The exclusion of the rights that an inclusive citizenship could ensure, despite its complexity, is in many cases seen as a consequence of lack of education, motivated both by economic difficulties that kept the subjects away from school as by lack of personal interest.

Since, however, almost all children aged 6 to 14 years have access to school, let us return to the school´s subjects. How may they experience the emptying of meaning that makes citizenship a strong and, at the same time, ambivalent principle around which the curriculum is articulated? And, how may they experience attempts to fix these meanings around a remarkably universal identity? We must remember that the experiences of these individuals are varied and not always linked to collective belongings such as social class, race or professional identity.

The strength of citizenship as a nodal point that articulates the curriculum national policies derives from a certain emptiness of meanings which facilitates the articulation of demands from different subjects. Beyond the strength of the concept of citizenship, such emptying implies also the non-fulfillment of any specific demand. All groups are represented in the ambivalence of the project of citizenship while they see their wishes on behalf of the articulation diluted. The project also becomes ambivalent in its interaction with the individuals who see themselves as citizens at the expense of a certain self-estrangement. Such movement is experienced not only by students but also by teachers within schools, and perhaps explains why the project of citizenship is both a project for everyone and for no one. The task of training for citizenship has been taken up by students and teachers, but, at the same time, there is some concern that this may entail adherence to an empty slogan. This mixture of acceptance and distrust has facilitated the assertion of the citizenship's idea with universal speeches as those present in policy documents and also in classrooms.

The longing for a safe answer about what would constitute training for citizenship is the context in which the universalisms gain strength. This longing is visible among teachers, but society in general seems to confirm this need when it nostalgically states that the school was once much better. This link with the past does not, however, take the centrality of education for citizenship, but justifies the importance of its coherence and authority with contents seen as universally relevant. On behalf of inclusive citizenship, a belief in universal knowledge penetrates into the curriculum. This is not possible without a more or less radical exclusion of some individuals.

The most obvious form of exclusion is experienced by students who are expelled from school. Of course, the high school dropout rates in Brazil have strong economic roots, but multiple repetitions have been a strong supporting factor in this process. It is common for children to hear, especially from parents of the popular classes and even children themselves, that they have a 'weak head', and therefore are not able to learn. In this case, it is worth not insisting on going to school. Insofar as there is a requirement, they make school enrollments every year, but they participate only for a few months of school activities. They tell themselves that citizenship, although for all, is not for them. They realize the selectivity of the term 'all' in public policies in Brazil, while living the deep experience of exclusion, not from school, but from the 'all' which refers to citizenship. This experience has been more common in lower social classes, but also for blacks and for children from the poorest geographical regions of the country (MEC/IBGE n.d.).

For those who stay in school, the experience of dealing with an ambivalent project of citizenship involves negotiating their identity attachments with the idea of becoming a Brazilian citizen. This negotiation is experienced differently by each individual and constitutes us all as hybrid subjects. In this way, teachers and students live the common experience, reinscribing it on their culture, but at the same time, giving up part of that culture. For black students and teachers, for example, this experience incorporates part of their demands as a group, while it leads them to an identification with a national citizen as it is proposed as a master identity. In the same way, national identity is presented to the working class as a horizon of formation that appears to be fictitious for them, as it is not lived in their daily lives. The ambivalence of the citizenship agenda confuses educators and teachers do not know how to recontextualize curriculum policies in their schools, and students estrange themselves, even while recognizing that parts of their demands are being attended to.

As I consider this project of citizenship, I must question how it affects the educational process that enables the other to be a singular other – not one that someone else has invented (Derrida 1989: 59). I am concerned about the politics of recognition in the citizenship agenda that 'the Other' from being other in full: that makes him a project of himself.

Although I am not referring to any particular identity, they end up in the center of the task of deconstructing the hegemonized discourses. Universalized discourses, as we have seen, have a symbolic force that makes them powerful fragments in the construction of the new text. They are defended by groups that have greater control of the apparatus of signification and, as a result, become more easily hegemonic. In that sense, those who have less opportunity of signifiXating, generate peripheral discourses, produced on the sidelines. Thus, in the case of national, plural and inclusive citizenship, the struggles of the minorities for the valorization of their demands expanded the notion of citizenship in such a way as to embody cultural plurality. At the same time, however, that plurality was integrated as a national trait and incorporated to the Enlightenment discourse of valorizing the knowledge accumulated by humanity. That is why the task of decentering the text that naturalizes citizenship as identity projected for everyone is urgent. I think that this is the possible contribution of the theoretical debate to the change. To deconstruct what displeases us, to denaturalize the obvious, although it may not be sufficient, is a condition necessary for subverting the mechanisms that prevent us from doing what is not foreseen on the agenda.

Notes

1 The National Curriculum Council was created by Law in 1995 with the aim of collaborating in the formulation of national education policy and to exercise regulatory functions, deliberative and advisory services of the Ministry of Education. Its members are appointed by the President of the Republic, but at least half its members must be chosen from among members appointed by civil society institutions related to education. The National Education Guidelines and Foundations Act determined that the development of national guidelines for all levels of education would be a function of this Council.

2 An empty signifier is a 'point inside the system of signification which is constitutively unrepresentable; which, in that sense continues empty, but is a vacuum that can be signified because it is a vacuum inside the signification' (Laclau 2008: 136).

3 As a subject of lack.

4 And other nodal points around which the curricular texts are constructed.

5 The myth of the three races, which spreads the idea that the fusion of black, white and indigenous people is the main element of identity that constitutes Brazilian nationality, makes the discussion of racism complicated. It is a myth built early in the twentieth century, based on questioning of theories that defined racial miscegenation as degeneration. Although from this perspective it can be seen as anti-racist, this myth conceals the deep hierarchy of the Brazilian social system with the idea of racial democracy that paradoxically can only exist because such hierarchies ensure the superiority of white as the dominant group (Matta 1971).

6 It is important to emphasize that the reforms of the 1930s ended up more strongly contributing toward forming a national elite.

7 From the 1950s to 1990, debates on the adaptation of national curriculums were intense. Although there were no national curriculums in the period, general legislation on education tended to blend common curricular bases with diversified activities.

8 Mercosur is the Southern Common Market comprising Argentina, Paraguay, Uruguay, Brazil and, recently, Venezuela.

9 The standards in action constitute a project for continued training of teachers for using the NCS and the national curricular references. They are in the format of study modules, with support from other media, in which collective activities are proposed for teachers. Although they are available for general access, the national ministry proposes to education departments of states and municipalities that they should use them in training courses. There are modules common to teachers as a whole and others organized by subjects.

10 This without mentioning that both the standards and the teacher training documents and the program of textbooks have, in their own titles, the national adjective.

11 Although the myth of the three races, which maintains that Brazil is formed by the contribution of the three races – whites, blacks and indigenous peoples – has been strongly criticized for several decades, it still prevails in the basis of affirmations like these.

12 That does not mean erasing the importance of the work, which continued, in some passages, to be an educative principle, in a Marxist reading widely disseminated in Brazil. As that reading is associated with the defense of knowledges socially accumulated as curricular content, which I will take up further on, I will not dwell on it.

13 I am not arguing that the perspective of (post-)modernized social efficiency, in which economic and social development would assume more individual patterns, is absent

from the documents, but that it does not happen via valorization of the school for direct insertion in the market.

14 The emphasis with which the school should treat socially relevant knowledge is defended in Brazil by countless authors, aggregated under the heading of critical-historical pedagogy. I feel, however, that here we can also see traces that are visible in various countries (Young 2009; Taylor *et al.* 1997) and which could be indicated as a return to the basic.

References

Anderson, B. (1983) *Imagined Communities: On the origin and spread of nationalism.* London: Verso.

Bauman, Z. (2005) *Identidade*, Rio de Janeiro: Jorge Zahar.

Bhabha, H. (2003) *O local de cultura*, Belo Horizonte: UFMG.

Brazil, Congresso Brasileiro (1988) *Constituição da República Federativa do Brasil*, Brasília: Presidência da República.

Brazil, Ministério da Educação, Secretaria de Educação Fundamental (1999) *Parâmetros Curriculares Nacionais em ação*, Brasília: MEC.

Brazil, Ministério da Educação, Secretaria de Educação Básica (2007) *Guia de livros didáticos PNLD: Ciências*, Brasília: MEC.

Brazil, Secretaria de Educação Fundamental (1998a) *Parâmetros Curriculares Nacionais: Introdução*, Brasília: MEC.

Brazil, Secretaria de Educação Fundamental (1998b) *Parâmetros Curriculares Nacionais: Temas Transversais*, Brasília: MEC.

Brazil, Secretaria de Educação Fundamental (1998c) *Parâmetros Curriculares Nacionais: Pluralidade Cutural*, Brasília: MEC.

Chaterjee, P. (2000) 'Comunidade imaginada por quem?', in G. Balakrishnan (ed.) *Um mapa da questão nacional*, Rio de Janeiro: Contraponto.

Derrida, J. (1989) 'Psyche: inventions of the Other', in L. Waters and W. Godzich (eds) *Reading de Man Reading*, Minneapolis, MN: University of Minnesota Press.

Hall, S. (2003) *Da diáspora: Identidades e mediações culturais*, Belo Horizonte: UFMG.

Harding, S. (2000) 'Gender, development and post-enlightenment philosophies of science', in U. Narayan and S. Harding (eds) *Decentering the Center: Philosophy for a multicultural, postcolonial and feminist world*, Indianapolis, IN: Indiana University Press.

Laclau, E. (1998) 'Desconstrucción, pragmatismo, hegemonía', in C. Mouffe (ed.) *Desconstrucción y pragmatismo*, Buenos Aires: Paidós.

Laclau, E. (2008) *La razón populista*, Buenos Aires: Fondo de Cultura Económica.

Laclau, E. and Mouffe, C. (2004) *Hegemonia y estratégia socialista,* Buenos Aires: Fondo de cultura econômica.

Matta, R. (1971) *Relativizando: uma introdução à Antropologia Social*, Petrópolis Vozes.

MEC/INEP (n,d,) *Mapa do analfabetismo no Brasil*, Brasília: INEP.

Shawver, L. (2010) 'Derrida's Concept of DifferAnce'. Online. Available HTTP: <http://users.sfo.com/~rathbone/differan.htm> (accessed 5 August 2010).

Taylor, S., Rizvi, F., Lingard, B., and Henry, M. (1997) *Educational Policy and the Politics of Change*, London/New York: Routledge.

Willinsky, J. (1998) *Learning to Divide the World: Education at empire's end*, Minneapolis, MN: University of Minnesota Press.

Young, M. (2009) *Conhecimento e currículo,* Porto: Porto Editora.

Zizek, S. (1990) 'Eastern Europe's republics of Gilead', *New Left Review*, 183: 51–62.

5   Conceptualising Curriculum Knowledge Within and Beyond the National Context[1]

Berit Karseth and Kirsten Sivesind

Introduction

In 2006, the world marked the 100th anniversary of the death of the Norwegian playwright Henrik Ibsen. Despite his continued popularity worldwide, recent curriculum debates in Norway reveal some concern that students may leave school without having read any of his works. There are even some claims that students in China read more Ibsen than Norwegian students! (Engelsen and Karseth, 2007). The Ibsen discussion emerges from an important and recurrent question pertaining to curricula: 'what knowledge is of most worth for the millennial citizen'? (Muller, 2000, p. 41). This issue is at the heart of every curriculum that is devised and the answers depend on the responses and claims that gain legitimacy within and beyond the national context.

In this article, we shall examine the possible implications of globalisation for curriculum design and how subject matter is defined so as to respond to new demands. Questions arise when aims, processes and outcomes detail historical and cultural dimensions of content as part of curriculum guidelines. Can a national culture be described through examples like Ibsen's plays, and will they embody values that are relevant for a global context? Is there a public legitimacy for the cultivation of national cultures as an overall purpose of the curriculum and how does this match ideas of qualifying students for life? These problems relate not only to the conceptualisation of subject matter, but also to its link to the outside world and the contexts of schooling.

This article discusses alternative routes for nations to respond to global demands, balancing cultivation and qualification as complementary parts of curriculum and schooling. The two last curriculum reforms in Norway serve as a point of departure. First, we shall briefly introduce global issues in curriculum theory. Second, we shall outline the methodology of our analysis. Then, we shall undertake a content analysis of curriculum policy and design and compare the two reforms in terms of how they approach global cultures through national reform. Finally, we shall study professional semantics which play a mediating role between reform efforts and schooling. By referring to both the North-Continental and Anglo-American curriculum theory, we shall attempt to merge different traditions and sophisticated theoretical arguments about the way knowledge is dealt with in curriculum policy and schooling.

National Curriculum Guidelines and Globalising Policies

The modern history of national curriculum guidelines for compulsory education in Norway dates back more than 100 years and is part of attempts for Norway to become a nation. Therefore, ideas of national culture are central in the construction of knowledge through reform and schooling, although contested and adjusted along the way.

An important force for change is political ideas and efforts to create what is known as a social democratic welfare state associated with the Scandinavian model (Talhuag *et al.*, 2004, p. 143).This model combines local requests and developments with a strong, active and interventionist State and has resulted in several national curricula (Gundem, 1993b; Sivesind, 2008). Moreover, institutions for professionalising teachers and supporting staff were established, influencing how curriculum was formulated, interpreted and put into practice (Bachmann, 2005; Skarpenes, 2004). However, both reform and the institutional design of curriculum and teacher education are being questioned, as are the professional semantics of Didaktik/didaktikk (Hamilton, 1999).[2] Daily news and other channels for public discourse report on the low quality of schooling and degrees of achievement in the last decades. National reform, schooling and teacher education are criticised for not satisfying societal expectations. International assessments, national tests, and research evaluations challenge not only the design of reform, but also public opinion about the curriculum and comprehensive schooling (Elstad, 2009; Hopmann, 2007a; Langfeldt, 2008).

On this basis, organisations such as OECD advocate a new political technology where formalised curriculum-making is ignored or even contested in favour of assessment and accountability systems. A probable consequence of the new recommendations is that national politics will transform the curriculum as part of an overall globalisation.This is supported by current research on reform and curriculum. According to John Meyer (2006), curriculum reform worldwide seems to follow common general ideas on how education should prepare the individual and the national state to become part of a world society. Based on an analysis of curriculum research in several countries, he argues that the modern world society builds on the idea of 'an expansive conception of the individual human person, being a member of a human society as a whole rather than principally as the citizen of a nation-state' (p. 264). This is reported along with other studies by Moritz Rosenmund in his comparison of curriculum guidelines from 100 countries collected by the International Bureau of Education, UNESCO. A general trend is that curriculum guidelines shift from being content-oriented to being learning-oriented and individuals are seen as self-regulated in their approach to knowledge and the curriculum (Rosenmund, 2006).

Although many nations create their own guidelines, they are changing with global demands. According to Meyer, curriculum researchers show significant variations in the implementation and management of reforms, but they do not legitimate these by references to national structures (p. 265). Hence, Meyer questions the role of states in creating a global heterogeneity through national reform. Formal curriculum documents refer to multiple contexts, from the global to the local.

There are several signs of an emerging standardisation which support Meyer's conclusion. In Norway, international studies like PISA play a significant role in legitimating new educational policy (Elstad and Sivesind, 2010). They offer new conceptualisations of subject matter as competences in and across subject areas, which are formally distinguished from national cultures and a school curriculum. Besides, a national system for quality assessment presumes goals of learnable knowledge and skills in accordance with formulas that are defined internationally. In the new frameworks for national testing, the content of schooling is redefined in terms of competence aims, detailing levels of achievement in certain areas. These evaluations partly contest the formal curriculum and become reactive to what is considered as the main purposes and aims of schooling (Lundgren, 2006).

Reformers have, as Gita Steiner-Khamsi (2009) puts it, 'come to accept the existence of transnational regimes in education' (p. 67). These regimes are based on a belief in the importance of evidence-based policy for development matters and the need to establish 'knowledge banks' with comparative data. Hence, there is a call for more R&D activities which produce a systematic knowledge base and could lead to more research-informed educational policies and practices (Burns and Schuller, 2007). The power of transnational actors is obvious as comparative data become a source of authority for assessing national educational reforms.

However, can we conclude that the history of national reform loses its relevance in the current interpretation of curriculum and culture? An alternative understanding is that continents and countries renew their traditions and curriculum designs to respond to global expectations and standards by adjusting their own policy to global requests and demands. Hence, they can also become active participants in a worldwide society by formulating and distributing texts as a central force in renewing curriculum and schooling globally.

Methodological Approach

Our analysis is based on an examination of core policy documents and curriculum guidelines from the two latest reforms between the early 1990s and the mid-2000s in Norway. The first is *Curriculum Guidelines for Compulsory School* (L97) (The Royal Ministry of Education, Research and Church Affairs, 1996) and the second is *Knowledge Promotion*, which is still under revision (LK06) (The Royal Ministry of Education and Research, 2006). Both start out with the Core Curriculum of 1993 (L93) (The Royal Ministry of Education, Research and Church Affairs, 1994), which describes the legitimating rationales and goals for comprehensive schooling in Norway.

All guidelines were formulated as main elements in reform design, involving many groups and persons who were assigned by the executive agency for the Ministry of Education and Research (which became The Norwegian Directorate for Education and Training in 2009). Their drafts of a new curriculum guideline were finally approved by the Ministry of Education and Research in 2005 after rehearsals which initiated political and public discussions. Green and white papers were produced, which are also referred to in this article.

Several strategies are promising for examining public documents of this kind (Andersen, 2003). This article uses a content analysis strategy which considers histories and the use of language as significant concerns. It is inspired by discourse analysis, since we study the way policy texts are shaped through the configuration of concepts and arguments in use. But such an analysis does not provide information about the consequences of policies, but about which policy problems and goals are brought to the fore and which are left aside (Saarinen, 2008). It can also conclude about the potentials of reform in terms of its use. However, the interpretations here will not only reject discursive practices, but also form and content, as they take shape in curriculum guidelines considered as texts. Such guidelines primarily describe programmes for education, with their specification of overall purposes, content and organisational arrangements, including evaluation (Reid, 1999).

In our content analysis, we apply a combination of a theory-driven and realistic-orientated text interpretation, where alternative configurations of concepts such as curriculum aims and subject matter are discussed. In the first part, we look for the way content matter is conceptualised in view of globalising concerns and how it is politically legitimated in white and green papers. The Core Curriculum is of particular interest in this regard, since it calls for a global heterogeneity through national reform and thereby defends a national cultural heritage in view of a globalising order.

In the next section, we compare the two formal curriculum guidelines of 1997 and 2006 and question whether they represent two designs or models of reform. Here, we use a comparative strategy to examine how curriculum knowledge is formulated to frame teaching and learning practices. As we will see, the texts refer not only to the overall visions of curriculum policy, but also to earlier texts which constitute an institutional force in representing their own histories and languages, such as professional semantics. Curriculum is, in these semantics, conceptualised in terms of theories which deal with paradoxes of schooling and reform beyond the national context.

In the last section, we discuss how theories and professional semantics deal with contradictions between a formalisation of curriculum and individuals' autonomy to decide upon their own values, cultures and meaning-making. Global requests for individualisation create possibilities for defining and redefining what constitutes the cultures of the world, but at the same time, make students responsible for their capacity to deal with what counts as subject matter.

In Norway, there is a long tradition of curriculum research of which documentary analysis of this kind is an integral part. Documents examined in this article have been the object of many research projects, reports and articles (Bachmann, 2005; Bachmann *et al.*, 2004; Engelsen, 2008; Engelsen and Karseth, 2007; Sivesind, 2002). This article refers to examinations and conclusions in earlier studies (Engelsen, 2008; Engelsen and Karseth, 2007; Gundem, 1995; Gundem, 1996) and adds new insights into the relationship between global changes and national curriculum reform as viewed from a North-Continental perspective.

Curriculum Policy: Approaching Culture and Content in National Reform

Promoting Global Cultural Heterogeneity Through National Reform

Most twentieth-century European curriculum reforms were developed by the nation-state, reflecting both the world and the *Bildung* of the population. *Bildung* in this context is regarded as something to approach by educating the individual as well as the public. Institutional arrangements like schooling are essential for this pursuit and relate to both cultivation and formation of individual and societal requests (Hopmann and Riquarts, 2000; Westbury, 2000). Moreover, since nation-states are the locus of change, they have also become the locus for citizens' identities (Keating *et al.*, 2009). Formal curriculum documents constitute this history, empowering states to regulate how the outside world will be reflected within a geographical territory, although not by sanctioning individuals in their views of the world. Hence, the rationale for reform in the 1990s and 2000s reflects not only a history of nation-building, but also a history of students' individual autonomy.

Although the nation-state was in a phase of transition in the 1990s, losing its clear-cut role as the place for government and reform-making, the Ministry of Education put forward arguments for developing a common history and a language of the nation (Gundem and Karseth, 1998, Gundem and Sivesind, 1996). Concerning formal curriculum making, this included content descriptions of what counted as subject matter in the daily practice of teachers and learners (Hopmann and Riquarts, 2000). Below, we quote a paragraph from the preface of L97 (English version) that underscores this cultural orientation:

> One of the most significant developments in the new curriculum is that greater emphasis has been placed on a central curriculum. This is intended to ensure a nation-wide education system with a common content of knowledge, traditions and values regardless of where the pupils live, their social background, gender, religion or their mental or physical ability. At the same time there is still room for local and individual choice and adoption, which is a long-standing principle in the Norwegian school policy (p. 5).

The content will not only be represented at large, but will contribute to the personal development of the citizen. Cultural heritage is considered as an important source in two respects. *Personal* identity is developed by becoming familiar with inherited forms of conduct, norms of behaviour and modes of expression to become cultivated. The curriculum should therefore develop the learner's familiarity with national and local traditions. One argument is that the bonds between generations are closer when they share experiences and insights, stories, songs and legends. In addition, if society is going to remain *democratic*, the curriculum must play a leading role in passing on the common cultural heritage.

However, the main arguments for a centralisation of content related to *equity and equal rights* adhere to a more subtle line of thought: in an increasingly specialised society, common frames of references must be the property of all in order to avoid differences in competence that may become *social inequality* and be abused by undemocratic forces. From this point of view, the political discourse revolves around the ideas of cultural integration and how to design good conditions for students to develop literal knowledge and skills.

One argument, according to Gundem, is that those who do not share the background information that is taken for granted in public discourse will often overlook the points in question and miss the meaning (Gundem, 1996). In this sense, *newcomers* to the country are more easily incorporated into society when implicit features of the *cultural heritage are made clear*, such as knowledge about past events and achievements. Professor Gudmund Hernes, who initiated the reform as the then Minister of Education and Research, argued for enculturation as important for citizenship. Highly inspired by what is known as cultural literacy, knowledge of the cultural heritage is important to become a world citizen (Hernes, 2008; Hirsch, 1985). Cultivation and civilization are considered as two sides of the same coin.

The capacity to communicate across cultures is also required in working life and within the public discourse. Without an overarching comprehension of culture the Ministry argues that it would be difficult for non-specialists to participate in decisions that affect their lives (The Royal Ministry of Education, Research and Church Affairs, 1994, pp. 26–27).

The curriculum policy asserts that the combination of new information technology and travel, together with the globalisation of the world economy, imply a rapid distribution of knowledge and innovation. Knowledge development is significant for the economic and technological balance and competitiveness between countries. In this situation, cultural heritage and traditions could stimulate knowledge creation and discovery.

From this cultural-economic point of view, new problems arise in policy as well as in society. A possible threat to globalisation and the use of new technology is *cultural convergence*, which leads to the following conclusion: a renewed focus on national identity is needed to ensure a *multicultural society*. National cultures contribute to the world culture by stimulating a multicultural language within a global context. Hence, the arguments for designing a curriculum which defines a common content of schooling seek to create a global cultural heterogeneity through national reform. These ideas were included in the new Core Curriculum, launched in 1993 and which was translated into Chinese, English, French, German, and Russian (The Norwegian Directorate for Training and Education, 1994). Not only were foreigners invited to read the overall vision of education, but the text was distributed globally to symbolise national policy and goals. It seeks to realise ideas of the 1990s policy in Norway, marketing Norway in the global society, yet it is also motivated by an ideals approach to create a global cultural heterogeneity through national language and reform.

Promoting Global Culture by Value and Competence

In the 2000s, reform strategies indicated a new orientation towards a global language of reform, focusing on competence aims, skills and capacities of learning. This new policy adjusts to strategies and concepts advocated by OECD and seems to be inspired by new forms of governance in what is conceptualised as the knowledge society. The following compares white and green papers from the two decades.

In both decades, a combination of cultural and instrumental purposes was formulated in policy documents, linking economic progress to moral and political values. The 1990 reform was legitimated by a societal approach, yet it maintained a normative foundation by focusing on interaction and companionship between people. It claimed to have a dialectical relationship between individuals' fulfilment of their own capacity legitimated by the aims of societal development 'towards democratic participation and solidarity, towards economic growth and force of development, towards cultural aptitude and compassion' (Report No. 40 to the Storting, 1990–91, p. 2). It also emphasised humanity as a facet of the interactive relationship between individuals: 'Knowledge is a resource that is not restricted when it is shared; humanity is a value, which increases when people fully exploit themselves in companionship with each other' (Report No. 40 to the Storting, 1990–91, p. 2).

Likewise, the policy at the turn of the century adheres to societal and valuable growth, but unlike in the former, the knowledge society is viewed as a changing arrangement which supports, but does not guarantee, self-fulfilment. It focuses on knowledge and creativity and on human capital: 'the most important input-factors in working life are not longer economical capital, buildings and equipment, but the humans themselves' (Report No. 30 to the Storting, 2003–2004, p. 23).

In both cases, knowledge is considered as increasing in value when it is shared, but according to the last report, not by companionships but by being shared and used. There are nuances in the conceptualisations of what a knowledge society means for citizens. In the first phase, individuals are considered as persons who deal and work with knowledge in different contexts, such as higher education, while in the second phase, knowledge is seen as becoming 'an increasingly important source and a driving force' for individual societal success within a society which is 'ever more complex and diverse'. It is stated that 'Since society constantly changes, schools cannot supply pupils with all the knowledge they will need as adult citizens. However, it is important that schools give pupils the basis they need for lifelong learning' (Report No. 30 to the Storting, 2003/2004, p. 23).

In the first run a Coleman-inspired orientation is evident. Individuals create and recreate societies in all their complexities, whilst in the next phase post-modern liberalism seems to take over, providing students with opportunities to develop and learn as individuals. Moreover, in the last phase, international test scores are referred to as an evaluation of the former policy, which implies this change.

It is stated in the report that few countries spend as much money on education as Norway. In our country, the report continues, there is 'broad political consensus about the objectives of education — to give children and young people opportunities for general education, personal development, knowledge and skills' (Report No. 30 to the Storting, 2003/2004, p. 3). All the same, the white paper goes on, Norwegian and international research show, that our school system has weaknesses. Many pupils underachieve and complete their education with poor results and there are large differences due to social background. Furthermore, education is not sufficiently customised and tailored to meet individual needs and the culture for learning is poorly developed. The report recommends improving these weaknesses by developing a national test system and increasing the competence of teachers, school leaders and administrators through the establishment of a *culture of learning*. A solution to this is differentiation through a decentralised policy where the single municipality and schools are considered as the sites for change (Hopmann, 2007a). Moreover, the individual student is the core object of change. According to this idea, training in skills should be the core of schooling, while a common content is ignored in favour of learning which is differentiated in regard to individual needs. The same idea seems to be advocated worldwide, pinpointing individualisation as a solution to curriculum change. Again we can ask: *What are the implications of a new global language for descriptions of culture and how can it be dealt with in national curriculum reform?*

Types of Curriculum Designs

We shall now compare subject curricula in the curriculum guidelines with regard to their way of formulating aims and content. The first reform specifies subject matter according to what content should be the base for students' learning (The Royal Ministry of Education, Research and Church Affairs, 1999). This content is described through topics, concepts and a cultural canon and specified by names of authors and artists and historical events. In the introduction to Arts and Crafts, we can read the following:

> In a society undergoing constant change, experience of art, architecture, design, applied arts and crafts — from past and present, from one's own culture and from others' — provides an important frame of reference for cultural insights. Roots in one's own culture make a secure foundation for identity and for respect for new and unfamiliar impressions and forms of expression
>
> (L97, p. 204).

The first reform emphasises topical interests and interdisciplinary work, as well as ways of working with the content. Very importantly, the principles and guidelines in this curriculum do not conceptualise methodical aspects which profile semantics of effective learning but specify the amount of subject-oriented teaching and project work at different levels.

However, a more learning-oriented approach is persistent in the new subject curricula in the reform of the 2000s, and forms of work described earlier in aims are excluded in favour of a general idea of individual learning strategies as a main principle to strengthen basic skills. In the new curriculum, the principle of learning is also built into the concept of how to improve learning by expressing oneself orally, writing, developing numeracy and using digital tools. Aims of learning relate to student activities which can be assessed within the school practice and centre on the improvement of knowledge and skills. This is a methodical aspect rather than an interactive approach and is more oriented towards learning outcomes than the former L97.

To describe content in terms of main subject areas, which structure but give no clear-cut descriptions of what to teach, is obviously the most radical change of LK06. This shift is, above all, a question of form and language, of how competence aims are defined in different grades. This change breaks away from the form that has been decisive to curricula in Norway since 1890 (Gundem, 1993a; Gundem, 1993b). However, does this new approach exclude content and a culture of knowledge as elements in the subject curricula? In the area of Arts and Crafts, we can read:

> The perception of art, design and architecture are along with raising the awareness of our cultural heritage in a global perspective, important aspects of the subject ... Understanding the arts and crafts of the past and the present in one's own culture and that of others may provide the basis for developing our multicultural society.
>
> (LK06, p. 1).

From this citation, it seems that the approach of L97 is still alive. Moreover, national culture is considered as the starting point for social deliberations relating to history and society. Still, it proclaims an old distinction by the use of us/our and the others/unfamiliar. This is a common trait of both reforms, as illustrated by the following example drawn from history in the latest reform where it is stated that the major aim of teaching is 'linguistic confidence and a belief in one's own culture as the basis for development of identity, respect for other cultures, active social participation and lifelong learning' (p. 1).

The subject curriculum in Norwegian (in LK06) considers subject matter as placed between the historical and the contemporary and the national and global. Paradoxes in reform are made evident as a consequence of the opposite environments of the curriculum. Considered historically, this tells us that formal curriculum is not considered as a buffer-zone for political values and conflicts.

Whereas the subject curricula of L97 present detailed descriptions of topics that pupils should learn from, LK06 describes what they should be able to do in more practical terms. For instance, while it is stated in L97 that pupils in grade 9 should have the opportunity to 'consider the ideological foundations of Fascism and Nazism so as to be able to develop reasoned attitudes to those ideologies and their modern offshoots' (p. 198), LK06 states that pupils after year 10 should be able to 'present a historic event based on different ideologies' (p. 6). Moreover, the new curriculum of the 2000s embraces a concept of standards or levels of goal achievement, although there are not yet descriptions of such levels within the subject curricula (Kunnskapsdepartementet and Utdanningsdirektoratet, 2006, p. 9).

How the learning aims are formulated varies across subjects. Some are defined precisely and are related to basic skills, e.g. 'the students should be able to count to 100' by the end of second grade (Mathematics). Others are more general and it is therefore more difficult to measure the learning outcomes. For instance, students at the end of the 7th grade should be able to discuss how language represents expressions and attitudes about individuals and groups (Norwegian).

Although the curricula texts represent descriptions of objectives and skills, the subject curricula represent a shift from the previous version. While the phrase framing the aims in the former curriculum is *Pupils should have the opportunity to* observe the principle, etc. (L97 English version), the new version uses the phrase *The aims for the education are that the pupil should be able to* observe the principle, etc. (LK06 English version). Likewise, whereas 'to learn about, work with and study' are verbs that are commonly used in former subject curricula to describe the objectives, the new curriculum uses verbs which indicate performance: to be able to elaborate on, to describe, to explain, to find.

To conclude, the two reforms prolong long-standing traditions related to subject matter in terms of contents. This is framed by the curriculum guidelines, which describe culture in terms of subject matter and are also conceptualised in the professional semantics of reform. Both curriculum guidelines from the two decades are content-oriented, although they represent this subject matter differently. Neither the role of the state, nor the vision of supporting individuals in their endeavour for cultivation and learning are very different. Moreover, our content analysis shows that both guidelines conceptualise national culture in relation to the past and passing on knowledge as a frame of reference. Curriculum making is then about the selection of what should be represented and its potential to encapsulate future pursuits of students and societies.

Since this knowledge is not evident by itself, the curriculum has been part of negotiations among different actors in the field of education (educational bureaucrats, teachers, students, politicians, parents, academic institutions, etc). They are all Norwegians, appointed by the government. As such, the curriculum is located within a geographic territory, limited by the nation-state.

The curriculum reflects a particular time in history and even *fixes* the history of knowledge to be dealt with in teaching and learning. In this sense, both reforms exemplify 'neo-conservative traditionalism' (Young, 2008). However, both guidelines are also conceptualised in terms of learning achievements, which could be considered as 'technical instrumentalism', following Young, where knowledge arguments behind the text do not describe education as a cultural project, but rather the imperative of education, forced by the needs of modern capitalism and instrumental concerns. This idea is also apparent in the two reforms as a purpose of qualification, but mixed with the idea of carrying over knowledge from the past.

Certain characteristics appear if we go into the rationales of the two reforms. While social integration is a fundamental value behind the core curriculum and the way the subject curricula in the 1990s are designed, utilitarianism has become essential for the curriculum in the 2000s. In both cases, however, paradoxes are to be solved, not only between politics and schooling, but in terms of how knowledge and culture are elaborated on in terms of subject matter in teaching and learning. This relates to the pedagogical paradox.

The Pedagogical Paradox of Education

We shall now address questions on how the recent curriculum reforms in Norway and international trends towards a global curriculum model pertain to the indispensable purpose of education found in the continental tradition of *Bildung* and the link between education (as enculturation and qualification) and human requests.

Moreover, traditional and instrumental concerns, all part of modernising society, enforce education reform towards instrumental concerns, reflecting interests in economic progress and social welfare associated with the industrialisation of the early twentieth-century (Weber, 1978 (1922)). Dealing with paradoxical concerns in knowledge-transition as well as knowledge-making has a much longer history however. We will consider it as a classical paradox, which is not only a philosophical problem, but explains the development and existence of professional semantics which deal with formalised content to guarantee individual freedom and autonomy. Following Kant, this paradox concerns the balance of constraining enculturation in guaranteeing individual self-determination which proclaims responsibility: 'How shall I cultivate freedom under conditions of compulsion? I ought to accustom my pupil to tolerate constraint upon his freedom, and at the same time lead him to make good use of his freedom' (Kant, 2008 (1903); Løvlie, 2007, p. 15).

In curriculum history, the pedagogical paradox explains how professional semantics deal with cultural knowledge in view of an open-ended idea of *Bildung*, which asserts individual cultivation and formation within society at large. Besides, these semantics relate to the idea of formalising a content of schooling connected to curriculum guidelines.

Didaktik is, as Stefan Hopmann points out, 'at the centre of most school teaching and teacher education in Continental Europe, but at the same time almost unknown in the English speaking world' (Hopmann, 2007b, p. 109). It concerns

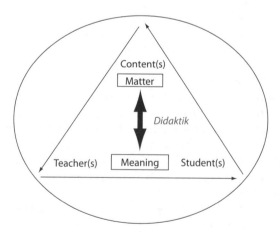

Figure 5.1   How matter relates to meaning within the tradition of *Didaktik* and according to the licence model (source: Hopmann 2007b: 116, see also Künzli 1998).

a theory of professions, or a professional semantic, developed through teacher education, and as such frames interpretations and understanding of teaching and learning. In addition, this semantic refers to the formal curriculum, linking school knowledge to the external world.

According to *Didaktik*, it is within the context of schooling that the meaning of objectified knowledge and self-determination are realised. Therefore, in the tradition of *Bildung*, content is not defined by heritage as such, or a concept of knowledge as having its own value, or even considered as a body of knowledge to be learnt. Content is not limiting but opens up a range of possibilities through reasoning and interactions. The educative meaning is thereby not defined in terms of a particular content described in the formal curriculum, but is dependent on the interpretation made by both teachers and students and their activities (Hopmann, 2007b). Despite the fact that the content of the curriculum is objectified, simultaneously ascribing to both the right of law and the right of individual *Bildung*, teaching and learning are defined through processes, framed by, but not explained by, formalised aims and standards. Moreover, disciplines and school subjects function as organising elements within this institutional framework where knowledge is predefined according to a given order, sequenced according to levels and grades, and eventually selected for pursuing educational purposes in teaching practices (Künzli, 1975; Künzli and Hopmann, 1998). However, this knowledge is not fixed as something learnt.

In conclusion, aims and contents are selected for educational and formative purposes and not just as ends in themselves. This leads to the following definition: 'Didaktik is a theory of the content of formation (*Bildung*) and of its structure and selection' (Gundem, 1998; Gundem, 2000). It is a guiding theory for both designing a formal curriculum and applying this and related documents in daily work with students. So, the paradox of enculturation frames the paradox, but still opens up for individual and societal *Bildung*, and moreover, it is not solved by the formal curriculum but the selection of knowledge and the practices of teaching and learning which are guided by a theory of *Didaktik*. Hence, *Didaktik* as a semantic construction comes to terms with the pedagogical paradox.

In accordance with Klafki, the first solution to the pedagogical paradox is to create a principle to guide the selection of content that would be significant to everyone (Klafki, 2000). Klafki declares: 'It is meant to be Bildung for all.' (Klafki, 2000, p. 89) According to this principle, predefined content should possess universal values or at least values that can be accepted by public interests, formed by society. It is here that globalisation requires reformulations of curriculum guidelines which connect to national identities rather than to objectified culture. Multicultural societies presume content which can be shared by a population which differs from before when it comes to cultural-individual backgrounds.

Another solution in continental *Didaktik* is to solve the pedagogical paradox by defining the substance of learning as beyond any objectified knowledge organised by the curriculum. Learning is configured through pupils' recognition of knowledge, contextualised in terms of different meanings (*gehalt*). These meanings are constructed through the course of schooling, exploring a particular content, but not considered as a result of teaching itself. As formulated by Hopmann:

In the perspective of Bildung and Didaktik there are no facts or objects of teaching as factum brutum ... Any given matter (Inhalt) can represent many different meanings (Gehalt), any given meaning (Gehalt) can be opened up by many different matters (Inhalt). However, there is no matter without meaning, and no meaning without matter.

(Hopmann, 2007b, p. 116)

Moreover, the idea of becoming *gebildet* embodies a lifelong course, where citizens continuously generate knowledge and virtue through their experiences with the world. In schooling, this means creating an educational process, not in terms of individualistic modes of learning, but by participating in a 'reciprocal exchange of information, consideration and argumentation' (Klafki, 2000, p. 93).

Both the content and rationale of the curriculum which developed in the first decades of the 19th century do not define a cultural heritage of its own. Moreover, content is not organised into constructs of knowledge to be reproduced in technical terms. It does not argue for training, although the curriculum informs the specific aims and content of teaching. Rather, the classical and neo-humanistic idea of *Didaktik* encapsulates constructs of how to trace contradictory values of curriculum and schooling in terms of *Bildung*.

The issue we address in the following and concluding part is how the continental approaches to curriculum and *Didaktik* presented above can be used to critically examine recent curriculum reforms and contribute to a dialogue on what counts as teaching matters and how these are to be formed by public documents such as curriculum guidelines. In this discussion, continental approaches to curriculum and *Didaktik* offer viewpoints to be included in theorising about curriculum, knowledge and learning. However, does the theory make sense in view of globalisation? The next section will discuss this question.

Discussion

The term curriculum has been given multiple definitions and can be seen as a product of different ways of understanding the relationship between schools, the state and society (Doyle, 1992; Westbury, 2008).When it is viewed as a social and cultural text, its content is neither a fixed, stable body of knowledge, nor a logical manifestation of a discipline or a well-defined political decision. Curriculum is about meaning-making and negotiation among different actors in different positions in the field of education (educational bureaucrats, teachers, students, politicians, parents, academic institutions, etc). Hence, the curriculum can be considered as social from the very outset (Moore, 2000) and the negotiations revolve around what counts as valid knowledge and values in particular historical and social settings (Goodson, 1997).

Emphasising the social and historical basis of school knowledge, however, does not mean that it is merely social (Moore, 2000, p. 13). We must not ignore the internal and cognitive dimensions of knowledge and school content (Moore and Young, 2001), and according to Moore (2000, p. 32), 'Knowledge is socially produced, but at the same time has the capacity to transcend the social conditions under which it is produced'.

Although the continental theory of *Didaktik* aimed at public requests from the beginning, regulated and formalised and constrained by formal guidelines, it also presumes a distinction about the processes in meaning-making as part of schooling, although always related to objectified matters of interpretation and meanings, and as such, knowledge. How does this theory make sense in contemporary times where standardisation processes are evident, framed by new curriculum guidelines which trace knowledge, cultures and individual learning as the main cores?

With reference to our analysis and the two reforms, we may ask whether the first reform of the 1990s is oriented towards classical ideas of enlightenment or towards facts and acts through a cultural canon? Is the objectified world of matters considered as a base for interpretation in creating new understanding? According to Lars Løvlie, the answer is clear when he argues that:

> We are used to thinking of the past 250 years — what we call modernity — in terms of Enlightenment rationality, more specifically as the proud realization of a scientific spirit which shattered superstition and prejudice, of a humanity which tolerated differences in religion and ethnic background, and of an idea of justice which makes all individuals equal under the law. The most obvious paradox is of course that the explicit re-affirmation of the European tradition and of national culture under the present political conditions proceeds by an actual emptying of such terms as freedom responsibility and solidarity.
>
> (Løvlie, 1998, p. 201).

The critique is that L97 falls short in its guide to weighing the importance of individual self-determination and autonomy to make independent and responsible decisions in a multicultural environment. By detailing content and not restricting itself to a reasonable project from a practical point of view, the curriculum fails to select and balance content matter (*Inhalt*) in view of different meanings (*Gehalt*) (Klafki, 2002). Moreover, if cultural heritage is to be conceptualised, the realities of cultures within a geographical territory must be taken into consideration. The curriculum guidelines of 1997 fail in these respects.

On the other hand, the LK06 reform has been criticised for representing an individualised curriculum. A learner-centred approach emphasises emancipation and individual choices. This asks for a 'Well-tempered Learner' (Muller, 2000, p. 95) and views education as something that is self-governed. In this sense, the question of whether students succeed or not becomes an individual issue, or as Bauman (2002, p. xv) formulates it: 'individualization' consists in transforming human 'identity' from a 'given' into a 'task' — and charging the actors with the responsibility for performing that task and for the consequences (also the side-effects) of their performance'.

Furthermore, according to Engelsen (2008), LK06's lack of content prescription and clarifications may give greater power to stakeholders as textbook authors and publishing companies in deciding what is worth knowing. This is also claimed by Bachmann in her studies on curriculum reform (Bachmann, 2004; 2005).

The curriculum fails to ask for deliberation about the boundaries between what knowledge to include and not to include in public schooling. There is, following an argument by Hopmann and Künzli (1997) 'no purposeful selection of what school and school alone should be offering and achieving. The so-called opening of the school places the school alongside all the other places of learning at society's disposal, instead of creating a culture of exclusively school-specific experience' (p. 263). This view demands for content-prescriptions in curriculum guidelines.

Klafki concludes that the *Bildung* theory, and in particular the theory of *Didaktik* relating to the philosophy of *Bildung*, emphasises personal uniqueness and does not consider factors that create isolation. Moreover, teaching is not a one-way method of instruction, rather the teacher communicates with students according to an objectified world of knowledge, as a subject matter for meaning-making. As such, content might be prescribed without hindering individualisation and emancipation. In Klafki's view, cultural studies provide unique historical examples of how the human being could use a combination of a productive and formative attainment of knowledge, not as an end in itself, but as a framework that students could use to acquire awareness about themselves (Klafki, 2002, p. 41). Therefore, one could think of a body of knowledge as something to be taught and skills to be learnt, but not as measurements of *Bildung*.

Certainly, global perspectives add new dimensions to today's orientation towards new experiences and systems that differ from before and for this reason need to be regarded as significant. As discussed in the introduction, individuals become the agents of a global history (McEneaney and Meyer, 2000, p. 196). Due to the ignorance of modern institutional boundaries, individuals are not protected against societal demands and are to a large extent expected to be their own care-takers and knowledge-makers. Hence, the nation-state and schooling weaken and with this the legitimacy of national curriculum guidelines.

However, there are no signs of a curriculum decline if one counts the number of curriculum documents and frameworks. In countries where curriculum history is institutionalised through national reforms, guidelines are still elaborated, and in other nations, inventions such as curriculum standards are formulated (Westbury, 2008). This mixing trend clearly shows how globalisation transforms curriculum policy, although it does not cancel the history of national culture, institutions like schooling, or curriculum guidelines as such. The question is then, what is considered as contributing to global cultures and institutions? Moreover, is cultural heritage of significance for what is conceptualised as a world culture? If so, how is the selection of this culture legitimised? The lessons drawn from curriculum history are that neither the order nor the selection can be legitimated without institutions and governments. Boundaries between the social and the individual must be conceptualised through the semantics which accompany formalised guidelines and documents.

Current policies and theories reconceptualise the curriculum as a pedagogical tool for learning rather than as a framing text for what to teach and learn, also reflected in curriculum theorising (Kelly, 2004). In this perspective, a globalising context redefines not only the boundaries between the state and the school, but also the relationships between teachers and learners. Nonetheless, this is still a paradox that one must be aware of.

Notes

1 This chapter was originally published in the *European Journal of Education*, 45, 1, 2010: 103-120.
2 David Hamilton specifies that the term *didactics* for an English-speaking audience denotes 'formalist educational practices which combine "dogma" with dullness'. This connotation is misleading according to the German and Nordic conceptions of *Didaktik(German)/didaktikk (Norwegian)*. In this article, we use *Didaktik* to avoid possible misunderstandings.

References

Andersen, N. Å. (2003) *Discursive Analytical Strategies: Understanding Foucault, Koselleck, Laclau, Luhmann,* Bristol: Policy Press.

Bachmann, K. (2004) Læreboken i reformtider — et verktøy for endring? in G. Imsen (ed.) *Det ustyrlige klasserommet. Om styring, samarbeid og læringsmiljø i skolen,* Oslo: Universitetsforlaget.

Bachmann, K. (2005) 'Læreplanens differens. Formidling av læreplanen til skolepraksis'. Dissertation for the Dr.Pol. degree, Pedagogisk institutt, Fakultet for samfunnsvitenskap og teknologiledelse (Norges teknisk-naturvitenskapelige universitet, NTNU).

Bachmann, K., Sivesind, K., Afsar, A. and Hopmann, S. (2004) *Hvordan formidles læreplanen? En komparativ evaluering av læreplanbaserte virkemidler — deres utforming, konsistens og betydning for læreres praksis,* Evaluering av Reform 97 — i regi av Norges forskningsråd, Kristiansand: Høyskoleforlaget.

Bauman, Z. (2002) 'Forward: individually, together', in U. Beck and E. Beck-Gernsheim (eds) *Individualization,* London: Sage Publications.

Burns, T. and Schuller, T. (2007) 'The evidence agenda', in T. Burns and T. Schuller (eds) *Evidence in Education: Linking research and policy,* Paris: OECD/CERI.

Comparative Education 18, Comparative Education Research Centre, The University of Hong Kong, Hong Kong: Springer.

Connelly, F. M. (ed.) (2008) *The SAGE Handbook of Curriculum and Instruction,* Toronto: Sage.

Doyle, W. (1992) 'Curriculum and pedagogy', in P. W. Jackson (ed.) *Handbook of Research on Curriculum,* New York: Macmillan Publishing Company.

Elstad, E. and Sivesind, K. (eds) (2010) *Pisa: visjoner og diskusjoner,* Oslo: Universitetsforlaget.

Elstad, E. (2009) 'Schools which are named, shamed and blamed by the media: school accountability in Norway', *Educational Assessment, Evaluation and Accountability,* 21, pp. 173–89.

Engelsen, B. U. (2008) *Kunnskapsløftet. Sentrale styringssignaler og lokale strategidokumenter,* Rapport nr. 1. Forskningsgruppen Læreplanstudier, forskningsprosjektet ARK (Det Utdanningsvitenskapelig Fakultet, Universitetet i Oslo).

Engelsen, B. U. and Karseth, B. (2007) 'Læreplan for Kunnskapsløftet — et endret kunnskapssyn?', *Norsk pedagogisk tidsskrift,* 5, pp. 404–15.

Goodson, I. (1997) *The Changing Curriculum,* New York: Lang.

Gundem, B. B. (1993a) *Mot en ny skolevirkelighet? Læreplanen i et sentraliserings-og desentraliseringspersektiv,* Oslo: Ad Notam Gyldendal.

Gundem, B. B. (1993b) 'Rise, development and changing conceptions of curriculum administration and curriculum guidelines in Norway: the national-local dilemma', *Journal of Curriculum Studies,* 25, pp. 251–66.

Gundem, B. B. (1995) 'The role of didactics in curriculum in Scandinavia', *Journal of Curriculum and Supervision,* 10, pp. 302–16.

Gundem, B. B. (1996) 'Core curriculum — cultural heritage — literacy: recent perspectives and trends in Norwegian education', in: E. Marum (Ed.) *Children and Books in the Modern World: An international perspective on literacy,* London: Falmer Press.

Gundem, B. B. (1998) *Understanding European Didactics — An Overview. Didactics (Didaktik, Didaktik(k), and Didactique), Report no. 4,* Oslo: Institute for Educational Research, University of Oslo.

Gundem, B. B. (2000) 'Understanding European didactics', in: B. Moon, M. Ben-Peretz and S. Brown (eds) *Routledge International Companion to Education,* London: Routledge.

Gundem, B. B. and Karseth, B. (1998) 'Norwegian national identity in recent curriculum documents'. Paper presented at the AERA Conference April 13–17, San Diego.

Gundem, B. B. and Sivesind, K. (1996) 'From politics to practice: reflections from a research project on curriculum policy and notes from (outside and inside) a national curriculum reform project'. Paper presented at AERA Conference March 24–28, 1997, Chicago IL, ERIC.

Hamilton, D. (1999) 'The pedagogic paradox (or why no didactics in England)', *Pedagogy, Culture and Society,* 7, pp. 135–52.

Hernes, G. (2008) 'The interface between social research and policy', *European Sociological Review,* 24, pp. 257–65.

Hirsch, E. D. J. (1985) 'Cultural literacy'. Paper presented at the National Adult Literacy Conference January 19–20, Washington, DC.

Hopmann, S. (2007a) 'Epilogue: no child, no school, no state left behind: comparative research in the age of accountability', in: N S. Hopmann,G. Brinek and M. Retzl (eds) *PISA zufolge PISA: PISA according to PISA* Schulpädagogik und Pädagogische Psychologie, Band 6, Münster, Wien: LIT Verlag.

Hopmann, S. (2007b) 'Restrained teaching: the common core of didaktik', *European Educational Research Journal,* 6, pp. 109–124.

Hopmann, S. and Künzli, R. (1997) 'Close our schools! Against current trends in policy making, educational theory and curriculum studies', *Journal of Curriculum Studies,* 29, pp. 259–66.

Hopmann, S. and Riquarts, K. (2000) 'Starting a dialogue: a beginning conversation between didaktik and the curriculum traditions', in I. Westbury, S. Hopmann and K. Riquarts (eds) *Teaching as a Reflective Practice: the German Didaktik tradition,* London: Lawrence Erlbaum Associates Publishers.

Imsen, G. (Ed.) *Det ustyrlige klasserommet. Om styring, samarbeid og læringsmiljø i skolen.* Oslo: Universitetsforlaget.

Kant, I. (2008 (1903) *Om Pedagogik,* Göteborg: Daidalos.

Keating, A., Ortloff, D. H. and Philippou, S. (2009) 'Citizenship education curricula: the changes and challenges presented by global and European integration', *Journal of Curriculum Studies,* 41, pp. 145–158.

Kelly, A. V. (2004) *The Curriculum: theory and practice,* London: Sage Publications.

Klafki, W. (2000) 'The significance of classical theories of Bildung for a contemporary concept of Allgemeinbildung', in I. Westbury,S. Hopmann and K. Riquarts (eds) *Teaching as a Reflective Practice: the German Didaktik tradition,* London: Lawrence Erlbaum Associates Publishers.

Klafki, W. (2002) 'Første studie. De klassiske dannelsesteoriers betydning for et tidssvarende almendannelseskoncept', in W. Klafki (ed.) *Dannelsesteori og didaktik: nye studier* (2nd ed), Århus: Klim.

Kunnskapsdepartementet and Utdanningsdirektoratet (2006) *Læreplanverket for kunnskapsløftet. Midlertidig utgave juni 2006.*

Künzli, R. (Ed.) (1975) *Curriculumentwicklung. Begründung und Legitimation,* München,:Kösel-Verlag).

Künzli, R. (1998) 'The common frame and the places of Didaktik', in B. B. Gundem and S. T. Hopmann (eds) *Didaktik and/or Curriculum.* New York: Peter Lang.

Künzli, R. and Hopmann, S. (eds) (1998) *Lehrpläne:Wie sie entwickelt werden und was von ihnen erwartet wird. Forschungsstand, Zugänge und Ergebnisse aus der Schweiz und der Bundesrepublik Deutschland,* Zürich: Rüegger.

Langfeldt, G. (2008) *Ansvar og kvalitet,* Oslo: Cappelen.

Lundgren, U. P. (2006) 'Political governing and curriculum change — from active to reactive curriculum reforms: the need for a reorientation of curriculum theory', *Studies in Educational Policy and Educational Philosophy,* 1, pp. 1–12. (http://www.upi.artisan. se/docs/Doc262.pdf)

Løvlie, L. (1998) 'Paradoxes of curriculum reform', in B. B. Gundem and S. Hopmann (eds) *Didaktik and/or Curriculum — an International Dialogue,* New York: Peter Lang.

Løvlie, L. (2007) 'Does paradox count in education?', *Education and Democracy,* 16, pp. 9–36.

McEneaney, E. H. and Meyer, J. W. (2000) 'The content of the curriculum: an institutionalist perspective', in M.T. Hallinan (ed.) *Handbook of the Sociology of Education,* New York: Kluwer Academic.

Meyer, J. W. (2006) 'World models, national curricula, and the centrality of the individual', in A. Benavot and C. Braslavsky (eds) *School Knowledge in Comparative and Historical Perspective: changing curricula in primary and secondary education,* Hong Kong: Comparative Education Research Centre, Springer.

Moore, R. (2000) 'For knowledge: tradition. Progressivism and progress in education — reconstruction the curriculum debate', *Cambridge Journal of Education,* 30, pp. 17–36.

Moore, R. and Young, M. F. D. (2001) 'Knowledge and the curriculum in the sociology of education: towards reconceptualisation', *British Journal of Sociology of Education,* 22, pp. 445–461.

Muller, J. (2000) *Reclaiming Knowledge: social theory, curriculum, and education policy.* Knowledge, Identity, and School Life Series 8, London: Routledge.

The Norwegian Directorate for Training and Education (1994) *The Core Curriculum in Five Languages* (The Royal Ministry of Education and Research).

Reid, W. A. (1999) *Curriculum as Institution and Practice: essays in the deliberative tradition,* London: Lawrence Erlbaum Associates Publishers.

Report no. 30 to the Storting (2003/2004) *Kultur for læring.* The Royal Ministry of Education and Research.

Report no. 40 to the Storting (1990/1991) *Fra visjon til virke. Om høgre utdanning.* The Royal Ministry of Education Research and Church Affairs.

Rosenmund, M. (2006) 'The current discourse on curriculum change: a comparative analysis of National Reports on Education', in A. Benavot and C. Braslavsky (eds) *School Knowledge in Comparative and Historical Perspective: changing curricula in primary and secondary education.* CERC Studies in Comparative Education 18, Comparative Education Research Centre, The University of Hong Kong, Hong Kong: Springer.

The Royal Ministry of Education and Research (1994) *Principles and Guidelines for the Structure,Organization and Content of the 10-year Compulsory School. Draft version in English.*

The Royal Ministry of Education and Research (2006) *Læreplanverket for Kunnskapsløftet.* Provisional printed version.

The Royal Ministry of Education,Research and Church Affairs (1994) *Core Curriculum for Primary, Secondary and Adult Education.*

The Royal Ministry of Education, Research and Church Affairs (1996) *The Curriculum for the 10-year Compulsory School in Norway,* Oslo: KUF.

The Royal Ministry of Education, Research and Church Affairs (1999) *The Curriculum for the 10-year Compulsory School in Norway,* Oslo: KUF.

Schuller T. (ed.) *Evidence in Education: linking research and policy,* Paris: OECD/CERI.

Sivesind, K. (2002) 'Task and themes in the communication about the curriculum: the Norwegian Compulsory School Reform in perspective', in M. Rosenmund,W. Heller and A.-V. Fries (eds) *Comparing Curriculum Making Processes,* Bern: Peter Lang.

Sivesind, K. (2008) 'Reformulating reform: curriculum history revisited.' Dissertation for the degree of Dr.Phil (Det utdanningsvitenskapelige fakultet, Universitetet i Oslo).

Skarpenes, O. (2004) 'Kunnskapens legitimering: en studie av to reformer og tre fag i videregående skole'. Dissertation for the degree of Dr.polit (Sosiologisk institutt Universitetet i Bergen).

Steiner-Khamsi, G. (2009) 'Knowledge-based regulation and the politics of international comparison', *Nordisk Pedagogik,* 29, pp. 61–71.

Saarinen, T. (2008) 'Position of text and discourse analysis in higher education policy research', *Studies in Higher Education,* 33, pp. 719–28.

Telhaug, A. O., Aasen, P., and Mediås, O. A. (2004), 'From collectivism to individualism? Education as nation building in a Scandinavian perspective', *Scandinavian Journal of Educational Research,* 48, pp. 141–158.

Weber, M. (1978 (1922) *Economy and Society,* Berkeley, CA: University of California Press.

Westbury, I. (2000) 'Teaching as a reflective practice:what might Didaktik teach curriculum?' in I. Westbury, S. Hopmann and K. Riquarts (eds) *Teaching as a Reflectice Practice.: the German Didaktik tradition,* London: Lawrence Erlbaum Associates Publishers.

Westbury, I. (2008) 'Making curricula: why states make curricula, and how', in F. M. Connelly (Ed.) *The SAGE Handbook of Curriculum and Instruction,* Toronto: Sage.

Young, M. F. D. (2008) *Bringing Knowledge Back In: from social constructivism to social realism in the sociology of education,* London: Routledge.

Part II

Curriculum, the Economy and Work

6 Values Education Amid Globalization and Change

The Case of National Education in Singapore

Jason Tan

Globalization in its economic, cultural and social manifestations has been the focus of many educators especially over the past few decades (see for instance Townsend and Cheng 2000; Hershock, Mason and Hawkins 2007). Economic globalization with its implications for national economic competitiveness has led numerous governments to re-examine their national education systems with a view to developing specific skills and attitudes that are supposedly essential for preparing young people for success within a knowledge economy. In addition, there is now an emerging literature on how the fruits of economic globalization have not been equitably distributed in various societies. If anything, existing inequities in income distribution have been exacerbated. On the cultural front, the advent of the internet and other forms of information technology, with its accompanying rapid spread of ideas across national boundaries, has been viewed as a potential threat to cultural, linguistic and religious homogeneity. Many governments have renewed calls for education systems to emphasize values education in a bid to strengthen social cohesion and maintain cultural continuity (see for instance Lee, Grossman, Kennedy and Fairbrother 2004). However, governments do not always find it easy to reconcile sometimes wildly contradictory functions of schooling. For instance, schooling systems often serve as key sorting or sifting devices to prepare students for their future roles in the workforce, which sometimes leaves them open to accusations of perpetuating social class inequalities. At the same time, in a bid to enhance educational outcomes, some governments have fostered market forces and inter-school competition at the risk of sidelining more humanitarian values.

Singapore, a former British colony with a multi-ethnic, multi-lingual and multi-religious population of just under five million, has made rapid economic progress over the past four decades since attaining political independence in 1965. By the early 1980s, it had become known as one of the four Asian tiger economic powerhouses and, alongside Brunei, enjoyed one of the highest per capita incomes in Southeast Asia. More recently, it has received international attention because of its students' outstanding performance in the Third International Mathematics and Science Study in 1997, as a result of which a small but growing number of school districts in the United States have adopted modified versions of Singapore mathematics and science textbooks.

Singapore exemplifies the case of a country whose government is well aware of the pressing imperatives for economic, cultural and societal change brought about by globalization (Velayutham 2007). It offers interesting lessons on how the tensions and pressures of globalization have played out in the arena of the education system over the past decade. On the one hand, schools and universities are constantly being urged to better prepare students for the challenges of the knowledge-based economy. An avalanche of education reforms has descended on various sectors of the school system in an attempt to promote certain skills, attitudes and behaviors. A wave of marketization initiatives has also swept through schools in the past two decades. Terms such as 'diversity', 'choice' and 'competition' are now commonplace. On the other hand, there are also attempts in the school system to shore up national identity and to preserve 'desirable' cultural traits and behaviors as a bulwark against the perceived undesirable effects of globalization on young people. This chapter highlights and discusses various issues pertaining to equity, as well as the inculcation of values and ethics, in a climate characterized by rapid globalization and change. It suggests that at times the values prescribed in the official values education curriculum appear at odds with the social context in which the schools are functioning. Furthermore, there are limits to a paternalistic, interventionist style of education policymaking.

Thinking Schools, Learning Nation

Singapore's ruling People's Action Party (PAP) has enjoyed uninterrupted political power for the past 51 years and has developed a paternalistic, interventionist style of governance. Almost every aspect of social policy has been harnessed single-mindedly in the pursuit of economic development in order that Singapore might emerge alongside other 'First World' nations (Wee 2007). The education system, in particular, has received particular attention as a prime instrument of socializing the populace into norms of behavior that might better suit the needs of economic development. In the early 1990s, the then Prime Minister Goh Chok Tong warned that the educational profile of Singapore's workforce trailed those of its chief economic competitors in East Asia. He also claimed that Singapore would not be able to compete effectively against the People's Republic of China and India, which offered abundant supplies of low-wage labor (*The Straits Times* 1993). The then Education Minister Lee Yock Suan echoed Goh's claims in 1995 and highlighted that the advent of rapid advances in information technology, coupled with increasing global economic competition, would invariably increase income disparities.

A few years later, Goh launched the Thinking Schools, Learning Nation (TSLN) initiative. Driven explicitly by official concern about Singapore's economic competitiveness within the global economy, TSLN included a reduction in curricular content from primary to pre-university levels to allow more time to be devoted to thinking skills and processes, and the revision of assessment modes. A whole list of desired outcomes, such as creative, critical, analytical and flexible thinking, the exercising of initiative, communication skills, problem solving, co-operative team work, and research skills, were announced. Goh claimed that TSLN had to instil a passion for learning among students instead of having them study merely for the purpose of obtaining good examination grades (Goh 1997a). Several skills, such as creativity, entrepreneurship, innovation, knowledge application, independent thinking, and the ability to work in teams, were subsequently listed in an official Education Ministry document that outlined the final desired outcomes of formal education for every Singaporean (Singapore Ministry of Education 1998). TSLN has since become a major policy umbrella encompassing multiple policy prongs such as Innovation and Enterprise, the Information Technology Masterplan, Ability-Driven Education (where every child's potential is supposed to be developed to its fullest), *Teach Less, Learn More*, the review of primary, secondary and pre-university curricula, as well as the revision of university undergraduate admission criteria.

Values Education

Along with this emphasis on thinking skills for economic ends, values education policies have also taken center stage over the past decade (as they have over the past five decades). Chief among them has been National Education, which was officially launched in 1997. Goh had in 1995 claimed that:

> [g]iving them [students] academic knowledge alone is not enough to make them understand what makes or breaks Singapore … Japanese children are taught to cope with earthquakes, while Dutch youngsters learn about the vulnerability of their polders, or low-lying areas. In the same way, Singapore children must be taught to live with a small land area, limited territorial sea and air space, the high cost of owning a car and dependence on imported water and oil. Otherwise, years of continuous growth may lull them into believing that the good life is their divine right … [students] must be taught survival skills and be imbued with the confidence that however formidable the challenges and competition, we have the will, skill and solutions to vanquish them.
>
> (*The Straits Times* 1995)

At the same time the former Prime Minister Lee Kuan Yew commented that:

> thirty years of continuous growth and increasing stability and prosperity have produced a different generation in an English-educated middle class. They are very different from their parents. The present generation below 35 has grown up used to high economic growth year after year, and take their security and success for granted. And because they believe all is well, they are less willing to make sacrifices for the benefit of the others in society. They are more concerned about their individual and family's welfare and success, not their community or society's well being.
>
> (Lee 1996: 30)

At a Teachers' Day rally in September 1996, Goh lamented the lack of knowledge of Singapore's recent history among younger Singaporeans, as reflected in the results of a street poll conducted by a local newspaper. The Ministry of Education had also conducted a surprise quiz on Singapore's history among 2,500 students in schools, polytechnics and universities. The results proved equally disappointing.

Goh claimed that the gap in knowledge was the direct result of a deliberate official policy not to teach school students about the recent political past and the events leading up to political independence. However, he felt that this ignorance was undesirable among the young people who had not personally lived through these events. He claimed too that these events, constituting 'our shared past', ought to 'bind all our communities together, not divide us ... We should understand why they took place so that we will never let them happen again' (Goh 1997b: 425). Goh highlighted the possibility that the young people would not appreciate how potentially fragile inter-ethnic relations could prove to be, especially in times of economic recession. Not having lived through poverty and deprivation meant that young people might take peace and prosperity for granted.

Calling on all school principals to throw their support behind this urgent initiative, which he termed National Education (NE), Goh pointed out that NE needed to become a crucial part of the education curriculum in all schools. Emphasizing the importance of nation building in existing subjects such as social studies, civic and moral education and history would be insufficient. More important was the fact that NE was meant to develop 'instincts' in every child, such as a 'shared sense of nationhood [and] understanding of how our past is relevant to our present and future'. NE was to make students appreciative of how Singapore's peace and stability existed amid numerous conflicts elsewhere around the world. This meant that what took place outside the classroom, such as school rituals and examples set by teachers, would prove vital in the success of NE. Goh announced the establishment of an NE Committee to involve various ministries, including the Education Ministry, in this effort.

The NE initiative was officially launched in May 1997 by the then Deputy Prime Minister Lee Hsien Loong. Lee claimed that countries such as the United States and Japan, with longer national histories, still found it necessary to have schools transmit key national instincts to students. Singapore, being barely one generation old, therefore needed a similar undertaking in the form of NE.

NE aimed at developing national cohesion in students through:

- Fostering Singaporean identity, pride and self-respect;
- Teaching about Singapore's nation-building successes against the odds;
- Understanding Singapore's unique developmental challenges, constraints and vulnerabilities; and
- Instilling core values, such as meritocracy and multiracialism, as well as the will to prevail, in order to ensure Singapore's continued success.

(Lee 1997)

Lee called on every teacher and principal to pass on six key NE messages:

- Singapore is our homeland; this is where we belong;
- We must preserve racial and religious harmony;

- We must uphold meritocracy and incorruptibility;
- No one owes Singapore a living;
- We must ourselves defend Singapore; and
- We have confidence in our future.

(Singapore Ministry of Education 1997a)

Several major means were suggested for incorporating NE in all schools. First, every subject in the formal curriculum would be used. Certain subjects, such as social studies, civics and moral education, history and geography were mentioned as being particularly useful in this regard. Social studies at the primary level would be started earlier, at primary one instead of at primary four. It would also be introduced as a new mandatory subject for all upper secondary students in order to cover issues regarding Singapore's success and future developmental challenges. The upper secondary history syllabus would be extended from 1963, where its coverage had hitherto ended, to include the immediate post-independence years up until 1971.

Secondly, various elements of the informal curriculum were recommended. All schools were asked to include a few major events on their school calendar each year:

- Total Defense Day, to commemorate Singapore's surrender under British colonial rule to the Japanese in 1942;
- Racial Harmony Day, to remember the outbreak of inter-ethnic riots in 1964;
- International Friendship Day, to bring across the importance of maintaining cordial relations with neighboring countries; and
- National Day, to commemorate political independence in 1965.

In addition, students would visit key national institutions and public facilities in order to feel proud and confident about how Singapore had overcome its developmental constraints. A further means of promoting social cohesion and civic responsibility would be through a mandatory six hours of community service for secondary and pre-university students each year. An NE branch was established in the Ministry of Education headquarters to spearhead this initiative.

To further demonstrate the importance of NE, the key NE outcomes were enshrined in the *Desired outcomes of education* document (Singapore Ministry of Education 1998). Civics and moral education syllabi at the primary and secondary levels have been revised twice in the past decade. Both syllabi were premised on the key values of respect, responsibility, integrity, care, resilience and harmony, and were supposed to be consistent with NE messages. In addition, elements of the *Singapore 21* Vision, which the government had promulgated in 1999, were incorporated in the civics and moral education syllabi (Singapore Ministry of Education 2006a, b). This Vision was yet another official attempt to manage the growing impact of income disparities by claiming that every Singaporean mattered and had a useful contribution to make to society (Government of Singapore 1999).

Contradictions and Tensions in Values Education Over the Past Decade

Behind the NE initiative, one can detect a pressing concern among the political leadership about how, on the one hand, to satisfy the growing desires among an increasingly affluent and materialistic population for car ownership and bigger housing amid rising costs of both commodities, and on the other, to maintain civic awareness and responsibility. A related concern is that the population might translate their dissatisfaction with unfulfilled material aspirations into dissatisfaction with the ruling party.

There is also official concern that social cohesion might suffer, should the economy falter and fail to sustain the high growth rates of the past few decades. Social stratification has assumed a growing prominence on the government's policy agenda, especially in the wake of the 1991 general elections, when the People's Action Party (PAP) was returned to power with a reduced parliamentary majority. Whereas the issue of income stratification was largely taboo in public discussions up till 1991, there has been growing acknowledgement on the part of the PAP government since then of the potential impact of income disparities on social cohesion. For instance, Goh Chok Tong has acknowledged on several occasions that not all Singaporeans stand to benefit equally from the global economy. He has also pointed out that highly educated Singaporeans are in a more advantageous position compared with unskilled workers and that there is a great likelihood of widening income inequalities and class stratification (Goh 1996, 1997b).

Goh has drawn an explicit link between income inequalities and the need to maintain social cohesion. However, he thinks that 'we cannot narrow the [income] gap by preventing those who can fly from flying ... Nor can we teach everyone to fly, because most simply do not have the aptitude or ability' (Goh 1996: 3). In the late 1990s, Goh introduced the terms 'cosmopolitans' and 'heartlanders' to illustrate the class divide between the well-educated, privileged, globally mobile elite, on the one hand, and the working-class majority, on the other (Parliamentary Debates 70(20), 1999, Col. 2284). A PAP Member of Parliament expressed his fervent hope that Singaporeans would not 'allow our system of education [to] create a bipolar society of cosmopolitans and heartlanders that will be destructive for nation-building' (Parliamentary Debates 71(2) 1999: Col. 87). More recently, these income gaps show no sign of closing and may in fact be widening (Loh 2007).

This tension between social inequalities and social cohesion permeates the underlying framework of NE. Different emphases are planned for students in various levels of schooling. For instance, students in technical institutes are to:

> understand that they would be helping themselves, their families and Singapore by working hard, continually upgrading themselves and helping to ensure a stable social order. They must feel that every citizen has a valued place in Singapore.

Polytechnic students, who are higher up the social prestige ladder, are to be convinced that 'the country's continued survival and prosperity will depend on the quality of their efforts, and that there is opportunity for all based on ability and effort'. Junior college students, about four-fifths of whom are bound for university, must have the sense that 'they can shape their own future' and must appreciate 'the demands and complexities of leadership' as future national leaders (Singapore Ministry of Education, 1997b: 3).

One sees in these differing messages, clear and unmistakeable vestiges of the stratified view of society espoused by Lee Kuan Yew more than thirty years earlier. Speaking to school principals in 1966, Lee stressed that the education system ought to produce a 'pyramidal structure' consisting of three strata: 'top leaders', 'good executives' and a 'well-disciplined and highly civic-conscious broad mass'. The 'top leaders' are the 'elite' who are needed to 'lead and give the people the inspiration and the drive to make [society] succeed'. The 'middle strata' of 'good executives' are to 'help the elite carry out [their] ideas, thinking and planning', while the 'broad mass' are to be 'imbued not only with self but also social discipline, so that they can respect their community and do not spit all over the place' (Lee 1966: 10, 12–13). It was clear in this message that Lee wanted the education system to act as a key sorting or sifting device to identify and nurture the tiny elite group, and to send clear messages to each student about his or her place in the 'pyramidal structure'. Lee also lamented the tendency among many Singaporeans to be more concerned with individual survival, rather than national survival, a theme that both he and Goh later repeated, within the setting of a much more materially prosperous society.

It is somewhat difficult to reconcile this stratified view of society, in which individuals are still being pigeonholed based on their academic achievement, on the one hand, with visions of a socially cohesive society, on the other. The claims of the *Singapore 21* Vision (Government of Singapore 1999) that 'every Singaporean matters' and of 'equal opportunities for all', as well as one of the secondary school Desired Outcomes 'believe in their ability' (Singapore Ministry of Education 1998), tend to be belied by the persistent reliance on academic achievement as a primary indicator of an individual's societal worth, as well as the longstanding belief of the former Prime Minister Lee Kuan Yew, who continues to play an active role in governance, in the primarily genetic basis of an individual's intelligence, creativity and leadership qualities (see for instance *The Straits Times* 1996, 2005; Parliamentary Debates 66(3) 1996: Cols. 331–345; Parliamentary Debates 70(14) 1999: Cols. 1651–1653). For instance, it is only recently that high-profile official attention has been paid to special needs education in mainstream schools.

At a more general level, the continued insistence on what some observers have termed a paternalistic, interventionist political system – one in which many citizens are 'denied self-designed forms of citizenship performance'; in which many citizens' mother-tongue languages such as Hokkien, Cantonese and Teochew, as well as the widely-spoken colloquial form of Singapore English have been marginalized by official language policies; and in which many citizens 'have never experienced how their views can have an influence' – has in practice 'disenfranchised' most citizens and contributed further to their obsession with consumerism (Woo and Goh 2007: 111).

The task of holding on to citizens' sense of loyalty and commitment will come under increasingly severe strain as globalization and its impact mean that

Singaporeans are exposed via overseas travel, the internet and news and print media to social and political alternatives outside of Singapore. Increasing wealth also means that individuals are able to send their children to be educated outside of Singapore, after which work opportunities beckon. Furthermore, the government itself has been calling upon Singaporeans to work outside of Singapore in order to further broaden the country's external economic competitive advantage. It has also been government practice for four decades now to sponsor top-performing students in the General Certificate of Education Advanced Level examinations for undergraduate studies in prestigious universities such as Oxford, Cambridge, Harvard and Stanford. It is perhaps ironic, if somewhat unsurprising, that the well-educated elite, in other words, the very individuals who have been accorded generous support and funding in their schooling in the hope that they will take on the mantle of national leadership, are the most globally mobile, and best placed to take advantage of economic opportunities around the world, to the point of contemplating emigration. This policy dilemma was exemplified in the late 1990s when parliamentarians debated the merits of publicly naming and shaming individuals who had been sponsored for their undergraduate and/or postgraduate studies in elite foreign universities, only to repay the government the cost of their studies upon completion of their studies instead of returning to Singapore to work for the government (Parliamentary Debates 68(7) 1998: Cols. 855–996). A few years later there were echoes of the 'cosmopolitans–heartlanders' issue in the wake of Goh Chok Tong's National Day rally speech which referred to two categories of individuals, the 'stayers' (Singaporeans who were 'rooted to Singapore') and the 'quitters' ('fair weather Singaporeans who would run away whenever the country runs into stormy weather') (Parliamentary Debates 75(8) 2002: Cols. 1110–1201).

Entangled with the question of class-based disparities is that of ethnic inequalities. Data from the population census in the year 2000 indicated that the ethnic Malay and Indian minorities, constituting 13.9 per cent and 7.9 per cent of the total population respectively, formed a disproportionately large percentage of the lower income strata and a correspondingly small percentage of the higher income strata vis-à-vis the majority ethnic Chinese. There is sufficient cause for concern that these disparities will not narrow as the effects of economic globalization make further inroads into Singapore society.

These ethnic disparities play out in the area of educational attainment as well. Ethnic Chinese are heavily over-represented in local universities and polytechnics, forming 92.4 per cent and 84.0 per cent of the respective total enrolments in 2000, as compared with their 76.8 per cent representation in the overall population. Ethnic Malays (2.7 per cent and 10.0 per cent, respectively), and Indians (4.3 per cent and 5.2 per cent, respectively) are correspondingly under-represented (Leow 2001: 34–36). Despite ethnic Malay and ethnic Indian students having made tremendous quantitative improvements in educational attainment over the past four decades, their public examination results continue to lag behind those of their Chinese counterparts (see for instance Singapore Ministry of Community Development, Youth & Sports 2007). A disproportionately large percentage of Malay and Indian students are streamed into the slower-paced streams at both primary and secondary levels. In other words, the educational gap is already present at the lower levels of schooling (Ministry of Education programs such as the Learning Support Programme notwithstanding) and perpetuates itself at the higher levels. This gap also translates into ethnic minority under-representation (and working class under-representation) in some of the most prestigious schools and a corresponding over-representation in some of the least prestigious schools.

There is evidence that four decades of common socialization in a national school system have still not managed to eradicate racial prejudice among school students (see for instance Lee *et al.* 2004). The existence of Special Assistance Plan schools, which are almost entirely ethnic Chinese in enrolment, has been the subject of periodic discussion because of their perceived ethnic exclusivity (see for instance Parliamentary Debates 55(4) 1990: Col. 371; 64(5) 1995: Col. 486; 70(9) 1999: Col. 1027; 76(10) 2003: Col. 1635). Moreover, the practice of streaming students into various tracks at the primary and secondary levels within the context of a highly competitive, high-stakes education system has, since its inception in 1979, contributed to prejudice on the part of students in faster-paced streams, and teachers as well, towards students in slower-paced streams (see for instance Kang 2004).

Exacerbating tendencies towards segregation and stratification of students across and within schools has been the marketization of schools since the early 1990s. This marketization drive, which is supposed to enhance the quality of education by increasing competition between schools (and supposedly fostering diversity and choice for parents and students), has been manifested in several key ways. One of them is the annual publication of secondary school ranking league tables that provide summary data of schools' performance in the annual national General Certificate of Education 'Ordinary' Level examinations. It took a number of years before the Education Ministry responded to public criticism about the way in which these ranking league tables had made a number of principals focus narrowly on boosting students' examination results. It announced in 2004 that it would be moving away from raw numerical rankings of secondary schools in favor of broad performance bands. Another response to public criticism of school ranking exercises has been instead to broaden the range of indicators upon which schools are to be assessed, through the use of the School Excellence Model (SEM). This quality assurance model, which was implemented in all schools in 2000, is meant to help schools appraise their own performance in various areas such as leadership, staff management, staff competence and morale, and student outcomes. Beginning in the year 2001, each school is supposed to subject its own internal assessment to external validation by a team headed by staff from the School Appraisal Branch of the MOE. These validations are to be carried out at least once every five years. Part of the SEM involves the awarding of Achievement Awards, Development Awards, Sustained Achievement Awards, Outstanding Development Awards, Best Practice Awards, School Distinction Awards and School Excellence Awards to individual schools. These awards reward achievement in various categories such as aesthetics, sports, uniformed groups, physical health, character development, NE, organizational effectiveness, student all-round development, staff well-being, and teaching and learning. It is arguable that the use of the SEM may result in some schools using more of the same covert strategies that they have been using thus far, this time in a wider spectrum of school processes and activities in order to boost their schools' performance in as many of the aspects that are being assessed as possible. For example, principals may narrow the range of available co-curricular activities in order to focus the schools' resources on those activities that are considered more fruitful in terms of winning awards in inter-school competitions. This phenomenon may have been exacerbated by the introduction in 2003 of the Enhanced Performance Management System used to appraise principals and teachers, a system that puts a premium on quantifiable indicators of personal achievement and contribution.

The competitive stakes have now extended to student recruitment after the Education Ministry initiated the practice of Direct School Admission (DSA) for secondary schools in 2004. The scheme allows schools to apply for full discretion to conduct selection interviews and devise their individual selection criteria to admit a certain percentage of their students before they sit the Primary School Leaving Examination. It will also likely intensify the tendency of some schools to narrowly focus on co-curricular activities that are proven award winners, to concentrate obsessively on student participation in activities more for competitive stakes than for intrinsic enjoyment, and to exclude students without a proven track record of competitive achievement from participation in niche cocurricular activities.

The marketization of education has further accentuated the stratification of schools within a hierarchy of prestige and the segregation of students along ethnic and class lines across schools. The government has claimed in the *Singapore 21* Vision that:

> Everyone has a contribution to make to Singapore. It is not only those who score a dozen 'A's, or those who make a lot of money who are important and an asset to the country … Each one of us has a place in society, a contribution to make and a useful role to play … As a society, we must widen our definition of success to go beyond the academic and the economic.
>
> (Government of Singapore 1999: 11)

However, the problem is that professional and managerial positions, which increasingly depend on one having acquired university-level qualifications, continue to be valued more highly and to receive superior remuneration than more traditional working-class occupations. This had led to a scramble, especially on the part of middle-class and upper-middle-class parents, to enroll their children in more prestigious schools. The more prestigious schools in turn have increasingly tried through such means as the DSA to maximize their chances of enrolling students from home backgrounds that are favorably predisposed to supporting academic achievement. Far from supporting some of the Desired Outcomes of Education, such as 'have moral integrity', 'have care and concern for others', and 'be able to work in teams and value every contribution', as well as the communication skills and team work required in TSLN and the key civics and moral education messages, the marketization of education has tended instead to foster a climate of self-centered individualism that views individuals more as 'assets' or 'liabilities' according to what they are perceived to be able to contribute tangibly to schools' academic and non-academic outcomes. The question then arises of the equity of the sorting mechanisms by which various students' life chances begin to be determined.

In the past few years, there have been belated policy reforms as part of a tacit official admission of the divisive impact of education policies. For instance, there have been moves to blur some of the boundaries across different academic streams at the primary and secondary levels; to encourage greater interaction between primary students enrolled in the Gifted Education Programme and their other schoolmates; and to provide some semblance of upward mobility from lower-prestige academic streams to higher-prestige academic streams.

The various tensions and dilemmas that have been discussed in this section have serious implications for efforts to impart the key values education messages in all students. Further compounding the situation in recent years has been a renewed heightening of awareness of religious differences, especially between Muslims and non-Muslims. In 1999 there was a public controversy over the future of privately-run Islamic religious schools following the publication of a Ministry of Education report recommending six-year-long compulsory education for all children in state-run schools. This was followed by events in the aftermath of the attacks on the World Trade Center in New York in September 2001 when, at the end of that year, Singapore authorities arrested several Muslim Singaporeans on suspicion of involvement in terrorist activities. The specter of militant Islamic terrorism is far from over, as exemplified by the further arrest of several Muslim Singaporeans in June 2007. In early 2002 another domestic controversy broke out over the Education Ministry's insistence that female Muslim students not be allowed to don Islamic head veils in state-run schools. In the midst of these potential flashpoints, government leaders have renewed calls for all Singaporeans to remain united, and for schools to play their role in fostering social cohesion.

In a sense, the Singapore government has never pretended that ethno-religious tensions have been swept away as a result of various educational policy initiatives (including civic and moral education) and other economic and social policies. In fact, certain government pronouncements may have served (unintentionally) to make the task of forging social cohesion more problematic. For example, the question of ethnic Malay representation in the Singapore Armed Forces (SAF) has continued to remain controversial ever since the establishment of the SAF in 1967. Government leaders have openly stated that Malays are not recruited into certain military units in case their religious affinities come into conflict with their duty to defend Singapore (Hussin 2002; see also Chua 2007). In addition, Lee Kuan Yew has stated publicly that Singapore needs to maintain current ethnic ratios in its population in order to ensure continued economic success. These ethnic-based controversies have been complicated in recent years by the influx of new immigrants and individuals on temporary work permits from such countries as the People's Republic of China and India. Permanent residents formed 10.1 per cent of the total population in 2005 (Singapore Department of Statistics 2006: 3), while 'non-residents' (which includes foreign students and transient workers, among other categories) comprised 18.3 per cent. These new immigrants have had at times to cope with resentment among some Singaporeans over perceived competition for jobs, a phenomenon that has been acknowledged by Goh Chok Tong (Loh 2007). The schools will have to grapple with the task of socializing the children of the new immigrants, as well as how values education ought to play out in the case of students whose parents may have no intention of seeking Singapore citizenship, but who have chosen nevertheless to enroll their children in Singapore schools. Even in the schools arena, there is worry among some parents, teachers and local students about the added competitive element that talented foreign students are perceived to represent (see for instance Quek 2005; Singh 2005).

At the same time, the question of national vulnerability in terms of resource constraints has leapt to the forefront of public consciousness in recent years, adding further urgency to the task of values education, and perhaps complicating the task of values education by fostering a perpetual siege mentality among the populace. In particular, the governments of Malaysia and Singapore have been unable to agree on the terms under which Malaysia will continue to supply the bulk of Singapore's water needs. The two governments continue to trade words over a disputed island, Pedra Branca, lying between the two countries.

On a more practical note, it is not always easy to get teachers and students to accord sufficient importance to values education amid the general scramble to prepare students for examinations within a highly competitive education system, a trend which shows few signs of abating even amid the TSLN rhetoric about critical and creative thinking. As Chew (1997: 90–91) has pointed out:

> ... there is a conflicting moral orientation in parts of the written curriculum that socialises Singaporean pupils to behave in a very individualistic and self-serving way in their relationships with other people. The message is clear: if an individual and a small nation-state are to survive in a highly competitive world, then they must work smartly and try to 'keep ahead of the pack.' Herein lies the strongest driving force in Singapore society, a force that encourages unbridled competition and selfish individualism, and one that is reflected in the education system. The school programme poses some dilemmas to its pupils. Given the reward structure of the wider society, pupils are responding in an expected way. In this sense, the whole educational system is geared towards sustaining a competitive ethos rather than an ethos of cooperation and caring for others. An important consequence is that much of the effort put in by the school to give pupils a balanced education is in danger of being nullified by the entrenched value system.

Attempting to quantify the success of values education initiatives (which essentially involve intangible emotional attitudes and beliefs) through the collection of hard data for the annual School Excellence Model reports, leads more often than not to students chalking up the necessary hours of community service or attending school-mandated activities for the sake of complying with school requirements rather than undertaking these activities in the genuine spirit of helping one's fellow citizens (see, for instance, Tan 2005). The Singapore government has over the years instituted a system of incentives and disincentives to goad citizens into complying with official policies (Lee 1966). There is therefore the danger that schools might treat community service as yet another means to compete for national trophies and awards for schools that have chalked up tangible, quantifiable indicators in terms of community service or for NE, and might not manage to evoke genuine, intrinsic passion for the objectives of NE or civics and moral education on the part of students.

Another concern with regard to values education in Singapore is exactly how comfortably it sits within the TSLN initiative. One might argue that the patriotic nature of NE, for example, requires a certain degree of convergence among teachers and students in terms of the emotions and passions that are officially deemed desirable. In other words, a common set of responses is deemed more worthy than all others. However, it might be said that this sort of convergence of thought is somewhat incompatible with the sort of critical thinking skills that TSLN would appear to encourage.

Conclusion

The Singapore case is instructive for other countries as they grapple with reforms to their values education programs in direct response to the challenges posed by globalization. Despite a whole flurry of values education initiatives – National Education, civics and moral education, for example – over the past decade, this chapter has shown how the rhetoric of these initiatives often appears at odds with the reality of school life in the light of other policy initiatives. Most fundamentally, the education system has not strayed far from the fundamental sorting and sifting function assigned it at the start of PAP rule five decades ago. Such a divisive function is hard to reconcile with rhetoric about inclusiveness and valuing every individual equally. The introduction of market values into schools has further served as a differentiating mechanism within and across schools, at times working against key values education messages rather than in consonance with them. Another lesson from Singapore is that despite the best efforts of an interventionist state that believes in a technocratic, state-directed manner of policy implementation, policy goals often remain elusive. This gives rise to repeated reform initiatives that very often sound repetitive in their rhetoric, which may lead over time to reform fatigue among school principals, teachers and students. In the meantime, the various challenges posed by globalization, such as the growing income stratification and the influx of large numbers of non-local-born residents, show little sign of disappearing from the public agenda.

References

Chew, J.O.A. (1997) 'Schooling for Singaporeans: The interaction of Singapore culture and values in the school' in J. Tan, S. Gopinathan and W.K. Ho (eds) *Education in Singapore: A book of readings*, Singapore: Prentice Hall.

Chua, B.H. (2007) 'Multiracialism as official policy: A critique of the management of difference in Singapore', in N. Vasu (ed.) *Social resilience in Singapore: Reflections from the London bombings*, Singapore: Select Publishing.

Goh, C.T. (1996) 'Narrowing the income gap', *Speeches*, 20, 3: 1–4.

Goh, C.T. (1997a). 'Shaping our future: "Thinking schools" and a "Learning nation"'. Online. Available HTTP: <http://stars.nhb.gov.sg/stars/public/viewHTML.jsp?pdfno=1997060209> (accessed 20 December 2007).

Goh, C.T. (1997b) 'Prepare our children for the new century: Teach them well', in J. Tan, S. Gopinathan and W.K. Ho (eds) *Education in Singapore: A book of readings*, Singapore: Prentice Hall.

Government of Singapore (1999) *Singapore 21: Together, we make the difference*, Singapore: Singapore 21 Committee.

Hershock, P.D., Mason, M. and Hawkins, J.N. (eds) (2007) *Changing education: Leadership, innovation and development in a globalizing Asia Pacific*, Hong Kong: Comparative Education Research Centre, University of Hong Kong.

Hussin, M. (2002) 'The socio-economic dilemma in Singapore's quest for security and stability', *Pacific Affairs*, 75: 39–56.

Kang, T. (2004) 'Schools and post-secondary aspirations among female Chinese, Malay and Indian Normal Stream students', in A.E. Lai (ed.) *Beyond rituals and riots: Ethnic pluralism and social cohesion in Singapore*, Singapore: Eastern Universities Press.

Lee, C., Cherian, M., Rahil, I., Ng, M., Sim, J. and Chee, M.F. (2004). 'Children's experiences of multiracial relationships in informal primary school settings', in A.E. Lai (ed.) *Beyond rituals and riots: Ethnic pluralism and social cohesion in Singapore*, Singapore: Eastern Universities Press.

Lee, H.L. (1997) *The launch of National Education*. Online. Available HTTP: <http://www1.moe.edu.sg/ne/KeySpeeches/MAY17-97.html> (accessed 8 February 2005).

Lee, K.Y. (1966) *New bearings in our education system*, Singapore: Ministry of Culture.

Lee, K.Y. (1996) 'Picking up the gauntlet: Will Singapore survive Lee Kuan Yew?', *Speeches*, 20, 3: 23–33.

Lee, W.O., Grossman, D.L., Kennedy, K.J. and Fairbrother, G.P. (eds.) (2004) *Citizenship education in Asia and the Pacific: Concepts and issues*, Hong Kong: Comparative Education Research Centre.

Leow, B.G. (2001) *Census of population 2000 statistical release 2: Education, language and religion*, Singapore: Department of Statistics.

Loh, C.K. (2007) 'Cracks in society are showing', *Today*, 17–18 November: 1, 3.

Quek, T. (2005) 'China whiz kids: S'pore feels the heat', *The Straits Times*, 13 February: 3–4.

Singapore Department of Statistics (2006) *General household survey 2005 release 1: Socio-demographic and economic characteristics*, Singapore: Department of Statistics.

Singapore Ministry of Community Development, Youth & Sports (2007) *Progress of the Malay community in Singapore since 1980*, Singapore: Ministry of Community Development, Youth and Sports.

Singapore Ministry of Education (1997a) *About NE*. Online. Available HTTP: <http://www1.moe.edu.sg/ne/AboutNE/SixMSGs.html> (accessed 8 February 2005).

Singapore Ministry of Education (1997b) *Launch of National Education*, Ministry of Education press release no. 017/97.

Singapore Ministry of Education (1998) *Desired outcomes of education*, Singapore: Ministry of Education.

Singapore Ministry of Education (2006a) *Civics and moral education syllabus primary 2007*, Singapore: Ministry of Education.

Singapore Ministry of Education (2006b) *Civics and moral education syllabus secondary 2007*, Singapore: Ministry of Education.

Straits Times (1993) '2 main challenges facing country', *The Straits Times*, 16 August: 24.

Straits Times (1995) 'Teach students to live with S'pore's constraints: PM', *The Straits Times*, 5 March: 1.

Straits Times (1996) 'Entrepreneurs are born, not made', *The Straits Times*, 11 July: 25.

Straits Times (2005) 'How Singapore grooms its leaders', *The Straits Times*, 18 November: 22

Singh, S. (2005) 'But Montfort principal says: We are improving local standards', *The New Paper*, 15 February: 2–3.

Tan, S.H. (2005) 'No vision? Youths need role models', *The Sunday Times*, 13 February: 26.

Townsend, T. and Cheng, Y.C. (eds) (2000) *Educational change and development in the Asia-Pacific region: Challenges for the future*, Lisse: Swets & Zeitlinger.

Velayutham, S. (2007) *Responding to globalization: Nation, culture and identity in Singapore*, Singapore: Institute of Southeast Asian Studies.

Wee, C.J.W.L. (2007) *The Asian modern: Culture, capitalist development, Singapore*, Hong Kong: Hong Kong University Press.

Woo, Y.Y. and Goh, C. (2007) 'Caging the bird: *TalkingCock.com* and the pigeonholing of Singaporean citizenship', in K.P. Tan (ed) *Renaissance Singapore? Economy, culture, and politics*, Singapore: NUS Press.

7 Preparing Students for the New World of Work

Critical Reflections on English Policy for Work-Related Learning in the Twenty-First Century

Ann-Marie Bathmaker

Introduction

How education prepares young people for the future, and in particular for their future working lives, has become an increasingly central concern both for national governments and for supra-national agencies such as the Organization for Economic Co-operation and Development (OECD) and the European Union (EU). The perception that a 'knowledge economy' places different demands on education systems, and that competitiveness in a high-skills knowledge economy is essential for post-industrial Western economies such as the UK, has led to expansion and reform of all forms of educational provision, with compulsory schooling at the heart of change.

This chapter examines how the vision of a changing world of work has influenced curriculum policy in England in the first decade of the twenty-first century. During this period, a wide range of policy initiatives have sought to strengthen connections between education and the economy, involving extensive reforms to the school curriculum. The chapter focuses on just one example of these reforms: Work-Related Learning. Although Work-Related Learning is not new, it only became a statutory component of education for 14–16 year olds in 2004 (UK Department for Education and Skills 2003).

The official definition of Work-Related Learning, as provided by the UK's Department for Children, Schools and Families,[1] is:

> Planned activity that uses the context of work to develop knowledge, skills and understanding useful in work, including learning through the experience of work, learning about work and working practices, and learning the skills for work.
>
> (UK Department for Children, Schools and Families 2009: 6)

The apparent simplicity of this definition glosses over a much more complex terrain. Work-Related Learning stitches together a diverse and ad hoc range of activities, qualifications, skills, attitudes and aptitudes. These have emerged over the past 30 years since the first wave of mass youth unemployment in England in the 1970s. The various forms of 'new' vocationalism introduced since this time, of which Work-Related Learning represents just one example, are associated with claims about the lack of technical and vocational skills developed by schools, leading to attempts to prepare young people for future work through various initiatives and vocational curricula which have come and gone over time, and which have received much critical attention (Avis 1991; Bates *et al.* 1984; Dale 1985; Ecclestone 2010; Gleeson 1990; Moore and Hickox 1994; Pring 1995; Yeomans 1998). There are clear continuities between current policy and the past. Huddleston and Oh (2004: 83) describe Work-Related Learning as a 'magic roundabout', suggesting that government policy continually repeats the same promise, that Work-Related Learning will be 'the elixir to cure some of the supposed failings of the education system', and will produce young people 'able and willing to fit the demands of the labour market' (2004: 85).

At the same time, changes to the wider economic and labor market context have refocused policy around two key goals. The first is raising levels of achievement amongst all school students for employment in a high skills economy. The second, somewhat contrasting goal, involves preparing young people for the uncertainties of the new world of work, where all must expect not just employment, but *un*employment and *under*-employment to be part of their future.[2] Both these concerns inform and shape current policy.

The chapter offers a critical analysis of English curriculum policy at a particular moment in time. Just after the chapter was completed a Conservative–Liberal Democrat government came to power in the UK, whereas the first decade of the twenty-first century was a period of New Labour government (1997–2010). Under New Labour, the connection between education and economic success was seen as central. Nevertheless, English Work-Related Learning policy over the past decade cannot simply be read as a reflection of New Labour policy. As various policy analysts have argued, there are considerable continuities between the earlier Conservative governments and New Labour (Ball 1999; Hill 2001; Hodgson and Spours 1999; Power and Whitty 1999). New Labour's tendency to combine continuity and change by adding new policy developments on top of old is a visible aspect of Work-Related Learning policy, creating an overload of often conflicting intentions and practices. Furthermore, national policy is increasingly framed by global discourses (Ball 1999). Grubb and Lazerson (2006) talk of an Education Gospel that pervades education internationally. They argue that there is a global trend towards the vocationalisation of schooling, based on 'an article of faith', whereby education will lead to 'social and individual salvation' (2006: 295), by enabling competitiveness and growth in a high-skills economy, along with upward individual mobility in the labor market.

While policymaking at macro level forms only one part of the policy construction process, an analysis of policy at this level plays an important role in critical policy analysis (Ball 1997). Policies project an image of how things should be and act as an operational statement of values (Ball 1990: 3). An analysis of policy formulation and policy statements therefore provides a means of holding policy values and visions up to scrutiny. However, the translations and transformations of policy through enactment play a significant part in constructing what policy is, and this chapter makes brief reference to examples of the reworkings of policy in local school contexts, based on an evaluation of Work-Related Learning in one region of England in 2008–2009 (James, Bathmaker and Waller 2010).

The analysis focuses on four key features of Work-Related Learning policy. Firstly, the wide diversity of practices, which are brought together under the umbrella of Work-Related Learning, render the concept of 'Work-Related Learning' and its meaning as a form of 'vocational' education almost impossible to define. Secondly, Work-Related Learning is overloaded with an increasing number of different and potentially competing aims; thirdly, current policy is based on a rationale which reflects a particular interpretation of work and work futures. In these three respects, Work-Related Learning demonstrates key long-term features of policymaking in the area of broad vocational education in England, where there is no strong version of, vision for, or agreement about what 'vocational' means in this context. Instead, there is a constantly shifting terrain, that reflects the interests of different stakeholders in different times and places.

A final aspect of Work-Related Learning considered in this chapter is the development of employability and enterprise skills. Both employability and enterprise have been key themes within vocational initiatives since the 1980s in England and elsewhere (see Smyth 1999). In England, they are now promoted within an overarching Work-Related Learning framework as essential components of the school curriculum for all students. Whereas the framework appears to allow for considerable diversity of interpretation, the reification of employability and enterprise suggests a more concerted attempt to achieve a 'colonization' change of secondary education (Ball 1997: 261). Ball, drawing on McLaughlin (1991), defines colonization change as 'major shifts in the cultural core of the organisation', where reforms change substantially the values, culture and practices of an organization. Understood in this way, the purpose of Work-Related Learning might be seen as orienting schools and young people towards business interests. What is at stake is the subject formation of young people in the interests of the economy, centered on notions of employability and enterprise.

Defining Work-Related Learning

Work-Related Learning as a means of preparing young people for the future of work is not confined to courses or subjects that are specifically vocational or occupational in orientation. Instead, Work-Related Learning in England is defined as 'a way of delivering learning' right across the curriculum (UK Department for Children, Schools and Families 2008a: 10). An official definition published by the UK's Department for Children, Schools and Families suggests that Work-Related Learning concerns activities that will directly prepare students for entry to the labor market, stating that every young person should be able to:

- Learn through work by direct experiences, such as a part-time job or work experience

- Learn about work by providing opportunities for students to develop their knowledge and understanding, for example through vocational courses and careers education
- Learn for work by developing employability skills, such as mock interviews and work simulations.[3]

However, the official Work-Related Learning Guide for schools (UK Department for Children, Schools and Families 2009) expands considerably on this definition, listing nine elements of provision and thirteen different types of activity that come under the umbrella of Work-Related Learning. These bring together a wide range of 'linkage mechanisms', intended to 'narrow the distance between education institutions and employment' (Grubb and Lazerson 2006: 300 and 299).

Firstly, there is careers information, advice and guidance, including mock job interviews, intended to inform students about employment and help them make choices. Secondly, there are opportunities to experience the 'real' world of work. These involve on the one hand students going out into the workplace, for work taster sessions, work shadowing and work experience. On the other, they involve employers coming into schools, to teach or lead discussions about the 'realities' of work, and to act as mentors to students. Thirdly, there are various forms of curriculum projects. Within school these are listed as business projects and challenges, work simulations and industry days to analyze and solve business-related problems, alongside practical and applied job-specific tasks within different curriculum subjects. Out of school, they involve curriculum-linked workplace visits, and world of work events, where the information and experience gained from the visit is incorporated into the student's learning. Finally, there is enterprise education as an area in its own right, which embraces enterprise skills, financial literacy, economic and business understanding, and understanding of entrepreneurship.

This diversity is reflected in the wide range of practices found during the course of an evaluation of Work-Related Learning conducted in one region of England between 2008 and 2009 (James, Bathmaker and Waller, 2010). Alongside work experience (usually one to two weeks for students at the age of 15), and careers advice and guidance work, there were examples of many different types of projects that linked the curriculum to the world of work. These included:

- a school with a fully-functioning community radio station on site, where students were given real responsibilities (up to and including being a radio presenter)
- a school where young people, as part of a Media program, carried out a commissioned project to make a film with a local history focus for a local community organization
- a school where young people following a Creative and Media course painted new murals outside the school buildings, and set up a website with a blog for student commentary on their course and links with industry
- an English teacher using communication in workplaces as a driver for organizing part of the curriculum, such as student visits to a range of settings used for in-class activities which classified and differentiated use of language

- a Maths teacher who visited businesses as well as using materials on dedicated websites to construct new, differentiated teaching plans and materials to locate Maths learning in the context of a garage, a pub and a hairdressing salon
- vocational conferences with a focus on vocational subjects such as Health and Social Care, Media, Performing Arts and Sport, where students could experience the range of occupations available, and do activities that generated evidence for their vocational qualification.

It was clear that the broad nature of Work-Related Learning allowed the schools in these examples to develop diverse and educationally worthwhile projects.

However, there were also examples where teachers floundered in trying to insert 'Work-Related' learning into the curriculum for their subject, and where establishing links with local employers and businesses was so time-consuming as to be of questionable value in relation to the outcomes that might be achieved for students. The evaluation also found that Work-Related Learning activities were regularly aimed at particular students, usually those who were below average achievers. This was partly in the hope of increasing the motivation of these students, but also to avoid jeopardizing the progress of more 'successful' students, with activities that might divert them from focusing on achieving high qualification grades. A further issue that arose related to the ever-changing succession of initiatives, with no obligation on the part of employers to participate or contribute, which meant that practices remained episodic, and had to be constantly re-invented, with little continuity or learning from past experience.

The Multiple Aims of Work-Related Learning

The wide diversity of practices outlined above is matched by the multiplicity of aims that the UK's Department for Children, Schools and Families claims for Work-Related Learning. These aims include:

- develop the employability skills of young people;
- provide young people with the opportunity to 'learn by doing' and to learn from experts;
- raise standards of achievement of students;
- increase the commitment to learning, motivation and self-confidence of students;
- encourage young people to stay in education;
- enable young people to develop career awareness and the ability to benefit from impartial and informed information, advice and guidance;
- support young people's ability to apply knowledge, understanding and skills;
- improve young people's understanding of the economy, enterprise, finance and the structure of business organisations, and how they work; and
- encourage positive attitudes to lifelong learning.

(UK Department for Children, Schools and Families 2009: 6)

This list reflects the diverse, sometimes competing aims that have gathered around broad 'vocational' forms of education over the past thirty years, where the goals of motivating 'disengaged' students to stay in education and achieve qualification outcomes take precedence, avoiding any serious consideration in national policy of what might constitute high quality, worthwhile vocational education (Ecclestone 2010; Pring *et al.* 2009; Young 2008).

One way of interpreting these extensive aims is to view Work-Related Learning as a condensation symbol (Troyna 1994), which brings together disparate interests and concerns in apparent agreement, and which taps into the idea of enabling all young people to succeed through improved motivation and achievement. It also taps into a wishful vision of a high skills economy, where individuals may learn their way into prosperity (or as Hayward and James (2004: 3) put it, 'learn their way out of poverty'), a vision which has been rehearsed regularly in English education policy documents.

The Policy Vision of Work and Work Futures for Young People

Throughout the past decade national policy discourses in England have combined arguments about the globalization of the economy with the need to increase skills levels in the population. These policy discourses construct a relational distinction between the past and the future. The future of work is presented in terms of a binary, which contrasts jobs that require high skills (the future) with jobs that do not (the past). The UK is positioned as competing with other countries for investment in high skills industries, and the strategy for success depends on the development of high skills in the population.

Education policy for secondary education continually reiterates this message, with the risks to the economy resulting from failure to develop high skills defined as growing ever greater. In 2001 a government education White Paper claimed that: 'To prosper in the twenty-first century competitive global economy, Britain must transform the knowledge and skills of its population' (UK Department for Education and Skills 2001: 5). By 2005, a subsequent White Paper stated:

> currents of economic change in other parts of the world can quickly affect this country and technology increasingly means that even service industries serving one country can be sited in another.
> (UK Department for Education and Skills 2005: 17)

Three years later, a further White Paper stressed that:

> Economic activity will move to wherever in the world it can be carried out most competitively. As the impact of this grows, the skills of the workforce will be a decisive factor in our continuing to be a high wage economy.
> (UK Department for Children, Schools and Families 2008b: 15)

The policy solution reiterated throughout is to achieve global economic competitiveness through high levels of education and training:

> If we are to continue to attract many of the high value-added industries to this country, and to compete effectively on the global stage, then we will need far more of our population to have high levels of education.
>
> (UK Department for Education and Skills 2005: 17)

The belief expressed in the demand for high skills has not waned in the face of the recession which hit the UK in 2008. Instead, the government's 2009 Work-Related Learning Guide for schools claims:

> In the current economic downturn, it is even more important to ensure that all young people gain the skills, qualifications and experience they need to meet the demands of the future workforce.
>
> (UK Department for Children, Schools and Families 2009: 5)

However, the Future of Work research program, undertaken during the same period as these policy claims were made (Nolan 2003), suggests that these assertions construct a future imaginary, which even before the recession in the UK, did not match up to analyses of the changing nature of the labor market offered elsewhere. Nolan uses the example of dot.com businesses to show that while such companies require software engineers and management consultants, they are not the main occupations that result from the dot.com industry:

> The priority list with respect to occupational growth is dominated by shelf-fillers, warehouse keepers, drivers and telephone operators, the employees that have prime responsibility for ensuring the delivery of the books, groceries and other tangible commodities that represent a primary element of the core business of e-commerce companies.
>
> (Nolan 2003: 478)

Researchers for the Future of Work program conclude that in practice 'the majority of the workforce do not depend on high skills to perform their occupational roles' (Brown *et al.* 2003: 109).

While the above policy constructions of work focus on skills needs, a further aspect of work futures rehearsed in current education policy documents concerns the uncertainty involved in changing patterns of employment, also presented in terms of a contrast between the old and the new. Firstly, the (former) idea of a job for life is juxtaposed with considerable movement between jobs:

> No longer is there an assumption that the sector in which a young person starts work is the one in which they will end their career. For most, movement between jobs is the norm; for many, movement between entirely different sectors of the economy a realistic prospect.
>
> (UK Department for Education and Skills 2005: 15–16)

Secondly, the developing shape of the labor market at the present time is defined in terms of a contrast between growing and diminishing forms of employment.

The future is said to involve more self-employment, and work in small companies, set against decreasing numbers of jobs in large firms or the public sector, once thought of as the 'good jobs', offering reasonable pay and security (Roberts 1993).

The Davies Review (2002), which has been influential in shaping current Work-Related Learning policy, paints the following picture of the UK labor market in the twenty-first century:

> The number of public sector jobs has fallen by almost two million, offset by four million new jobs in the private sector. The fastest growth has been amongst small businesses which now account for over 4 in 10 of business jobs, and in self employment which accounts for almost one in eight jobs in the economy as a whole.
>
> (Davies 2002: 15)

Past responses to labor market uncertainty and lack of employment for young people have been various forms of vocationalism, which have been criticized for doing little more than 'warehousing' young people, until job opportunities arise (Ainley 1999). Despite past experience the changing nature of work is used by policymakers once again to underline the need to strengthen the link between education and the economy, and to establish particular priorities for schools, linked to an economic agenda. The top priority is the achievement of credentials, as a proxy for high skills. The second priority is the need for employability and enterprise 'skills', as preparation for a constantly changing and flexible labor market.

Constructing Enterprising and Employable Subjects

Enterprise and employability have formed key threads in English Work-Related Learning policy since the rise of the 'new' vocationalism at the end of the 1970s. Discourses surrounding both concepts are associated with a number of assumptions about young people and schooling, which are reiterated in the present policy context, particularly in reports from the UK's Confederation of British Industry (CBI 2007) and the Davies Review (2002), commissioned by the UK Treasury, which have been influential in shaping recent policy.

Firstly, young people are defined as lacking the skills required by employers. So, for example, the CBI's 2007 report on employability and work experience states:

> Time and again, UK businesses have expressed frustration with the competencies of many of the young people emerging from full-time education. Most recently, in the 2006 CBI Employment Trends Survey, over 50% of employers reported that they were not satisfied with the generic employability skills of school leavers, and almost a third had the same issue with graduates.
>
> (CBI 2007: 8–9)

Secondly, young people are described as lacking 'enterprise'. In current formulations, this means the capacities that will enable them to be enterprising in the face of insecure work futures. According to the Davies Review, young people have 'a limited ability to handle uncertainty and manage risk effectively' (Davies 2002: 26).

Thirdly, schools are seen as not adequately preparing young people for work futures, both in terms of 'generic employability skills' (CBI 2007: 11) and in relation to developing 'enterprise capability'. There is, according to the Davies Review 'too little activity that specifically aims to develop young people's enterprise capability' (Davies 2002: 25).

These discourses reiterate a long-standing rhetoric that constructs a deficit view of young people and schools. What has altered in current iterations, is that the future of work is defined as having undergone major changes, which are used to justify renewed efforts to embed employability and enterprise within the curriculum. The Davies Review argues:

> we have given the development of enterprise capability particular attention. This is because we believe that it could play a bigger role than at present in preparing all young people for the changing economic and technological environment, and in developing the confidence and self-reliance they need to manage their own careers in this context, whatever their career choices (not only those who choose to start up their own business).
>
> (Davies 2002: 20)

Current constructions of enterprise and employability are heavily influenced by the voices of particular business interests, notably the UK's Confederation of British Industry, whose influence has become dominant in vocational policy (Raggatt and Unwin 1991). The definition of employability is quoted directly from this organization (CBI 2007) which states:

> 'Employability' is a set of attributes, skills and knowledge that all labour market participants should possess to ensure they have the capability of being effective in the workplace – to the benefit of themselves, their employer and the wider economy.
>
> (UK Department for Children, Schools and Families 2009: 32)

The CBI framework for employability is then presented in full (see Table 7.1), consisting of a mixture of what appear to be basic skills in numeracy, literacy and information technology, alongside soft skills such as problem-solving, and the management – or perhaps control – of the self, through 'self-management'.

Enterprise involves a different but overlapping collection of skills, concepts, attitudes and qualities, all taken from the Treasury-sponsored Davies Review (2002: 17–18), comprising the following elements:

- know and understand important enterprise concepts
- demonstrate enterprise skills, including decision making, leadership, risk management and presentation

- demonstrate enterprise attitudes, including a willingness to take on new challenges, self-reliance, open-mindedness, respect for evidence, pragmatism and commitment to making a difference
- demonstrate enterprising qualities, including adaptability, perseverance, determination, flexibility, creativity, ability to improvise, confidence, initiative, self-confidence, autonomy and the drive to make things happen.

(QCA 2008: 21)

These two sets of attributes, attitudes, skills, and knowledge move a considerable way beyond Work-Related Learning as a means of delivering learning across the curriculum. They propose curriculum priorities which entail a form of 'social literacy' (Gleeson 1990: 191), oriented to the development of knowledge, behaviors and attitudes that, it is claimed, are desired in the business world. Whereas Ball (1990: 72) has in the past suggested contradictions in the schools/industry discourse between 'the encouragement of assertive, independent entrepreneurs, who would found their own businesses, as against fostering attitudes of deference within a body of potential employees', now enterprise and employability appear as complementary aspects of Work-Related Learning policy, functioning together to construct an ideal, 'enterprising' and 'employable' subject. This ideal subject is not necessarily employed, but must be always 'employable'.

Table 7.1   The CBI's seven-point framework for employability

The attributes, skills and knowledge that make up 'employability'	
Self-management	Readiness to accept responsibility; flexibility; resilience; self-starting; appropriate assertiveness; time management, and readiness to improve own performance based on feedback/reflective learning.
Team working	Respecting others; co-operating; negotiating/persuading; contributing to discussions, and awareness of interdependence with others.
Business and customer awareness	Basic understanding of the key drivers for business success, including the importance of innovation and taking calculated risks, and the need to provide customer satisfaction and build customer loyalty.
Problem-solving	Analysing facts and situations and applying creative thinking to develop appropriate solutions.
Communication and literacy	Application of literacy; ability to produce clear, structured written work, and oral literacy, including listening and questioning.
Application of numeracy	Working with numbers and general mathematical awareness and its application in practical contexts (e.g. measuring, weighing, estimating and applying formulae).
Application of information technology	Basic IT skills, including familiarity with word processing, spreadsheets, file management and use of internet search engines.

Source: UK Department for Children, Schools and Families 2009: 33.

Beneath the condensation symbol of Work-Related Learning therefore, which foregrounds increased motivation and achievement through practical and applied learning, one way of understanding current policy is linked to a deeper project of orientation to 'employability' and 'enterprise' as defined by business interests, which are presented as essential features of preparation for the future of work.

Old Solutions for New Times

Despite claims about the changing nature of work in new times, the solutions offered in English Work-Related Learning curriculum policy at the start of the twenty-first century are far from new. Instead, they might best be described as a repackaging of old solutions, which have been the subject of critical concern amongst researchers for many years.

Enterprise education was first introduced in England under the Conservative regime of the 1980s and 1990s, as part of attempts to promote 'enterprise culture'. It was associated with a project of cultural reconstruction, involving a process of changing norms, attitudes and values, and re-imagining society in terms of entrepreneurial and neo-liberal principles (du Gay 1996; Peters 2001), seeking to move individuals from a culture of dependency to a culture of self-reliance. Yet research has questioned not just the intentions of enterprise culture, but the effects of the initiatives that were introduced in the past. A study by MacDonald (1991) in the 1980s highlights how young adults who attempted to join the enterprise culture by setting up new, small businesses met with very varied degrees of success. Coffield's (1990) research into enterprise initiatives in the same period disputes whether there is such a thing as a generic skill of enterprise whose essence can be distilled and taught, and a study by Ashford and Bynner (1991) found that despite efforts to promote enterprise values in the 1980s, young people sought good pay and prospects in preference to the pursuit of 'enterprise'.

The introduction of 'employability' skills, attributes and attitudes as part of the curriculum for young people has also raised serious concerns. Keep and Payne (2004; Keep 1999) have questioned the meaningfulness of 'skill' in relation to employability in England over a long period. Payne (2000) argues that recent usage of the term skill, particularly core or key skills (now also known as functional skills), is more applicable to a vision of a low-skill rather than a high-skill economy. Other researchers have argued that the introduction of generic and transferable skills to replace dedicated occupational skills training has more to do with developing the attitudes, behaviors and dispositions desired by employers, than developing the skills that might be needed in employment (Halsall 1996; Holt 1987). Nevertheless, enterprise and employability continue to be presented as a magic elixir (Huddleston and Oh 2004), which will prepare young people for the future of work.

Conclusion

Preparing young people for the future of work is a significant concern in English education policy at the beginning of the twenty-first century, and Work-Related

Learning represents just one of a whole range of approaches intended to address this concern by creating stronger linkages between school and employment. However, an analysis of policy reveals the myriad, conflicting purposes and functions associated with Work-Related Learning, which is overloaded with a plethora of attributes, behaviors, skills, and knowledge that are supposed to be developed. While there is a broad claim that these will contribute to young people's preparation for work futures, the extensive range of goals and intentions in current policy adds to long-standing difficulties in constructing any meaningful definition of work-related 'vocational' education.

Whilst some aspects of Work-Related Learning policy are concerned with gaining specific work-related skills, considerable emphasis in the detail of policy texts is placed on developing appropriate dispositions and attitudes towards participation in education and the labor market, as preparation for the (uncertain) prospect of the future of work. In particular, the pursuit of enterprise and employability, which form a core part of Work-Related Learning, may be seen as attempts to change the values, culture and practices of formal education, orienting both schools and young people towards an unquestioning and uncritical acceptance of business and industry interests.

There are important implications here for educational practice, particularly if education is to enable young people to actively shape their future working lives. Firstly, the lack of a strong definition of what work-related vocational education means leads to very uneven practices. It allows Work-Related Learning to slip easily into ways of motivating 'disaffected' students through more practical and applied activities, where the development of general personal and social dispositions and attributes for work and life become prioritized over the learning of meaningful vocational knowledge. Secondly, the emphasis on skills and attributes that employer representatives claim are needed in the workplace leads to a completely uncritical view about the world of work, and the values and practices therein. Thirdly, the framework specification of what Work-Related Learning involves translates quickly into a set of requirements to be checked off as part of management and inspection regimes (see Ofsted 2004; QCA 2004; 2007).

Finally, while policy rhetoric combines an optimistic and 'consensual' notion of a high-skills, knowledge economy (Brown *et al.* 2003) with an agenda of motivating students to achieve qualification outcomes as a basis for future prosperity, this does not match the likely future of work facing many young people in schools today. A belief in what appear to be very basic 'employability' skills, coupled with can-do 'enterprising' attitudes and behaviors, which will supposedly enable all young people to prepare successfully for the future of work, is both simplistic and unhelpful. Yet by acting as a condensation symbol, which brings together diverse interests and concerns in apparent agreement, dissent about Work-Related Learning becomes very difficult. This allows more subtle shifts to take place without challenge, so that schools become increasingly oriented to the values of business and the economy, with little debate about how these construct a particular and impoverished understanding of the roles and purposes of education in the twenty-first century.

Acknowledgements

The ideas for this chapter were developed out of a Work-Related Learning evaluation project, and I am indebted to the co-members of the team, David James and Richard Waller. Helen Colley and Kathryn Ecclestone provided invaluable advice on earlier drafts of this chapter.

Notes

1 The UK Department for Children, Schools and Families was replaced in June 2010 by the Department for Education.
2 Under-employment here refers to the under-utilisation of skills (or over-qualification for jobs) and also to patterns of part-time working and moving in and out of work, not out of choice, but due to a shortage of full-time employment.
3 UK Department for Children, Schools and Families website. Online. Available at: http://www.dcsf.gov.uk/14-19/index.cfm?go=site.home&sid=46&pid=404&ctype=None&ptype=Contents (accessed 20 August 2009).

References

Ainley, P. (1999) *Learning Policy. Towards the Certified Society,* Basingstoke: Macmillan.
Ashford, S. and Bynner, J. (1991) 'Whither the enterprise culture: An examination of young people's job values', *British Journal of Education and Work*, 4, 3: 53–62.
Avis, J. (1991) 'The strange fate of progressive education in Education Group II', in Department of Cultural Studies, University of Birmingham (eds) *Education Limited. Schooling, Training and the New Right in England since 1979*, London: Unwin Hyman.
Ball, S.J. (1990) *Politics and Policy Making in Education. Explorations in Policy Sociology,* London: Routledge.
Ball, S.J. (1997) 'Policy sociology and critical social research: a personal review of recent education policy and policy research', *British Educational Research Journal*, 23, 3: 257–273.
Ball, S.J. (1999) 'Labour, learning and the economy: a "policy sociology" perspective', *Cambridge Journal of Education*, 29, 2, 195–206.
Bates, I., Clarke, J., Cohen, P., Finn, D., Moore, R. and Willis, P. (eds) (1984) *Schooling for the Dole? The New Vocationalism*, London: Macmillan.
Brown, P., Hesketh, A. and Williams, S. (2003) 'Employability in a knowledge-driven economy', *Journal of Education and Work*, 16, 2: 107–126.
CBI (Confederation of British Industry) (2007) *Time Well Spent*. Online. Available HTTP: <www.cbi.org.uk/pdf/timewellspentbrief.pdf> (accessed 10 February 2010).
Coffield, F. (1990) 'From the decade of the enterprise culture to the decade of the TECS', *British Journal of Education and Work*, 4, 1: 59–78.
Dale, R. (ed.) (1985) *Education, Training and Employment: Towards a New Vocationalism?*, Oxford: Pergamon Press.
Davies, H. (2002) *A Review of Enterprise and the Economy in Education,* Norwich: HMSO. Online. Available HTTP: <www.dfes.gov.uk/ebnet/DR/DR.cfm> (accessed 26 August 2009).
Du Gay, P. (1996) 'Organizing identity: Entrepreneurial governance and public management', in S. Hall and P. du Gay (eds) *Questions of Cultural Identity*, London: Sage.
Ecclestone, K. (2010) *Transforming Formative Assessment in Lifelong Learning,* Buckingham: Open University Press.

Gleeson, D. (ed.) (1990) *Training and its Alternatives,* Buckingham: Open University Press.

Grubb, W.N. and Lazerson, M. (2006) 'The globalization of rhetoric and practice: the education gospel and vocationalism', in H. Lauder, P. Brown, J.A. Dillabough and A.H Halsey (eds) *Education, Globalization and Social Change*, Oxford: Oxford University Press.

Halsall, R. (1996) 'Core Skills: the continuing debate', in R. Halsall and M. Cockett (eds) *Education and Training 14–19. Chaos or Coherence,* London: David Fulton.

Hayward, G. and James, S. (2004) 'Producing skills: conundrums and possibilities', in G. Hayward and S. James (eds) *Balancing the Skills Equation. Key Issues and Challenges for Policy and Practice,* Bristol: Policy Press.

Hill, D. (2001) 'The Third Way in Britain: New Labour's neo-liberal education policy', paper presented at Congres Marx International III. Le capital et l'humanité, Université de Paris-X Nanterre-Sorbonne, September 2001.

Hodgson, A. and Spours, K. (1999) *New Labour's Educational Agenda. Issues and Policies for Education and Training from 14+,* London: Kogan Page.

Holt, M. (ed) (1987) *Skills and Vocationalism: The Easy Answer*, Milton Keynes: Open University Press.

Huddleston, P. and Oh, S.A. (2004) 'The magic roundabout: work-related learning within the 14–19 curriculum', *Oxford Review of Education, 30, 1: 83–103.*

James, D., Bathmaker, A.M. and Waller, R. (2010) *Evaluation of the Learning and Skills Council (West of England) Work Related Learning Project. Final report for the Learning and Skills Council.*

Keep, E. (1999) 'UK's VET policy and the "third way": Following a high skills trajectory or running up a dead end street?', *Journal of Education and Work*, 12, 3: 323–346.

Keep, E. and Payne, J. (2004) '"I can't believe it's not skill": the changing meaning of skill in the UK context and some implications', in G. Hayward and S. James (eds) *Balancing the Skills Equation. Key Issues and Challenges for Policy and Practice,* Bristol: Policy Press.

MacDonald, R. (1991) 'Risky business? Youth and the enterprise culture', *Journal of Education Policy*, 6, 3: 255–269.

McLaughlin, R. (1991) 'Can the information systems for the NHS internal market work?', *Public Money and Management,* Autumn: 37–41.

Moore, R. and Hickox, M. (1994) 'Vocationalism and educational change', *The Curriculum Journal*, 5, 3: 281–293.

Nolan, P. (2003) 'Reconnecting with history: The ESRC Future of Work Programme', *Work Employment Society*, 17, 3: 473–480.

Ofsted, (2004) *Learning to be enterprising: an evaluation of enterprise learning at key stage 4,* HMI 2148. Online. Available HTTP: <http://www.ofsted.gov.uk> (accessed 15 November 2009).

Payne, J. (2000) 'The unbearable lightness of skill: the changing meaning of skill in UK policy discourses and some implications for education and training', *Journal of Education Policy*, 15, 3: 353–369.

Peters, M. (2001) 'Education, enterprise culture and the entrepreneurial self: A Foucauldian perspective', *Journal of Educational Enquiry*, 2, 2: 58–71.

Power, S. and Whitty, G. (1999) 'New Labour's education policy: First, second or third way?', *Journal of Education Policy*, 14, 5: 535–546.

Pring, R. (1995) *Closing the Gap. Liberal Education and Vocational Preparation*, London: Hodder and Stoughton.

Pring, R., Hayward, G., Hodgson, A., Johnson, J., Keep, E, Oancea, A., Rees, G., Spours, K. and Wilde, S. (2009) *Education for All. The Future of Education and Training for 14–19 Year Olds*, London: Routledge.

QCA (2004) *Work-related Learning Baseline Study 2004*, London: Qualifications and Curriculum Authority.

QCA (2007) *Work-related Learning at Key Stage 4. First replication study*, London: Qualifications and Curriculum Authority.

QCA (2008) *Career, Work-related Learning and Enterprise 11–19. A Framework to Support Economic Wellbeing*, London: Qualifications and Curriculum Authority.

Raggatt, P. and Unwin, L. (1991) 'Introduction: a collection of pipers', in P. Raggatt, and L. Unwin (eds) *Change and Intervention. Vocational Education and Training*, London: Falmer.

Roberts, K. (1993) 'Career trajectories and the mirage of increased social mobility', in I. Bates and G. Riseborough (eds) *Youth and Inequality*, Buckingham: Open University Press.

Smyth, J. (1999) 'Schooling and enterprise culture: pause for a critical policy analysis', *Journal of Education Policy*, 14, 4: 435–444.

Troyna, B. (1994) 'Critical social research and education policy', *British Journal of Educational Studies*, 42, 1: 70–84.

UK Department for Children, Schools and Families (2008a) *The Work-Related Learning Guide – First Edition*, Nottingham: Department for Children, Schools and Families Publications.

UK Department for Children, Schools and Families (2008b) *Raising Expectations. Enabling the System to Deliver*, Cm 7348, Norwich: The Stationery Office.

UK Department for Children, Schools and Families (2009) *The Work-Related Learning Guide (Second Edition)*, Nottingham: Department for Children, Schools and Families Publications.

UK Department for Education and Skills (2001) *Schools Achieving Success*, Cm 5230, Annesley: DfES Publications.

UK Department for Education and Skills (2003) *14–19: Opportunity and Excellence*, Annesley: DfES Publications.

UK Department for Education and Skills (2005) *14–19 Education and Skills*, Cm 6476, Norwich: HMSO.

Yeomans, D. (1998) 'Constructing vocational education: from TVEI to GNVQ', *Journal of Education and Work*, 11, 2: 127–149.

Young, M. (2008) *Bringing Knowledge Back In. From Social Constructivism to Social Realism in the Sociology of Education*, London: Routledge.

8 The Curriculum of Basic Education in Mainland China

Before and After the Reform and Opening Up

Miantao Sun and Jiang Yu

The year 1978 is a year of historic significance in China's history. In that year, the Third Plenary Session of the Eleventh Central Committee of the Communist Party of China (CPC) made the important decision of the Reform and Opening Up and from that year, China embarked on the road of Reform and Opening Up. The Reform and Opening Up is a huge turning point in the history of China, which put mainland China into a new stage of socialist modernization. The Reform and Opening Up made earth-shaking changes in China's political, economic and cultural fields. In terms of politics, the central task was shifted from class struggle to economic construction. In terms of the economy, the economic system was shifted from a highly centralized planned economic system to a socialist market economic system full of vigor and vitality. In terms of culture, the culture was shifted from single culture to multi-culture in its orientation. From that time, mainland China has been engaged in a process of changing from a closed and semi-closed society to an open society and education is seen as playing a great role in promoting this development. Education must cultivate a new generation for the changing society.

After the Reform and Opening Up the CPC Central Committee and the State Council put forward the strategy 'rejuvenating the country through science and education' (CPC Central Committee State Council 1995: 14) and the 15th Party Congress of CPC determined that education should be given priority to be developed to underpin this strategy. Because the objectives and values of education are mainly reflected and implemented through curriculum, curriculum reform is at the core of the basic education reform.[1]

The basic education curriculum reform in mainland China after the Reform and Opening Up has had a profound impact on schools, making schools shift from an emphasis on exam-oriented education to an emphasis on quality-oriented education, from an emphasis on passing on knowledge to an emphasis on the training of qualified citizens. Schools have been re-oriented from being 'educational factories' towards being 'learning communities'. Based on this understanding, hereinafter we briefly analyze the curriculum of basic education in mainland China before and after the Reform and Opening Up from the perspective of curriculum reform.

The Curriculum of Basic Education in Mainland China Before the Reform and Opening Up

From the founding of the People's Republic of China (1949) to the Reform and Opening up (1978), under the guide of Marxism-Leninism and Mao Zedong Thought, China set the basic goals and tasks of curriculum as: teaching students basic knowledge and the basic skills of culture and science; developing students' cognitive abilities and physical strength; and cultivating students' world view of dialectical materialism and communist moral qualities. Of these, teaching students basic knowledge and the basic skills of culture and science was the central task of classroom teaching. In this period the curriculum guidelines for primary and secondary schools went through roughly three stages.

The first stage was from 1949 to 1957 and had a strong focus on political and moral formation. In 1950 the state enacted the first primary and secondary teaching plan which abolished the 'citizen' and 'military training' curriculum of the previous KMT (Kuomintang) government. The teaching plan provided that secondary schools offered politics, Chinese language, mathematics, biology, physics, chemistry, history, geography, foreign languages, physical education, music, art and graphics: in total 13 courses. Primary schools offered eight subjects: Chinese language, arithmetic, nature, history, geography, physical education, drawing and music. In 1952, the secondary school teaching plan was adjusted, reducing the total class hours of secondary school and dividing politics curriculum into: General Knowledge of the Chinese Revolution, Basic Knowledge of Social Science, Common Policy Framework, Current Events and Policies.

During the first Five-year Plan period from 1953 to 1957, teaching plans and teaching programs changed frequently in order to meet the needs of national economic development. The 1957 educational policy required the educated to develop in moral, intellectual and physical aspects and become workers with a socialist consciousness and culture. A manual labor curriculum was added to the primary school curricula and production education was added to the secondary school curricula. In that period the secondary school curriculum system was a typical discipline-centered curriculum: it emphasized discipline-based study rather than activity curricula and preferred compulsory curricula to elective curricula. Reforms were focused on streamlining curriculum content, and strove to combine improving education quality with reducing the heavy burden on students in order to promote students' health.

The second stage was from 1958 to 1965 and had a stronger economic productivity focus. At this stage, affected by the Great Leap Forward (an economic movement launched in 1958 that involved overly high productivity demands), the curriculum was in chaos and the normal order of teaching was under attack, causing a decline in the quality of education. In 1963 the primary and secondary school teaching plans and teaching programs were revised again. The teaching requirements on primary school mathematics and Chinese language were increased; in secondary schools class hours of Chinese language, mathematics, foreign languages, physics, chemistry, etc. were increased and the class hours of history and geography were decreased. (At this stage, the tendency of valuing the sciences and neglecting the humanities began to appear.) The curriculum plan stressed that all subjects should pay attention to the teaching of basic knowledge and basic skills; and allowed senior secondary schools to offer some elective curricula, breaking through the uniform compulsory curricula of the 1950s. Production Knowledge, a subject introducing the basic knowledge and skills required in industrial and agricultural production, was added to both primary school curricula and secondary school curricula as a new curriculum.

In conclusion, at this stage, led by the principle that 'education must serve proletarian politics and must be combined with productive labor' (P.R. China, The CPC Central Committee, State Council 1959: 5), the primary and secondary school curriculum system changed in terms of curriculum objectives, structure, implementation and evaluation. The most significant change was the prominence given to political curricula and labor skill curricula and the weakened status of culture curricula. Influenced by ultra-leftist political thought, reforms reflected ideas that 'schools should be combined with social large-scale production and students don't have to learn but have to work' (China National Institute for Educational Research 1984: 225) and 'the number of curricula can be halved' (Party Literature Research Office of the CPC Central Committee 1996: 22).

The third stage was from 1966 to 1976 and intensified these political directions. This stage is the period of China's Cultural Revolution. From 1966, the Education Minister and the Deputy Minister were criticized or suspended, halting the educational administration function of the Ministry of Education. The normal teaching order of primary and secondary schools was destroyed. From this time until 1978, there were no national uniform school curriculum plans or textbooks, and local schools edited their own textbooks. Although the textbooks edited by local schools did not have a uniform format, the spirit and content of the textbooks was very similar. Not only were literature books replaced by Quotations from Chairman Mao, but so were science and engineering subjects. Physics, chemistry and even mathematics also became politicized. The previous mathematics curriculum did not link with any political factors and only emphasized the various inferences, axioms and formulas of mathematics, which resulted in students, having learned mathematics, not knowing whom they should serve. But the mathematics curriculum at this time started with counting the exploited account of workers and poor peasants and strengthened students' concept of class struggle, solving the problem of whom students should serve after learning mathematics.

The characteristics of primary and secondary school curricula during the Cultural Revolution were these:

1   The curriculum was highly streamlined. Some subjects such as foreign languages were canceled, and some were combined. For example politics and Chinese language were merged into Political Culture Curriculum or Mao Zedong Thought. Music curriculum and art curriculum were also combined into Revolutionary Art Curriculum.

2   The curriculum was highly politicized. The politics curriculum was not only made the most important curriculum, but without exception, other curriculum also indoctrinated political factors in an indirect way. Music,

art and other cultural curricula became a 'revolutionary literature and art curriculum'; the slogan of Military and Sports Curriculum 'one, two, three, four' was replaced by Quotations from Chairman Mao; and even the basic culture curriculum of Chinese language was combined with Mao Zedong Thought as a political curriculum (Cao Yanjie 2005: 18).

3   The curricula highlighted practicality and had an obvious pragmatic tendency. Phrases such as 'it is useless to read more books', 'learning by doing' and 'learning by using' were very popular. For the art curriculum, students mainly read Chairman Mao's works, wrote critical essays and did practical things. For the science curriculum, a large number of practical problems and knowledge in industrial and agricultural production was added, for example, the curriculum 'Basic Knowledge in Industry' mainly introduced the knowledge of tractors, diesel engines, motors, pumps and the like.

In short, the school curriculum during the Cultural Revolution was an extreme social activity curriculum and was a reaction to a discipline-centered curriculum. The historical value of this curriculum is that it is an effective correction to the discipline-centered curriculum which was divorced from reality, however it went to the other extreme. It despised and even abandoned the disciplinary system and theoretical knowledge, and attempted to replace the indirect experience that had been accumulated for thousands of years with the direct experience of practical reality. Practice has shown that this was very wrong because it abandoned history, which meant giving up the future. Its direct consequence was that a large number of young students abandoned their studies, and as a result there were not enough trained young men and women ready to take over from older experts, creating a poverty of thinking. The narrow empiricism was popular for many years and it created a huge negative impact on science and culture education.

The teaching processes of this period from the founding of the People's Republic of China (1949) to the Reform and Opening Up (1978), were highly didactic. Depending on the teaching task and content, classes were divided into the following types: new classes, recitations, exercise classes, laboratory classes, test classes and integrated classes. The teaching process of a class was structured as: organizing, reviewing old lessons, teaching new lessons, or consolidating new courses and assignments. This had the positive effect of enhancing classroom teaching order and enabled teaching tasks to be completed on time. Meanwhile, this teaching process theory was consistent with students understanding the general rules of the external objective things and it was feasible and easy for teachers to accept and master.

However, this approach also had some negative influences on school teachers' instruction. School teachers just considered students as teaching objects, neglected the students' subject position in classroom teaching and made too many restrictions and constraints on students, which seriously affected students' enthusiasm, initiative and creativity. Criticism, reprimand, prohibition and punishment were used as basic educational tools. The relationship between teachers and students was unequal and things like distrusting and disrespecting students often happened and even humiliation and corporal punishment occurred in disguised forms.

The curriculum preferred the teaching of basic knowledge and basic skills to the cultivation of students' ability and individuality. This resulted in students lacking innovation and hands-on ability.

This curriculum preferred discipline to self-consciousness. Students were not guided to form habits of self-discipline, self-education and self-management from childhood and there was an insistence that the stricter teachers were the better it was for students. This led students to lack the quality and capacity to judge independently, and have self-control, self-discipline and self-reliance. The curriculum also preferred uniformity to diversity. Uniformity was demanded in terms of teaching plans, teaching programs and teaching methods. The individual differences among students were not acknowledged and the uniqueness and difference of students was ignored. As a consequence, classroom teaching was monotonous and rigid. Students' interests, hobbies and needs were not fully respected or developed.

The curriculum preferred teaching to inquiry. In the classrooms, teachers instilled blindly and monopolized everything. It was insisted that the more teachers taught the more students knew, which meant that students were not good at thinking independently and lacked the ability to understand, analyze and solve problems.

The Implementation of Curriculum Reform of Basic Education in Mainland China After the Reform and Opening Up

After the Cultural Revolution, mainland China ended a decade-long turmoil. In 1978 the Third Plenary Session of the Eleventh Central Committee of the Communist Party of China sounded the clarion call of the Reform and Opening Up. China entered into a new historical period of prosperous development.

> The main theme of the times was reform and opening up and earth-shaking changes took place in China. Political system, economic system, science and technology system and educational system had started their reform one after another. Many areas of social life had undergone profound changes of the transformation of the new and old system.
>
> (Tian Huisheng and Zeng Tianshan 1997: 16)

In the economic field, the new system of a socialist market economy was established and mainland China faced the historical task of constructing socialism in all aspects of society with economic construction as the center. Among these, the task for education was particularly difficult. On the one hand socialist modernization was in urgent need of professionals in all aspects; on the other hand, after ten years of chaos, the academic structure and curriculum were destroyed, the majority of teachers were destroyed, students had abandoned their studies and their cultural and scientific knowledge seriously declined. In this lean situation, the revitalization of education became the basis for comprehensive restoration and the development of the national economy. For this reason, Comrade Deng Xiaoping repeatedly warned that the Communist Party of China should pay attention to primary and secondary education, and he personally worked on the recovery and reconstruction of the educational system and curriculum. School curriculum reform was thriving with vitality.

Curriculum reform of basic education since the Reform and Opening Up to the outside world has gone through four stages: renovation and starting off (1978–1985); springing up and further developing (1986–1992); deepening all-round (1993–1999); and innovation and scientific development (1999–present).

In the first stage of reform (1978–1985), the main change was to re-emphasize the importance of education. This first basic education curriculum reform followed the framework and model of the previously used primary and secondary school curriculum. There was no great change although a few selective curricula were added. Curriculum still was structured with a high degree of unity, a lack of flexibility in implementation and a mismatch between the content of teaching materials and children's psychological logic.

In the next stage (1986–1992) of developing these reforms, the promulgation and implementation of the 'Compulsory Education Law of the People's Republic of China' (1986) set objectives for high-quality curricula and priority to the implementation of compulsory education. The main features of curriculum reform at this stage was that on the one hand, curriculum objectives were more specific, clearer, and the range of curriculum objectives was expanded, and on the other there was some expansion of curriculum subjects and activities, and selective curricula were for the first time offered in junior secondary schools since the founding of P.R. China.

An important further educational idea in mainland China, namely, the idea of 'quality-oriented education' was raised during the third stage of reform (1993–1999). The idea of 'quality-oriented education' now took the place of 'exam-oriented education' in the conception and training objectives of primary and secondary education in mainland China. The two main features of this stage were the emphasis on students' innovative and practical abilities in curriculum objectives and the conversion of the curriculum administration system, namely, the implementation of a three-level administration system – central government, local government and school.

Further large-scale adjustment and reforms were made in curriculum objectives, structures, content, implementation and evaluation during the fourth stage of curriculum reform (1999–present). The core idea of the curriculum reform at this stage is 'for the development of each student' and the ultimate pursuit is 'a whole person education' which is the basic value orientation of curriculum reform in the present period. 'A whole person education' is student-oriented and insists on all-round development. Besides allowing students to obtain professional knowledge, it makes them understand and develop their self-confidence, self-positioning, attitude towards life, judgment, interpersonal skills and the like. Education should be concerned about students' physical and mental conditions, intelligence, emotion, and personality.

The most significant feature of the curriculum reform at this stage was its student orientation, and focus on the all-round development of students, requiring all students to have comprehensive development in contrast to the principles of authoritarianism and elitism. School curriculum objectives included the following new features: an emphasis on students' all-round development; attention to the learning of basic knowledge and improving students' basic quality; a focus on the development of students' individuality; a focus on the future and attaching great importance to ability development; a stress on the cultivation of students' good moral character; and emphasis on strengthening education in international awareness of students. This current reform was the most innovative, the most influential and the largest one since the founding of the People's Republic of China.

After the Reform and Opening Up, basic education curriculum reform in mainland China was led by the State Education Ministry and provincial educational administrative departments. The State Education Ministry was in charge of the leadership and overall management of the curriculum reform; provincial educational administrative departments were responsible for leading and planning provincial (autonomous regions and municipalities) implementation.

Basic education curriculum reform upheld the principles of democratic participation and scientific decision-making. Experts and scholars from universities and colleges and teachers from primary and secondary schools were all involved and some normal universities set up 'Research Centers of Basic Education Curriculum', to carry out research work on the curriculum reform, often working in conjunction with primary and secondary schools. Parents and different sectors of the community also participated in curriculum construction and school management and the news media played a positive role, guiding all social sectors in further discussing, caring about and supporting curriculum reform.

Major Changes of Basic Education Curriculum Reform in Mainland China After the Reform and Opening Up

After experiencing conscious reflection on the practice of denial and violation of cultural and scientific knowledge during the Cultural Revolution, mainland China deeply realized the strengths and values of cultural and scientific knowledge. The curriculum reform of this period resumed respect for knowledge, and then made more comprehensive quality requirements on students. Curriculum objectives have become more specific, comprehensive and systematic. And the reform has moved away from a single and narrow curriculum structure.

Activity curriculum, elective curriculum and integrated curriculum are now offered and the allocation of class hours among academic curriculum has been adjusted, lightening students' heavy study load and improving the all-round development of students' individuality and quality. The past curriculum structure, which emphasized the discipline-base too heavily, had too many subjects and lacked integration, has been changed. The new curriculum structure reflects balance, integrity and selectivity.

A nine-year integrated curriculum has been set up. The curricula offered at primary schools have mainly been integrated curricula. Lower primary school grades offer morality and life, Chinese language, mathematics, physical education and art. Higher primary school grades offer morality and society, Chinese language, mathematics, science, foreign languages, Comprehensive Practical Activities, physical education and art.

Junior secondary schools offer both subject curricula and integrated curricula, mainly including moral education, Chinese language, mathematics, foreign languages, science (or physics, chemistry and biology), history and society (or history, geography), physical education and health, art and Comprehensive Practical Activities. The teaching of writing has been strengthened in the curriculum in the same way as Chinese language and art were strengthened during the compulsory education period.

The curricula offered at senior secondary school have been mainly subject curricula. Curriculum Standards provide requirements of different levels, and both compulsory subjects and elective and technical curricula are offered, in order to enable students to develop according to their interests and individuality.

From primary school to senior secondary school Comprehensive Practical Activities are offered as a compulsory curriculum. The main content of Comprehensive Practical Activities includes: information technology education, research learning, community service and social practice as well as labor and technology education. Comprehensive Practical Activities emphasizes that through hands-on practice students enhance their sense of exploration and innovation, learn scientific research methods and develop the ability to synthetically use knowledge. These activities have enhanced the close ties between school and community and cultivated students' social responsibility. In the process of curriculum implementation, information technology education has been strengthened and students have been trained to have the awareness and ability to use information technology.

In rural areas, secondary school curriculum has served local socio-economic development. Under the premise of meeting the basic requirements of national curriculum, rural areas have set the curricula to fit in with local needs according to modern agricultural development and the adjustment of industrial structures in rural areas. Through Green Certificate education and other technical training, rural schools have enabled students in rural areas to obtain Double Certificates, namely general high school diploma and agricultural technical certificates (Green Certificates).

In summary then, the curriculum after the Reform and Opening Up has strengthened the links between curriculum content, students' lives, contemporary society, science and technology development, has paid close attention to students learning interests and experiences and has selected the basic knowledge necessary for lifelong learning and skills.

Since the Reform and Opening Up, curriculum reform in mainland China has been dedicated to the integration of curriculum unity and flexibility. It has changed the highly unified curriculum management and used the three-level administration of central government, local government and school to enhance the adaptability of curriculum to locality, schools and students. Schools can develop and use curricula that are suitable to the characteristics of schools themselves, while at the same time implementing national and local curricula.

An evaluation system that promotes the comprehensive development of students has also been established. Evaluation now not only stresses students' academic performance, but also discovers and develops a wide range of potentials that students' have, understands the development needs of the students, and helps students understand themselves and develop confidence. The evaluation system has played an educational function and promoted students' development on the basis of previous levels.

An evaluation system that promotes the continuous improvement of curriculum has been established. This system allows for periodical analysis and assessment of the curriculum implementation of schools and the problems that occur during curriculum implementation, adjustment of curriculum content and improvement of teaching management, and forms a mechanism through which curriculum can continuously innovate. At the same time there is in the current approach more interest in research and in referring to the experiences and lessons of curriculum reform in Hong Kong, Taiwan and abroad.

Basic education curriculum reform in mainland China after the Reform and Opening Up has had a profound impact on school teachers' instructional practices. In particular, teachers have been set an awareness of individuality in education. The new curriculum takes each student into account, particularly students of diverse backgrounds. The requirements teachers place on students in the classroom are no longer uniform, but reflect respect for individual differences and diversity. Teachers can teach students in accordance with individual differences. In order to respect the individuality and diversity of students, teachers are required to respect each student's dignity and value, especially those with mental retardation, poor academic performance, those isolated and rejected, and those who hold different views from others. Teachers are asked to guide students according to their individual differences, allowing students the right to choose their needs, interests and hobbies. Teachers are exhorted to fully explore every student's creativity and enthusiasm, stimulate students' psychological desire for development and cultivate students' special talents.

The curriculum objectives after the Reform and Opening Up have shifted from 'focusing on knowledge' to 'focusing on students'; curriculum design has shifted from 'passing knowledge' to 'causing activities'. Past curriculum implementation is seen as having placed too much emphasis on receptive learning, rote memorization and mechanical training. Teachers are now asked to promote students who actively participate and are willing to explore and to cultivate students' ability to collect and process information, acquire new knowledge, analyze and solve problems, communicate and cooperate. To develop students' innovative consciousness, teachers are expected to create a democratic and harmonious atmosphere in classrooms, create problem situations, stimulate students' curiosity and interest in innovative thinking, develop problem awareness and encourage students to query boldly and dare to challenge authority. Teachers are expected to develop a good class environment and use collective activities to improve the self-management ability of students.

The philosophy of the current changes reflects a transition from 'learning according to teaching' to 'teaching according to learning'. In terms of the arrangements of specific teaching processes, there is more democracy, less monopolization, more instruction, coaching and guidance, less explanation, which fully mobilizes the enthusiasm of students in independent learning.

The curriculum reform of basic education in mainland China has made considerable achievements and has brought vigor to the development of mainland China's basic education. At the same time there are still some problems.

1   Problems of teacher training. Teachers are an important guarantee for the success of basic education curriculum reform. However, teachers' conceptions and practical skills are far from enough. This is reflected in two respects: on the one hand, it is difficult for some teachers to change their traditional teaching conceptions. They are accustomed to the traditional curriculum ideas, objectives, content and methods. Old things are deeply rooted in their minds, so when facing the new curriculum reform they feel that it is 'too sudden', 'at a loss', and find it difficult to adapt to it. Yet the new curriculum places higher demands on teachers' quality. Although some teachers have been trained in the new curriculum reform philosophy, they still lack teaching methods and do not know how to convert theory into an operable method, so they cannot adapt to the new curriculum.

2   Not enough resources and support for implementing curriculum reform. Enough resources and support such as policy and outlay support are important prerequisites for the smooth implementation of curriculum reform. However, a very prominent problem that the basic education curriculum reform in mainland China since the Reform and Opening Up has encountered is insufficient resources and support. This is particularly obvious in rural areas.

3   There are significant differences between urban and rural areas in the process of curriculum reform. There is a certain degree of difficulty in rural areas. Because of the differences between urban and rural schools with regard to infrastructure, teaching environment, teacher levels and student foundations, curriculum reform has advanced relatively smoothly in urban schools, while there are difficulties in rural areas. 'In some schools in rural experimental areas, teachers lack of basic IT teaching methods, which combined with funding problems makes curriculum reform in rural schools face many difficulties' (Ma Yunpeng 2009: 8).

To sum up, the curriculum of basic education in mainland China before and after the Reform and Opening Up has experienced remarkable changes in terms of curriculum objectives, structure, content, implementation, administration and evaluation. The curriculum of basic education in mainland China before the Reform and Opening up emphasized teaching students basic knowledge and the basic skills of culture and science and just considered students as teaching objects, neglecting their subject position in classroom teaching and making too many restrictions and constraints on them, which seriously affected enthusiasm, initiative and creativity. It emphasized a collective and uniform political set of values that students should acquire, but weakened their scientific knowledge and ability to innovate. The Reform and Opening Up has led to a social transformation in mainland China and has also led to profound changes to the curriculum of basic education in mainland China. The new curriculum is directed towards developing students to learn to learn, to learn to cooperate, to learn to survive and to learn to be. It is concerned about students' 'whole person' development, and intended to cultivate students with social responsibility, good personalities, creative spirits, practical abilities and a desire and ability for lifelong learning. The function of the curriculum now is seen as not just about passing on discipline-based knowledge, or preparing for future labor, but about developing citizens who can be creative and innovative and can adapt to the social, technological and economic development of the twenty-first century. In doing this, the curriculum reform in mainland China has absorbed and learned from the experience of curriculum reform around the world, aligning with the world trend of curriculum reform. Mainland China has found a road of curriculum reform with Chinese characteristics and has achieved comprehensive and rapid development of the curriculum of basic education.

Note

1   This chapter draws throughout on the Chinese curriculum guidelines and policy documents listed in English at the end of this chapter.

References

(1) Chinese Policy Documents

P.R. China, The CPC Central Committee, State Council (19 September 1959) 关于教育工作的指示(The Instructions on Educational Work), in *A Collection of Educational Documents and Decrees 1958*, Beijing: General Office of the Ministry of Education of the People's Republic of China.

P.R. China, Ministry of Education (18 January 1978) 全日制十年制中小学教学计划（试行草案) (Full-time Ten-year Primary and Secondary School Teaching Plan (Trial Draft)); reprinted in Wu Luping (2001) *A Collection of Curriculum Standards and Teaching Programs of the People's Republic of China during the 20th Century* (Volume of Curriculum and Teaching Plans), Beijing: People' Education Press: 325–329.

P.R. China, Ministry of Education (17 April 1981) 全日制六年制重点中学教学计划（试行草案)(Full-time Six-year Key School Teaching Plan (Trial Draft)) ; reprinted in Wu Luping (2001) *A Collection of Curriculum Standards and Teaching Programs of the People's Republic of China during the 20th Century* (Volume of Curriculum and Teaching Plans), Beijing: People' Education Press: 338–342.

P.R. China, Ministry of Education (17 April 1981) 全日制五年制中学教学计划试行草案的修订意见 (Full-time Five-year Secondary School Teaching Plan Revisions to the Trial Draft); reprinted in Wu Luping (2001) *A Collection of Curriculum Standards and Teaching Programs of the People's Republic of China during the 20th Century* (Volume of Curriculum and Teaching Plans), Beijing: People' Education Press: 342–343.

P.R. China, The CPC Central Committee (27 May 1985) 中共中央关于教育体制改革的决定 (The Decision of the CPC Central Committee on Educational System Reform). Online. Available HTTP: <http://www.moe.edu.cn/edoas/website18/18/info3318.htm> (accessed 23 July 2010).

P.R. China, State Education Commission (20 September 1988) 义务教育全日制小学、初级中学教学计划(试行草案) (Compulsory Education Full-time Teaching Plan of Primary and Junior Secondary Schools (Trial Draft)); reprinted in Wu Luping (2001) *A Collection of Curriculum Standards and Teaching Programs of the People's Republic of China during the 20th Century* (Volume of Curriculum and Teaching Plans), Beijing: People' Education Press: 351–354.

P.R. China, State Education Commission (6 August 1992) 九年义务教育全日制小学、初级中学课程计划(试行) (Nine-Year Compulsory Education Full-time Curriculum Plan of Primary and Junior Secondary Schools (Trial)); reprinted in Wu Luping (2001) *A Collection of Curriculum Standards and Teaching Programs of the People's Republic of China during the 20th Century* (Volume of Curriculum and Teaching Plans), Beijing: People' Education Press: 372–379.

P.R. China, The CPC Central Committee, State Council (13 February 1993) 中国教育改革和发展纲要(Chinese Education Reform and Development Outline). Online. Available: <http://www.moe.edu.cn/edoas/website18/34/info3334.htm> (accessed 23 July 2010).

P.R. China, The CPC Central Committee, State Council (6 May 1995) 中共中央国务院关于加速科学技术进步的决定 (The CPC Central Committee and the State Council's Decision on Accelerating the Progress of Science and Technology), in The Department of Policy, Regulation and System Reform of the Ministry of Science and Technology of the People's Republic of China (2003) *A Selection of Laws, Regulations and Policies of Science and Technology of the People's Republic of China*, Beijing: Law Press: 14.

P.R. China, Standing Committee of the National People's Congress (17 March 1996) 中华人民共和国国民经济和社会发展九五规划和 2010 年远景目标纲要 (The Ninth Five-Year Plan for National Economic and Social Development and the Outline for the Long-term Goals for the Year 2010 of the People's Republic of China). Online. Available HTTP: <http://www.npc.gov.cn/wxzl/gongbao/2001-01/02/content_5003506.htm> (accessed 23 July 2010).

P.R. China, State Education Commission (26 March 1996) 全日制普通高级中学课程计划(试验) (Full-time General Senior High School Curriculum Plan (Pilot)); reprinted in Wu Luping (2001) *A Collection of Curriculum Standards and Teaching Programs of the People's Republic of China during the 20th Century* (Volume of Curriculum and Teaching Plans), Beijing: People' Education Press: 397–402.

P.R. China, State Education Commission (24 December 1998) 面向21世纪教育振兴行动计划 (The Action Plan for the Revitalization of Education for the 21st Century). Online. Available HTTP: <http://www.moe.edu.cn/edoas/website18/37/info3337.htm> (accessed 23 July 2010).

P.R. China, State Council (29 May 2001) 国务院关于基础教育改革与发展的决定 (State Council's Decision on Curriculum Reform and Development of Basic Education). Online. Available HTTP: http://news.china.com/zh_cn/domestic/945/20010614/10045441.html (accessed 23 July 2010).

P.R. China, Ministry of Education (8 June 2001) 基础教育课程改革纲要（试行） (The Outline of the Curriculum Reform of Basic Education (Pilot)); reprinted in Zhong Qiquan, Cui Yunkuo and Zhang Hua (2001) *For the Renaissance of the Chinese Nation and the Developing of Every Student: Unscrambling The Outline of the Curriculum Reform of Basic Education (Pilot)*, Shanghai: East China Normal University Press: 3–13.

(2) Other References

Cao Yanjie (2005) 'Retrospection 50: The Grouping Track of PRC Curriculum in General Middle School', unpublished thesis, East China Normal University.

China National Institute for Educational Research (1984) *Educational Chronicle of the People's Republic of China (1949–1982)*. Beijing: Educational Science Publishing House.

Ma Yunpeng (2009) 'The Implementation Process, Characteristics Analysis and Promotion Strategy of Curriculum Reform of Basic Education', *Curriculum, Teaching Material and Methods*, 29, 4: 8.

Party Literature Research Office of the CPC Central Committee (1996) *Mao Zedong's Manuscripts since 1949*, volume 11. Beijing: Central Party Literature Press.

Tian Huisheng and Zeng Tianshan (1997) *The Reform and Experiments of Curriculum and Teaching Material of Primary and Secondary Schools*. Chengdu: Sichuan Education Publishing House.

Part III

Curriculum and Knowledge

9 Curriculum Policies for a Knowledge Society?

Michael Young

> The time is out of joint: O cursed spite,
> That ever I was born to set it right!
> *(Hamlet*, Act 1 Scene V)

Introduction

In this chapter[1] I want to outline and comment on the implications of what I see as a tension in current curriculum policies of both national governments and international organizations. My argument will be that current policies are in danger of neglecting and even undermining the most basic education issue facing policy makers, teachers and researchers – how do we enable a higher proportion of each cohort of young people to gain access to 'powerful knowledge' (Young 2009), that it is the specific role of schooling to 'transmit'? Later in this chapter I will return to several issues that my question raises – what is powerful knowledge and why is it important? And what is meant by schools 'transmitting knowledge', if we recognize that transmission cannot be a one-way process as the metaphor implies but will always involve the active engagement of learners and the mobilization of their interests and experiences.

The tension I have referred to can be expressed in the following way. On the one hand most current policies take as a priority the extension of access to and the widening of participation in formal education (Young 2010). In other words these policies recognize the importance of extending the time young people spend in formal education and the proportion of each cohort that have this opportunity. However the same policies neglect what this access is *to*,[2] and what it is assumed students are encouraged to participate *in*. It is as if an *organizational criterion* – whether students are attending school or college and gaining certain certificates – is replacing an *educational criterion* which would refer to the intellectual development of students and whether, in the process they acquire that knowledge – powerful knowledge – that enables them to generalize from their experience and move beyond it. At the same time, there is little doubt that the transmission of 'powerful knowledge' is at the forefront of the goals of elite institutions, especially those which rely on parents paying full-cost fees. It follows that in so far as if access to 'powerful knowledge' is not the priority of national curriculum policies, such policies are likely to perpetuate and even exacerbate existing educational inequalities.

The question is how has this tension emerged and what form does it take? It arises, I suggest, from the pressures in all countries to expand public education with limited resources on the basis of what began as highly elitist upper secondary and higher education systems with their origins in a pre-industrial and Church-dominated era. This expansion has led in most countries, to unresolved questions as to how this expansion should take place. Should it involve (a) extending elite knowledge to the mass of students? (b) replacing concepts of knowledge associated with elite forms of education on the assumption that they are out of date, socially divisive in outcomes and primarily geared to preserving the privileges of the elite? or (c) developing a diversified system of education that is suited to what are claimed to be the needs, interests and capabilities of different groups in a modern society? These alternatives need some elaboration.

It is widely agreed that today, all societies should be moving towards what is referred to as a 'knowledge (or post-industrial) society'. The meaning given to such a society is usually that it is one in which an increasingly high proportion of jobs demand high levels of skill and knowledge. On the other hand there appears to be very little discussion concerning (a) what knowledge is being referred to, (b) what specifically is distinctive about employment in a 'knowledge society', (c) what it is that distinguishes high from low skills, and (d) why most societies continue to perpetuate an under-class of low achievers who, when they become adults, are trapped (both them and their children) in a culture of low achievement. It is as if the idea of a 'knowledge society' is a kind of unspecified but taken-for-granted goal to aim for. Differences between high and low skills are equated with the levels of a qualifications framework that are defined in terms of a hierarchy of learning outcomes (Allais, Raffe and Young 2010).

One consequence of these assumptions is that, in the absence of any more explicit specification, the educational goals of a knowledge society are reduced to a list of 'measurable' outcomes. In other words, by default, these policies appear to be leading us towards what is better described as a 'credentialist' rather than a 'knowledge' society, with all the problems associated with credential inflation and people gaining worthless qualifications with neither use value nor exchange value. These problems are not new and were of course addressed by the American sociologist, Randall Collins, in his book *The Credential Society* (1979).[3] However the new context where employment prospects are uncertain and the new policies for expanding post-compulsory education give Collins's analysis a new relevance and urgency.

Curriculum Policies for a Knowledge Society

Curriculum policies which invoke the idea of a knowledge society typically identify three related problems. The first, which I have already referred to, is the persistent and increasingly vulnerable under-class of low achieving, early leaving adolescents. They are frequently, but not always, from ethnic minorities who all too easily become unemployed and in many cases unemployable adults. The second is the rigidity and inflexibility of current systems of education and training and their inappropriateness when it is assumed that much higher levels of occupational mobility will be needed in future knowledge societies. The 'flexible workers' of the future, it is argued, will need to be prepared to move seamlessly from one sector, one region and even one country to another, and perhaps several times during their career. The third problem is that at the pace at which new knowledge increases, the knowledge acquired in school is seen as quickly becoming out of date. This raises questions as to the viability of curricula differentiated into subjects, domains, and disciplines (Young and Muller 2010). Each of these assumptions has influenced the type of curriculum policies that are currently proposed. In the next section I will discuss each briefly.

A New Educational Under-Class

An under-class of low achieving young people can be identified in most countries. However the educational questions are how to explain the persistence of this under-class and what strategies do we have for reducing its size. This relates directly to the dilemmas of 'massification' that I referred to earlier. Let me put the question more precisely: are low achievement and early leaving educational problems that must be dealt with by schools and colleges, and if so what strategies can schools adopt? Or are they primarily social and economic problems that no new curriculum can solve on its own?

The research literature emphasizes two points about persistent under-achievement. One is that it cannot be separated from the family and community circumstances of the learners concerned. Successful learning – and in particular acquiring what Vygotsky called the 'theoretical concepts' which are the basis of all higher forms of thought – relies on the cultural support of families and the close collaboration of families with teachers; these are conditions that are invariably absent in the circumstances of low achievers as the pioneering research in the 1960s and 1970s of Bernstein (1971) and Bourdieu and Passeron (1977) demonstrated. The second point that I draw from the research is that lack of skills and knowledge is almost always a *demand* problem located in the labour market rather than a *supply* problem located in the schools. As successive reports from the SKOPE[4] team of researchers such as Ewart Keep, based at the University of Cardiff have documented in the UK case, a significant section of private companies profit by employing those with few skills or qualifications on low wages to produce low quality but saleable products; the retail trade and summer fruit farming are the most obvious examples. With limited demand for middle level skills and opportunities divided between low paid un-skilled work and being unemployed and on benefits, it is hardly surprising that young people from poor families with little cultural or material support have little incentive to acquire higher level skills and knowledge. In other words, it is the failure of at least some industrial economies to create employment that demands new skills and knowledge that are realistically attainable by low achievers that is a major factor in the continued existence of a low achieving under-class. Any significant reduction of this under-class will mean either changes in the production priorities and human resource policies of employers or a more radical transformation of Western capitalism. It is only in the context of such economic changes that new curriculum strategies are likely to be effective.

A Curriculum for the Flexible Worker of the Future

The second issue that I want to consider is the inflexibility/immobility diagnosis of existing education systems and its curriculum implications. First two questions need to be asked: who exactly are the existing 'mobile'/'flexible' workers in a typical knowledge economy and in what sectors are they most likely to be found? I suspect that they are a far from homogeneous group which means there are no simple implications for the curriculum. However, it is likely that one type of flexible worker will be the currently mobile high achievers in fast-developing sectors like IT and the cultural industries. They are certainly mobile; however, they represent at best a small proportion of any national workforce and will have developed the cultural resources to manage their own flexible careers either in their previous work or in the education system. We need to be aware however, that even within this relatively privileged group, new forms of stratification are emerging that are expressed in the recruitment policies of international companies. Christopher Newfield (2010) coined the evocative term 'cognotariat' to describe how even those with doctorates – the elite of 'knowledge workers' – are being 'proletarianized'; in other words they have less and less control over their work. An almost polar opposite type of 'mobile worker' are the low wage employees and job seekers who move from low skill job to low skill job, some casual, some seasonal and sometimes from country to country. In Europe their jobs vary from cab driving to cleaning and security and farm work, whereas in the Middle East and wealthier Asian countries like Singapore, they are more likely to be in construction. The question is whether there is a curriculum that relates to the learning needs of this highly stratified, diverse and increasingly mobile group. Is it a more flexible education system based on modularization and higher levels of choice that encourages students to 'pick and mix' in often arbitrary sequences? I have profound reservations about this solution. If the 'knowledge economy' theorists are right in predicting the trend to increased flexibility and mobility, this is a complex situation for young people entering employment and a flexible curriculum which maximizing student choices is not necessarily the answer, especially for those who lack the necessary cultural resources from their homes and families to know the implications of their choices. More fundamentally, are we confident that mirroring the context of employment, with all its uncertainties, is the most reliable curriculum principle?

Knowledge and the 'Knowledge Society'

The third feature of many curriculum proposals that claim to be responding to the demands of a 'knowledge society' is that although they emphasize knowledge and knowledge workers, they invariably lack any specificity about what the knowledge is that is being referred to. Somewhat ironically, as I shall suggest, such proposals make this lack of specificity into a virtue. This leads to four priorities for the curriculum: (i) a 'generic' approach which plays down specific knowledge contents in favour of general and 'content-free' competences and skills, (ii) the idea that it is individual learner choice rather than curriculum prescription that should play a major role in how the sequencing of learning is structured, (iii) increasing the importance of (and where possible accrediting) informal or 'non-school' learning and experience and, (iv) shifting the basis for curricula from syllabuses to learning outcomes. The remainder of this section discusses these four developments and their possible implications for the curriculum.

Genericism

As a curriculum concept, *genericism* refers to the idea that specific contents (in particular subject-specific contents) – whether knowledge or skills – are becoming less important in a world where the pace of knowledge change is increasing. The new emphasis, it is argued, must be on what is 'generic' – in other words what is not specific to particular contents or (in the case of skills) contexts. There are many examples of the form that this 'genericism' is expected to take. One of the most well known and in many ways most insightful examples is Robert Reich's *four C's* (Reich 1991) – the ability to criticize, to conceptualize, to connect and to compare. These are the capabilities, Reich argues, of the new group he calls the 'symbolic analysts'. Their capabilities cut across many different occupations and not only characterize leaders in all fields but will also enable all those who develop them to make sense of an increasingly complex world. No one would deny the importance of Reich's four capabilities as a way of conceptualizing what kinds of 'thinking' might be important in the new workplaces. It is also possible that they could act as guides for those planning curricula and pedagogic strategies in many different fields and subjects. The problem is when such generic principles are separated from any content or context and seen as a basis for deriving specific programmes. When this happens, thinking becomes separated from what thinking is about; learning from what you are learning, and problem solving from the contexts in which particular problems arise or are posed. It is like learning to criticize literary texts independently of the texts themselves (a feature of some undergraduate programmes in Cultural Studies). As a consequence, Reich's set of capacities become categories which claim to map the world in an apparently coherent way without needing any knowledge of the specific case being mapped. This may make them a useful resource for a management consultant seeking a contract from a company whose specific business he knows very little about. However it is no basis for organizing teaching or learning – whether in the workplace or the school. For example, students learn to compare novels, societies, equations or rock formations; they don't learn to 'compare' as some kind of trans-disciplinary generic skill. It is the contents that give meaning and purpose to the conceptual process of 'comparing' – not vice versa.

The Increased Emphasis on Individual Choice

This idea has a number of origins. The first is the idea of choice arising from market economics and the increasing tendency for this to be seen as a model for good decision making of any kind. In the process learning (in another case it might be health) is reduced to a form of consumption – a world where choice reigns supreme. Of course except within a 'market logic' and in a very superficial sense, we understand very little about learning if we see it as a form of consumption; much learning, especially learning in school involves a pedagogic relationship, which like all professional relationships involves authority and the specialist knowledge of teaching which the learner does not have.

The most familiar application of the idea of choice to the curriculum is modularization – the curriculum is broken up into what the Dearing Report (Dearing 1997) set up by the UK government referred to as 'bite-sized chunks' – a classic example of the extension of the consumption metaphor.

In this model of the curriculum the teacher becomes a facilitator for helping learners to move from module to module and acquire a collection of module outcomes which go towards a certificate. The teacher is no longer the transmitter of knowledge to those who want or need to know. The organizing principle of the curriculum shifts decisions about the forms of sequencing and selection of knowledge from the teacher and her/his specialist knowledge to the choices and interests of learners – a kind of curriculum supermarket.

What the emphasis on learner choice plays down is that there may be objectively better ways of acquiring certain types of skills and knowledge and that relying on learner choices is unlikely to be one of them. Engagement by the learner in the curriculum is crucial; however engagement in a curriculum, as in any specialist field (for example law or medicine) is not the same as choice. As with the other trends I have referred to in this chapter, the most likely outcome of extending learner choice is to increase opportunities for those whose choices are best supported by their families – for those without such support, choice is a recipe for new inequalities.

The Emphasis on Experience and Informal Non-School Learning

Largely in the wake of the emphasis in the early 1990s on lifelong learning, there has been an increased emphasis, both in educational research and in curriculum policy on tacit, informal, and experiential skills and knowledge. One way this shift from the explicit and the codified to the implicit and the experiential can occur is through the claim that these latter forms of 'knowledge' can be equated with the former and with what is learned formally (in school) through a system of accreditation – the process known as the Accreditation of Prior Experiential Learning.

No one would deny the importance of these forms of learning. They were the only form of learning for most people in societies throughout history which did not have schools (except in some cases for a tiny elite). However it is quite another step to argue that there are no differences between the knowledge that can be acquired in school and the knowledge that is acquired informally, or that experience is some kind of hidden cultural resource which, if accredited can compensate for lack of success in school. As the French educational sociologist Bernard Charlot puts it, school is different,

> [it] is a place where the world is treated as an object and not as an environment, place of experience. At times, this object of thought has a referent outside school,

in the environment of the pupil's life. But in this case the relationship with the object of thought should be different to the relationship with the referent. The Lisbon that the Geography teacher talks about should not be confused with the Lisbon in which the pupils live. To a certain extent, it is the same city, but their relationship with it is not the same in the two cases: the latter is a place of experience, the former an object of thought. When the pupils do not manage to make the difference between the two and relate to the former as if it was the latter, they will have problems at school. For example, the teacher asks what the functions of the city of Lisbon are, which requires that the city is thought of in its role as the capital, and the pupils respond narrating how they, their parents and their friends live in the city.

(Charlot 2009: 91)

If students are to progress in their learning, it is vital that they are aware of the differences between school and everyday knowledge; not that one is better than the other but that they have different purposes. The idea of tacit knowledge, 'that we know more than we can say' was first discussed by the philosopher of science Michael Polanyi (1962). However as a former research chemist interested in the philosophy of science, Polanyi studied the work of scientists and how the tacit knowledge that they needed to create the codified or formal knowledge that we recognize as science was hidden and often not recognized – especially in the positivist accounts of science that were so common in his time. For Polanyi the tacit aspect of knowing was not as a kind of knowledge of its own that could be identified in isolation; it was an integral part of the process of creating and acquiring new knowledge.

In the case of informal learning we see another example of a policy that neglects the most fundamental purposes of any curriculum – the acquisition of knowledge that takes the learner beyond their experience. As a result, albeit unintentionally, such an emphasis can lead to new inequalities. Not only is there very little evidence of learners progressing by having their experience accredited, but the process of accreditation can even undermine someone's experience without necessarily providing them with access to new knowledge.

The Shift to Outcomes

The idea that educational programmes can be best expressed in terms of a set of 'written learning outcomes' and that such outcomes are a better alternative for developing curricula to subject-based or occupationally specific syllabuses, is increasingly widely supported by governments and international organizations (CEDEFOP 2009). Lists of written learning outcomes are a feature of many recent curriculum developments and are seen as achieving a number of purposes. For learners, it is claimed that a curriculum expressed in outcomes is a more open, transparent and democratic basis for them to access education. Learners, it is argued, can see before they start a programme, what will be expected of them and what they will know if they complete the outcomes. Outcomes are, in other words, presented as an instrument for promoting transparency that replaces the 'hidden mysteries' that characterize many syllabus-based models.[5] Secondly, listing learning outcomes, it is claimed, enables anyone to have their knowledge and skills assessed for a certificate regardless of whether or not they have attended a course. Again we see an example of the underplaying of the distinct kinds of knowledge and skills that can be acquired through formal education.

Despite the continuing support by governments and international organizations for programmes based on learning outcomes, there is virtually no evidence that learning outcomes realize the claims made for them (Allais, Raffe and Young 2010). In separating outcomes from the processes that lead to them, learning is also separated from any standards by which specialist skills and knowledge are recognized. In offering a route to qualification that is independent of institutions, outcomes-based approaches mislead those who have been unsuccessful at school or who have been denied access to institutional learning, into thinking that there is a genuine non-institutional alternative.[6]

Common Assumptions About These Curriculum Trends

It may be useful at this point to summarize the common features of the trends I have described in the previous sections. Firstly, they assume that the activities involved in learning and teaching can be treated independently of what is being taught or learned; in other words that these activities are in some way 'content free'. Secondly, they imply and are sometimes quite explicit that the teacher must become a facilitator rather than a transmitter of knowledge and that students will somehow acquire knowledge on their own if teachers do not intrude into what is seen as an almost natural process. Thirdly, they give much emphasis to the need for learners to develop the capacity to 'learn to learn'. Taken to an extreme, the focus on 'learning to learn' is saying that as learners we must always be ready to reject what we know and see every new experience as a 'learning opportunity' – the 'pedagogization of society', as the English sociologist Basil Bernstein called it. To put it another way, today's students and employees must learn that what they know will always be quickly out of date. The corollary is that because all knowledge is fluid, changeable and changing, they must have little sense of the worth and value of what they already know. The question that this raises is what is the basis for their identity as learners, if they are expected to dismiss what they already know so readily? What gives them the grounds for accepting or rejecting new learning opportunities and deciding whether new knowledge is really new or just the reformulation of an old idea? Fourthly, these trends all share a belief symbolized by the slogan of the 2008 conference of BECTA, the British Educational Computing Agency, 'Learning Everywhere'. What the BECTA slogan was seeking to convey (apart from the unquestioned educational befts of digital technologies), is that the learning that is not associated with educational institutions – work-based, community-based, family-based learning – is just as important as what it is possible to learn at school or college.

What Kind of Educational Future Do These Trends Envisage?

Considering these trends together led me to a broader set of questions. If informal, tacit, experiential, un-codified learning is so important, what is formal education – attending school, college, or university – for? Why do we want to increase participation in formal education, or raise the age that young people stay in full-time education? Is there nothing distinctively *educational* about learning in formal education that sets it apart from other forms of learning that people always have engaged in and always will? Should teachers only be facilitators or should they also be – to use an unfashionable term – 'transmitters of knowledge'? And if not how will young people acquire new knowledge, or even the knowledge developed by the previous generation?

I want to suggest that underlying these trends is an assumption that societies are changing in ways which can be expressed by the concept *de-differentiation*. De-differentiation refers to a process in which institutions, sectors, forms of knowledge, and types of learning are becoming more and more like each other. This is almost a complete reversal of the process of *differentiation* that has been a feature of social change in industrializing societies during the last 200 years. In relation to the curriculum the parallel assumption is that the institutional and knowledge differentiation that underpins most education systems is a set of barriers that inhibit learning and must be broken down. This conclusion leads to a number of questions – is the process of de-differentiation happening on a global scale? If so what does it mean for those working in and responsible for schools, colleges and universities? Does it follow that if occupational boundaries are breaking down we should necessarily encourage the breaking down of boundaries between subjects and disciplines in the curriculum and the broader boundaries between school and society? Maybe educational and knowledge boundaries have a purpose that does not necessarily apply to occupational boundaries? The final section of this chapter begins to explore these questions.

A Curriculum for the Future: The Educational Case for the Differentiation of Knowledge From Experience

In the earlier sections of this chapter I have identified a number of global strands in curriculum policy. They can be summarized as follows:

1   Most governments and international agencies assume that the most important goals of education are economic. Little room is left for the idea that education is first and foremost about promoting the intellectual and moral development of young people. Indeed a good argument can be made that only if the intellectual development purposes of education are given priority is there any chance of economic goals being realized.
2   The resolution of the 'massification' dilemma discussed earlier is seen largely in terms of an emphasis on a framework of generic outcomes.
3   An increasingly boundary-less future is envisaged where the differences between formal and informal, distinct subjects and disciplines and even the roles of teacher and taught are steadily eroded.

4   Knowledge as a set of relatively stable and systematically related concepts or ideas sustained and challenged by specialist communities is seen as part of the past rather than something to be extended for the future.

5   A flexible, optimistic, innovative, democratic, and at least theoretically egalitarian, future is envisaged. It is a future that is consistent with many of the post-modernist, social constructivist and relativist trends in the social and educational sciences, and not the least in curriculum studies (Young 2008). It appears to fit with the new opportunities for internet access to information (increasingly equated with knowledge).

Why might it be important for curriculum theorists to challenge this scenario? I think there are two main reasons, closely linked but separate. The first is epistemological – the new curriculum policies disregard much that we reliably know about the nature of knowledge and how it is acquired and produced. If the trends in policy discussed in this chapter were to become 'policies in practice', they would, I suggest, lead to the slowing down of innovation and the gradual collapse of economic growth in all countries adopting them. The sources of new knowledge and the structures for transmitting existing knowledge would be steadily undermined. However such policies are more likely to remain 'policy rhetoric' than 'policy in practice' and are only likely to be implemented in programmes for those with no power to resist. There is considerable evidence, at least in the UK, that private fee-paying schools, which educate 7 per cent of the children of the wealthiest group in the population, are rejecting these policies that are associated in varying degrees with the reformed National Curriculum in favour of content-specific syllabuses and examinations. This can only lead to new divisions and new forms of inequality. As a consequence, knowledge, in at least one country trying to become a 'knowledge society' will remain 'knowledge of the powerful' and 'knowledge for the powerful' despite its fundamentally universal character.

However, what is referred to as the realist sociology of knowledge and the social realist curriculum theory (Moore 2007; Muller 2000; Wheelahan 2010) based on it suggests that there is an alternative. It starts with the proposition first articulated by the French sociologist and educationalist, Emile Durkheim (1984) that one critical feature of human societies is that they are based on the *differentiation* of knowledge from experience. Our knowledge of the world draws on our experience but has different social origins, different structures and different purposes. This differentiation can be traced back to the small-scale societies with no schools where the differentiation was between the sacred (knowledge pertaining to God and the afterlife) and the profane (the everyday knowledge all societies draw on – initially to obtain food and shelter). What Durkheim argues is that this differentiation was the basis for the development of science and indeed all intellectual pursuits as more and more of the 'sacred' is secularized. It is this *differentiation* that was institutionalized in the first schools and in all examples of formal education that succeeded them historically. Without recognizing this *differentiation,* we can have no principles for distinguishing a curriculum from the everyday experiences that students bring to school. This principle of differentiation is expressed in two kinds of boundaries that are crucial for any curriculum that is going to achieve its emancipatory aims. These are the boundaries between school and non-school knowledge and the boundaries between knowledge domains, subjects or disciplines.[7] The curriculum principle of *differentiation* reverses the argument about de-differentiation and instead of encouraging the 'evacuation' of knowledge content in the curriculum on the grounds that it is always changing, re-inserts content in a new way and with new purposes. Content is no longer 'for its own sake' and to be memorized as in the old elite curriculum; it is an integral part of engaging with theoretical concepts which are the basis of understanding. Evacuating content also involves a denial of access to concepts and therefore leads to excluding learners from the possibility of an objective understanding of the world. It is here that the curriculum issues and the social justice issues, so often treated quite separately in the research literature, come together (Wheelahan 2007; 2010).

Instead of seeing differentiation and boundaries as barriers to greater access and equality, a social realist approach sees them as *historical* but *not arbitrary* conditions for accessing and producing new knowledge and hence as a resource for future progress and greater equality. Instead of seeing schools as mere agencies of reproduction (which in part they always are), it sees them also as an opportunity for the world to be treated as an object and not just as an environment and a place of experience (Charlot 2009); they are in other words a specialist site for the kind of learning that is rarely possible in homes and communities. In our unequal societies, only the few, rather than the many, take up these opportunities that schools offer; although at least many more have them and take them up than in earlier historical periods.

The purposes of schooling are in contradiction with the inequality-generating tendencies of modern capitalist societies. School, through its professed goals – the intellectual development of young people – is in principle, though due in part to flawed curriculum policies, not always in practice, a universalizing institution in a non-universalizing environment of unequally distributed wealth and power. The role of curriculum theory is to expose this contradiction not just by a critique of the inequalities perpetuated by all schooling. It is by demonstrating the specific activities of schools that enable at least some to acquire 'powerful knowledge' (Young 2008) and pointing to the external forces that limit this possibility. This approach has quite different implications from the current curriculum developments I have discussed. By evacuating the knowledge content of the curriculum they reduce the possibility of schools widening access to 'powerful knowledge' and in effect and despite their intentions, complement the wider reproductive processes of society.

Formal education (school, college and university) has an emancipatory purpose which is why those in power have devised a multitude of ways to limit access to it to the few. Despite the problems facing all modern school systems, this emancipatory role remains (and has even been extended). In capitalist societies, as sociologists such as Bourdieu have argued, formal education is a largely passive site for the social and cultural reproduction of inequalities, and for disciplining young minds and bodies to fit into an unjust social order. However it is a mistake to see schooling as only doing this. It is also a unique opportunity for students to acquire – through subjects and their link to discipline-based knowledge – the knowledge that they would not have access to at home or at work. If schools were solely agencies of reproduction of social class inequalities, it would not be possible to explain how it is that at least some students from lower social classes and without the necessary cultural capital have succeeded and still do. Likewise reproduction theories are unable to account for the fact that in many countries girls achieve significantly better results than boys (Marrero 2007).

Concluding Comments

There are two serious problems with the curriculum developments I have discussed in this chapter. The first is that in their response to the dilemmas of mass schooling and the uncomfortable fact that many children from disadvantaged backgrounds continue to fail, they have lost confidence in the emancipatory role of the schooling and how it enables some learners from all communities and from all social classes, whether boys or girls (albeit often in some cases the numbers are small) to acquire powerful knowledge that takes them beyond their experience. This has led policy makers and some curriculum theorists to argue that the curriculum should focus on the experience of young people and what is immediately relevant to them rather than on the knowledge that they need if they are to make sense of the world and have some control over their own lives.

The second problem is that in weakening the content of the curriculum, in seeking to break down boundaries because they are at odds with learners' experiences, and in celebrating learner choice and informal learning, they are reducing the possibility of schools realizing their emancipatory role. That is why we need a new principle for the curriculum and a new curriculum theory as this century moves into its second decade. It should not be one that expects students to be compliant and submissive as did the 'curriculum of the past' or be restricted only to an elite. It should be a theory which takes knowledge, its objectivity, its openness and how it is best acquired as its starting principle. At the same time, educationalists and curriculum theorists in particular need to remember that a new curriculum based on new principles is not going to remove structured failure and inequalities. That is a longer term and fundamentally political project that will fail without an adequate curriculum theory.

Acknowledgements

I would like to thank the editors of this handbook, Lyn Yates and Madeleine Grumet, for their encouragement and helpful comments on earlier drafts of this chapter.

Notes

1 This chapter draws on a number of recent papers which take further some of the issues discussed (Young 2009; 2010; Young and Muller 2010).
2 Elsewhere I have suggested that curriculum policies need to focus not just on 'access' but also on 'epistemic access' (Young 2010).

3 In his book *The Credential Society*, Collins (1979) challenges the assumption that increases in the credential requirements for entry into prestigious professions is a consequence of increases in knowledge. He argues that expansion of educational credentials is better understood as arising from a conflict between status groups seeking ways of maintaining or enhancing their privileges. One conclusion from his study is that as more and more people gain credentials, they inevitably lose their value.

4 See http://www.skope.ox.ac.uk/publications.

5 It is a case of knowing what you will know before you know it rather than waiting to know what you know when you do know it.

6 Here I exclude well-resourced distance learning programmes such as the UK's Open University; they have many of the features of institutional learning.

7 What Bernstein referred to as 'the classification and framing of educational knowledge' (Bernstein 1971).

References

Allais, S., Raffe, D. and Young, M (2010) *Researching NQFs: some conceptual issue*s, Working Paper 44, Geneva: International Labour Organisation.

Bernstein, B. (1971) *Class Codes and Control*, Volume 1, London: Routledge and Kegan Paul.

Bourdieu, P. and Passeron, J.C. (1977) *Reproduction in Education, Society and Culture*, London: Sage Publications.

CEDEFOP (European Centre for the Development of Vocational Training) (2009) *The Shift to Learning Outcomes: policies and practices in Europe*, Luxembourg: Office for Official Publications of the European Communities.

Charlot, B. (2009) 'School and the pupils' work', *Sísifo. Educational Sciences Journal*, 10: 87–94.

Collins, R. (1979) *The Credential Society: an historical sociology of education and stratification*, New York: Academic Press.

Dearing, R. (1997) *Report of the National Committee of Inquiry into Higher Education*. Online. Available HTTP: https://bei.leeds.ac.uk/Partners/NCIHE/ (accessed 6 August 2010).

Durkheim, E. (1984) *Pragmatism and Sociology* (translated J. Alcock), New York: Cambridge University Press.

Marrero, A. (2007) *Educacion y Modernidad Hoy*, Valencia: Germania.

Moore, R. (2007) *Sociology of Knowledge and Education*, London: Continuum.

Muller, J. (2000) *Reclaiming Knowledge*, London: RoutledgeFalmer.

Newfield, C. (2010) 'The structure and silence of the cognotariat'. *Globalisation, Societies and Education*, 8, 2: 175–189.

Polanyi, M. (1962) *The Republic of Science*, Chicago: Roosevelt University.

Reich, R. (1991) *The Work of Nations*, London: Heinemann.

Wheelahan, L. (2007) 'How competency-based training locks the working class out of powerful knowledge: a modified Bernsteinian analysis', *British Journal of Sociology of Education*, 28, 5: 637–651.

Wheelahan, L. (2010) *Why Knowledge Matters in Curriculum: a social realist argument*, London: Routledge.

Young, M. (2008) *Bringing Knowledge Back In: from social constructivism to social realism in the sociology of education*, London: Routledge.

Young, M. (2009) 'Education, globalisation and the "voice of knowledge"', *Journal of Education and Work*, 22, 3: 193–204.

Young, M. (2010) 'Alternative educational futures for a knowledge society', *European Journal of Education*, 9, 1: 1–12.
Young, M. and Muller, J. (2010) 'Three scenarios for the future: Lessons from the sociology of knowledge', *European Journal of Education*, 45, 1: 11–27.

10 Knowledge, Knowers and Knowing

Curriculum Reform in South Africa

Ursula Hoadley

Introduction

With the transition to democracy in South Africa in 1994 came the imperative to reform what was a highly inequitable system of education provision. Changing the curriculum was regarded as a crucial lever for fostering the ideals of the new nation – for creating a new citizenry and for re-inserting South Africa into a global context. The new curriculum that was constructed departed radically from what had gone before. It was underpinned by strong social goals which aimed to address past inequalities and foster human rights and democracy in every sphere – including what was learnt and how. While the political project of the new curriculum was very clear, its pedagogical shortcomings soon became evident. Within a short time this new curriculum was revised. And once again, within a relatively short period of time after the implementation of the revised curriculum, the national curriculum was once again reviewed. This chapter considers these processes of curriculum reform, considering the nature of the changes and the underlying logic of the shifts that were made in the course of the reforms.

The chapter traces the curriculum changes in relation to the notions of knowledge, knowers and knowing. In this way I attempt to show how the ultimate goal of achieving social justice has over time shifted from a focus on knowers and knowing, or the learner and learning, to one that privileges knowledge, or what is to be learnt. The three central moments in curriculum reform since the transition to democracy in South Africa in 1994 were alluded to above. Curriculum documents and review reports at three reform moments are considered in this chapter in tracing the reform process. The first reform moment was the construction and implementation of a new curriculum in 1998 for a new post-apartheid nation – called Curriculum 2005. The second reform moment was a review of Curriculum 2005 two years later. The result of this review was the construction and implementation of a revised National Curriculum Statement (NCS) in 2002. Finally, the third reform moment considered in the analysis below was in 2009, when the NCS was reviewed and another substantial revision of the national curriculum was proposed in the report issuing from this review. By considering these three reform moments in relation to how knowledge, knowers and knowing is constituted by and constitutes the curriculum, focus is drawn to the crucial distinction between curriculum and pedagogy. The chapter concludes by drawing out some of the implications of the distinctions for curriculum-making and the shaping of pedagogy in South Africa over the past 15 years. The chapter begins by briefly sketching out what apartheid curriculum and pedagogy entailed in order to provide a context for the discussion of the reform that followed its demise.

Apartheid Curriculum and Pedagogy

Under the highly racially segregated system of apartheid, different departments of education were set up to control education for different population groupings based on race classification. White departments produced a 'core' curriculum, which departments for other racial groupings adapted, often amounting to a watering down of the 'white' curriculum. The curriculum was content-driven with very stringent prescriptions for the sequencing and scope of contents. The selection of content reflected the tenets of the philosophy underpinning the system, known as Christian National Education, which was essentially an expression of Afrikaner nationalism. The curriculum was white- and male-oriented (NEPI 1992). Curricula for black students especially emphasized teaching based on drill and practice, and little elaboration of concepts and skills, but rather a strict focus on content to be memorized. Teachers were issued with syllabuses that often contained highly prescriptive teacher manuals with detailed work plans. In African schools, teachers were overseen by a highly autocratic and bureaucratic system of inspection that appeared to be used punitively and vindictively against teachers (Chisholm *et al.* 2005). Christian National Education had an attendant theory of pedagogy, or 'science' of education known as 'fundamental pedagogics'. This was an authoritarian pedagogical philosophy, where the child was regarded as ignorant and undisciplined, in need of guidance from the teacher, whose authority was derived from the God of the Dutch Reformed Church (Ensor 1999). It also promulgated a pedagogy devoid of analysis and critique (Enslin 1984), emphasizing rote memorization.

During the 1980s and 1990s there were two curriculum reform efforts. The one formed part of the range of movements for alternative proposals against apartheid education collectively known as 'People's Education'. Drawing on Freirian notions of education for empowerment, this movement tried to shift the focus of teaching and learning from a strong transmitter model and a given body of knowledge to one that stressed the politically potent role of education and the importance of students' experience and local context. The impact of People's Education was extremely limited. What predominated in schools under a strong inspection regime, and with teachers who were very poorly trained, was a pedagogy consisting largely of drill and rote routines, with '... teachers adopting authoritarian roles and doing most of the talking, with few pupil initiations, and with most of the pupil responses taking the form of group chorusing' (Chick 1996: 21).

At the same time the apartheid government was also engaged in its own process of curriculum revision, the 'Education Renewal Strategy', in an effort to rationalize and modernize curricula, and make them more relevant (especially in terms of economic demands and that of the labour force). This last apartheid state reform effort responded to some of the curriculum developments in the USA and the UK, most notably drawing on ideas around constructivism and progressivism developed there. But essentially, under the apartheid curriculum regime, strong control was exerted over knowing, knowledge and knowers, informed by an autocratic theory of pedagogy and clear content selection along white, Christian, nationalist lines.

Reform Moment 1: Knowers and the Conflation of Curriculum and Pedagogy

The shift from the apartheid regime to a democratic state in South Africa in 1994 entailed a negotiated settlement between old and new rulers. This negotiated settlement had particular implications for education and the construction of a post-apartheid curriculum. Fundamentally what it entailed was an eschewal of the definition of content to allow for a proliferation of sites for learning, and also the avoidance of explicit prioritizing of knowledge distribution to any particular group. The process of curriculum construction at this time was influenced by a number of foreign consultants, particularly those promoting outcomes-based education (OBE) as a curriculum alternative fostering generic skills for a new global economy. Policy-makers were also influenced by the increasing popularity of national qualification frameworks, which were identified as a way of integrating education and training and introducing equivalences into a system with a large number of disparate qualifications and unequal institutional capacity. South Africa termed its approach 'transformational OBE', and as educationally unsound as it proved to be, it presented a strong political argument for a curriculum for rapid social transformation. Transformational OBE was defined in official documentation thus:

> No thought is given to the existing curriculum. Instead schools (or local districts) are told they can choose any content and use a wide range of teaching methods as long as these develop citizens who display the agreed-upon critical outcomes.
>
> (South African Department of Education 2000b: 19)

These 'critical outcomes' were derived from the constitution and described the kind of citizen that the curriculum aimed to create, as well as broad, cross-curricular, generic skills underpinning the curriculum, for example, 'identify and solve problems by using creative and critical thinking' (South African Department of Education 1997: 16). The benefit of the approach of leaving out specific content, it was argued, was that 'This allows educators to relate teaching direct [sic] to their local contexts and also to change syllabus content rapidly' (South African Department of Education 1997: 16). The response here to the highly prescriptive curriculum of apartheid is obvious. But further, what the new curriculum signalled was a move to erode a number of boundaries – between education and training, between academic and everyday knowledge, and between different forms of knowledge, disciplines or subjects. This was to be achieved through a strong programme of integration, involving the collapsing not only of knowledge, but of political and economic boundaries as well:

An integrated approach implies a view of learning which rejects the rigid division between 'academic' and 'applied', 'theory' and 'practice', 'knowledge' and 'skills', 'head' and 'hand'. Such divisions have characterised the organisation of curricula and the distribution of educational opportunity in many countries of the world, including South Africa. They have grown out of, and helped to reproduce, very old occupational and social class distinctions. In South Africa such distinctions in curriculum and career choice have also been closely associated in the past with the ethnic structure of economic opportunity and power.

(South African Department of Education 1995: 15)

Ensor (1997) points out that this erosion of boundaries was expected to result in the collapse of a fourth: the social boundaries between groups on the basis of race and class. The strong political project of creating a new nation and a new citizenry meant that pedagogical and epistemological questions were subordinated to strong ideological notions around the kinds of persons to be formed for the new democratic era.

In 1997, the new post-apartheid curriculum, Curriculum 2005, was launched. As described above, Curriculum 2005 was informed by a number of trajectories within education, both locally (People's Education; the integration of education and training) and globally (outcomes-based education, competency-based curriculum) (Cross *et al.* 2002; Kraak 1999). Curriculum 2005 was defined in relation to the past. It was referred to as a paradigm shift in curriculum, from the traditional apartheid curriculum to a new outcomes-based curriculum. Curriculum 2005 was also designed in relation to the new National Qualifications Framework (NQF) launched in 1996, which was an attempt to create equivalencies between education and workplace learning by placing all qualifications on the same grid, and breaking them down into unit standards which could interchangeably make up different qualifications. The strong influence of Labour, and an economic discourse is evident in the quote above, but was also seen in an emphasis on the recognition of prior learning, access and portability which were the key ideas underpinning the creation of qualifications. There is general agreement in the literature that the construction of Curriculum 2005 was largely a product of Labour's needs, and their demands for a skills-based curriculum linked to an NQF. At the heart of this was the *outcome*, a discrete, generic, demonstrable performance required of the learner.

The curriculum had several progressive features. It placed an emphasis on group work, relevance, local curriculum construction and local choice of content. There was also a shift away from strong disciplinary boundaries, to a horizontal integration of traditional curriculum subjects. Learning areas, which were clusters of subjects, were introduced to support integration. Phase organizers also introduced themes that directed programmes of learning across different learning areas. Learning outcomes were generic, and most of the subject-specific content from the curriculum was removed.

Curriculum 2005 was driven by a strong pedagogical project. Learner-centredness was the cornerstone of this new project, and the teacher (now termed 'educator') was to *facilitate* acquisition through the selection of the appropriate knowledge, including that of the learners' own local cultures, to enable the learner to reach the 'competency' which was expressed as an outcome. The pedagogy was based on a reading of constructivist and progressive principles, strongly advocating a pedagogy that directly challenged that of fundamental pedgagogics. A well-known table at the time explained the desired shifts – see Table 10.1.

Another table in official documentation further spelt out the changes in terms of knowledge and pedagogy in the shift from 'a content-based to an outcomes-based approach' (South African Department of Education 1997: 5) – see Table 10.2.

The curriculum was thus built around a strong (though often theoretically muddled) project of knowing, and Tables 10.1 and 10.2 show the ardent concern with the stipulation of pedagogy in this project. But in responding to the repressive pedagogy of apartheid, Curriculum 2005 changed the curriculum. The assumption made in the constructivist vein was that learning disciplinary content knowledge (the what) could be replaced by learning the procedures and methods of the discipline (the how). What was entailed in this was a displacement of the ontological with the epistemological, which in a sense captures the shift from traditional to constructivist pedagogies that Curriculum 2005 attempted to accomplish. Curriculum 2005 conflated curriculum and pedagogy, emphasizing

Table 10.1   Shift from traditional to constructivist classroom

Traditional classroom	*Constructivist classroom*
Curriculum is presented part to whole, with emphasis on basic skills	Curriculum is presented whole to part with emphasis on big concepts
Strict adherence to fixed curriculum is highly valued	Pursuit of learner questions is highly valued
Curricular activities rely heavily on textbooks and workbooks	Curricular activities rely heavily on primary sources of data and manipulative materials
Students are viewed as 'blank slates' onto which information is etched by the teacher	Learners are viewed as thinkers with emerging theories about the world
Teachers generally behave in a didactic manner, disseminating information to students	Educators generally behave in an interactive manner, mediating the environment with learners
Teachers seek the correct answer to validate student learning	Educators seek the learner's points of view in order to understand learners' present conceptions for use in subsequent lessons
Assessment of student learning is viewed as separate from teaching and occurs almost entirely through testing	Assessment of learner learning is interwoven with teaching and occurs through educator observations of learners, learner observation of learners at work and through learner exhibitions and portfolios
Students primarily work alone	Learners primarily work in groups

Source: South African Department of Education (2000b: 12).

Table 10.2   From a content-based to an outcomes-based approach

Old	New
Passive learners	Active learners
Exam-driven	Learners are assessed on an ongoing basis
Rote-learning	Critical thinking, reasoning, reflection and action
Syllabus is content-based and broken down into subjects	An integration of knowledge, learning relevant and connected to real-life situations
Textbook/worksheet-bound and teacher centred	Learner-centred; teacher is facilitator; teacher constantly uses groupwork and teamwork to consolidate the new approach
Sees syllabus as rigid and non-negotiable	Learning programmes seen as guides that allow teachers to be innovative and creative in designing programmes
Teachers responsible for learning; motivation dependent on the personality of teacher	Learners take responsibility for their learning; pupils motivated by constant feedback and affirmation of their worth
Emphasis on what the teacher hopes to achieve	Emphasis on outcomes – what the learner becomes and understands
Content placed into rigid timeframes	Flexible timeframes allow learners to work at their own pace
Curriculum development process not open to public comment	Comment and input from the wider community is encouraged

Source: South African Department of Education (1997: 6–7).

the everyday knowledge of students, in other words *knowers,* and silencing knowledge with a strident theory of knowing.

Reform Moment 2: Towards a Knowledge Project

Curriculum 2005 was reviewed in 2000. Although muted at first, the criticism generated by the first post-apartheid curriculum was significant. Prominent critiques focused on training and implementation, system failures and curriculum design. Jansen (1999: 147) in his 'Why outcomes-based education will fail' offers as a principal reason the idea that curriculum was driven by policy imperatives with no conception of the realities of classroom life. Later Jansen (2001) went on to argue that policies developed in the first five years of democracy served the purpose of 'political symbolism', helping to mark the shift from apartheid to post-apartheid education and establish the ideological and political credentials of the new government. In short, although the political project of Curriculum 2005 had been clear, the pedagogical one was far from graspable.

Further research related to Curriculum 2005 involved a series of empirical classroom-based studies. The report on the studies (Taylor and Vinjevold 1999) claimed convergence in findings from the research around a number of issues, most importantly around teachers' extremely poor conceptual knowledge. They also found that teachers lacked the knowledge base to interpret Curriculum 2005, and were unable to deal with integration and 'ensure that the everyday approach prescribed by the new curriculum will result in learners developing sound conceptual frameworks' (Taylor and Vinjevold 1999: 230). Researchers found that although teachers were implementing their understanding of forms of 'learner-centred' practice and co-operative learning, very little learning was taking place. Another key contribution to critique at this time was Harley and Parker's (1999) analysis of outcomes-based education, the National Qualifications Framework, and competency models. They point out the conflicts in the system generated from incompatible frameworks – such as competence-based and outcomes-based assessment.

In the light of the criticisms, a review team was set up to consider the curriculum and make recommendations regarding the 'strengthening and streamlining' of Curriculum 2005. It was in this *Curriculum 2005 Review Report* (South African Department of Education 2000a) that a key argument entered official discourse. It was based on a critique developed by Muller (2000) around the conceptual design of the curriculum, arguing that while the socio-political rationale for integration was clear, the pedagogical purposes were not. The fact that the curriculum had removed most of the content for subjects, and replaced it with outcomes expressed as generic skills, meant that teachers were expected to select the appropriate content and design 'learning programmes' themselves. Muller summed up the class implications of this kind of curriculum:

> A success can be made of such an under-stipulated curriculum, but only if the teacher has a well-articulated mental script of what should be covered, and if the pupils come from homes where they have been well prepared to respond to such putative freedom, in other words, only in schools by and for the middle class.
>
> (Muller 2000: 14)

There was also a strong critique at the time of the radical constructivism which underpinned the curriculum, identifying that 'by ignoring the boundary between school and everyday knowledges, radical modes increase the difficulties that working-class children will have in trying to acquire formal discourses' (Taylor and Vinjevold 1999). These arguments derived from a number of seminal papers on the distinction between everyday knowledge and school knowledge (Dowling 1995; Ensor 1997; Davis 1996; Muller and Taylor 1995) which asserted the necessity for distinguishing between knowledge types. The work, grounded in Bernstein's (1990) theory of pedagogic discourse, emphasized the importance of recognizing the *boundary* between knowledge types. Through the review team report, these academic arguments around the distinction between everyday knowledge and school knowledge, and the implications of integration entered the formal domain in a way that was understandable to a broader readership, including some in government. The arguments focused centrally on the unequal distribution of types of knowledge to different students, often on the basis of social class. Dowling's (1998) research in particular showed how the working-class and lower-ability student 'paradoxically, is left free to be a local individual but a failed mathematics learner' as Muller (2000: 68) put it.

Drawing implicitly on Bernstein's theory of knowledge then, the authors of the *Curriculum 2005 Review Report* took a realist view of knowledge, and of school knowledge as having an objective conceptual structure (especially in terms of the selection and sequence of knowledge). The major design flaw of Curriculum 2005 was identified as its having no conceptual sequence and hence no learning progression path. 'It is true that different learners approach learning in different ways, and might even learn concepts in a non-prescribed sequence. But this non-prescribed sequence must be an alternative route up the same conceptual ladder. There is no such thing as an alternative ladder, of optional and replaceable concepts' (South African Department of Education 2000a: 44).

The *Curriculum 2005 Review Report* strongly recommended reduced integration and clearer specification of contents. Greater simplicity to the design of the curriculum and language was also recommended. Significantly, under pressure from the unions (Chisholm 2005), outcomes were retained in the design of the curriculum. As a result certain pedagogical and curriculum features *associated* with outcomes would also be retained. These were identified by the *Curriculum 2005 Review Report* itself. It states that outcomes-based education asserts the dominance of outputs over inputs, but it also contains features of curriculum reform the world over, which are:

- the active learner and ideas of uniqueness and difference
- the active teacher who, rather than following a prescriptive syllabus, makes decisions about what to teach and how to teach it
- the relative importance of activity and skills as a basis for knowing and knowledge
- the relative importance of induction over deduction

(South African Department of Education 2000a: 47)

Thus although the knower mode went into retreat with the review of Curriculum 2005, and knowledge was foregrounded, knowing remained pronounced. It was clear that the hold over pedagogy was to be sustained, mitigating a slide back into 'traditional forms'. The four pedagogical aspects bulleted above are features of progressive and constructivist pedagogies and in the argument of the *Review Report* are associated with outcomes-based education. There is some contradiction in the retention of outcomes in relation to the treatment of knowledge. Although the *Curriculum 2005 Review Report* provided a clear and coherent critique around knowledge and the need for greater conceptual coherence and progression, knowledge stipulation and attention to disciplinary structure, the pedagogical project of Curriculum 2005 was to a certain extent retained along with the retention of outcomes thus reasserting local choice of content, a skills-based approach and an emphasis on the everyday (by asserting inductive approaches).

Over time, outcomes, constructivism and progressivism became entwined, and because of their conceptual conflation it became difficult to disentangle them

(Morrow 2000; Harley and Wedekind 2003). Similarly, the conflation of curriculum and pedagogy was not dealt with in the *Curriculum 2005 Review Report*. The how remained entangled in the what, and Davis' (2005) comment on this conflation is apposite: that it is curious that those who argue for an emphasis on relevance and real-world problem-solving demand that the curriculum should organize and package curriculum in an already-integrated way.

Fataar (2006) links the shifts signalled in the *Curriculum 2005 Review Report* towards knowledge differentiation and stipulation to changes in the economy: 'by the time of the second election in 1999 the state had authorized a fiscally conservative development path, and had put leftist elements such as the unions and civic movements on the ideological retreat' (2005: 650). What happened in the development of the new curriculum based on the review of Curriculum 2005 was that the curriculum was wrested back from Labour into the hands of a particular group of academic educationalists whose concern was with knowledge and the 'boundary' alluded to above. Notions of knowledge differentiation emerged strongly, undergirded by the key conceptual critique of Curriculum 2005 around disciplinary probity and conceptual coherence. Fataar's more subtle argument was that the decline of the influence of Labour in curriculum construction 'can be found in the ambiguous constructivism that informed the curriculum design. The epistemological shortcomings upon which its knowlegability was constructed contained the seeds for its displacement' (2006: 657). In other words, an emphasis on a kind of radical constructivism, which was theoretically unstable, was the ultimate undoing of Labour's influence.

When considering some of the compromises and contradictions in the *Curriculum 2005 Review Report* (see also South African Department of Education 2009), it is clear that what was likely to emerge was a compromise curriculum, which could be read in a number of ways, and which would be underpinned by conceptual unease. Also, despite arguments to the contrary, the strong ideological arguments about changing the knowledge of the school to grant access to previously marginalized groups (rather than facilitating greater access to specialized knowledge) still dominated, particularly in parts of the bureaucracy involved in the mediation of curriculum to teachers (Chisholm 2005). Integration was also retained in the organization of traditionally separate subjects in 'learning areas'.

Implementation of the National Curriculum Statement was begun in schools in 2002. The first final school-leaving certificate based on the new curriculum was written in 2008. The following year the process of revision started up again.

Reform Moment 3: Subduing Knowing

In 2009 the new Minister of Education called for a new review of the curriculum, again couched as a review of the 'implementation' of the curriculum, rather than of the curriculum itself. The call for the review came from two main sources: on-going criticism in the media of outcomes-based education, and the persistent poor performance of South African learners on national and international standardized tests. In particular, some of the international comparative standardized tests had shown South Africa out-performed not only by other developed countries, but also by developing countries with a lower GDP and lower spend on education (van der Berg 2008). Over time, since the introduction of OBE and the NQF, education and training had separated out institutionally, both in terms of provision, qualifications and curriculum. The formal schooling sector had managed to untether itself from some of the strictures of the National Qualifications Framework (Allais 2006). A new government took office in 2009. This new administration was committed in word at least to greater efficiency, more openness around mistakes made in the past and less insistence on approaches that were not working. The question of OBE had become not only an educational issue but also a political one and the focus of numerous attacks on the government's failure in the sphere of education. The new minister indicated no adherence or loyalty to approaches that had failed in the past, and was intent on a review which considered what could be done to enhance the curriculum and address some of criticisms of and inefficiencies in the schooling system (Motshekga 2009). As Fataar (2006) had pointed out earlier, the pressure on education from Labour had also all but dissipated in relation to formal schooling.

Again a review committee was constituted, this time with significant government representation, as well as union and to a lesser extent academic membership. The emphasis was on strengthening implementation once again, and on teachers' experiences. A series of provincial teacher hearings attended by hundreds of teachers across the country were held, forming the basis for the recommendations made in the report (South African Department of Education 2009).

As in the previous review, but more directly, the *NCS Review Report* makes a strong call for a knowledge-based curriculum. Once again, the theory of knowledge in the report rests on a Bernsteinian conception of knowledge structuring. In this vein, the *Report* invokes Michael Young's (2007) notion of 'powerful knowledge' in making its arguments around the social justice implications of an under-specified curriculum:

> What we have learnt is that, despite the good intentions of past efforts, an underspecified curriculum advantages those who are already advantaged – those who already have access to the knowledge needed to improve their life chances.
>
> (Young 2007: 61)

The *Report* also takes direct aim at the discourse of knowing, and the dominance of a constructivist approach specifically:

> Though all learners do engage in the construction of knowledge in terms of coming to understand certain concepts, skills and content, it has generally been accepted that these aspects inhere within the subject and not in the minds of learners in the first place.
>
> (South African Department of Education 2009: 24)

Further the *NCS Review Report* deals directly with the sustained emphasis on group work in classrooms and on an integrated approach to learning, often realized through theme-based learning. The *Report* explicitly recommends that some of these understandings from the past (including the subordination of textbooks and on-going emphasis on integration) associated with OBE be challenged. It argues that in many instances these approaches are not ones that are privileged in official thinking, but persist at levels of the system concerned with implementation, especially districts (South African Department of Education 2009: 45).

What the *NCS Review Report* deliberately attempts to do is define curriculum in terms of a specification of 'the what' of knowledge. It presents a comprehensive critique of outcomes-based education, recommending its discontinuation and alluding to the confusion between OBE and various tenets of progressivism mentioned above. In particular, the *Report* argues that outcomes inhibit a clear specification of what is to be learnt, suggesting that outcomes be replaced with 'clear content, concept and skill standards and clear and concise assessment requirements' (South African Department of Education 2009: 45). The critique in the report draws on the work of others (Muller 2000; Jansen 1999; Allais and Taylor 2007; Donnelly 2005; Young 2002) arguing that OBE, by focusing on attitudes, dispositions and competencies, fails to give adequate specification of essential learning. Further, by focusing on outcomes, inputs, content, or the means for achieving these outcomes are left open and unspecified. In particular, the South African version of outcomes focuses on *skills* statements, more appropriate to some subjects than others, and also insists on the same set of outcomes from Grade 1 to Grade 12. The latter necessitates that the outcomes are specified at a high level of generality, rendering them largely generic and insufficient as a guide for what is to be learnt. The result of the OBE-based curriculum, the *NCS Review Report* argues, is 'curriculum and assessment descriptors that are often vague, ambiguous, difficult to measure and low in academic content' (South African Department of Education 2009: 38).

At the time of writing this chapter the curriculum was undergoing revision in the light of the recommendations made in the *Report*. In parliament the Minister declared that she had 'signed OBE's death certificate' (Motshekga 2009). In the revised version of the curriculum no specification of particular pedagogic approaches was to be made, and no indication of a particular theory of knowing is included in the templates for writers. All references to learning outcomes are to be removed. The clear intention is to draw the process away from residue emphases on knowers and knowing to one that addresses the concern of curriculum primarily as a 'structuring and organisation of knowledge' (Moore 2004). The process is current and the outcome thus indeterminate. Although the intention of the reform move is clear, the argument that the discourse of knowers and knowing has been subdued in this reform is speculative and based primarily on the intentions of the *Report* and not on the curriculum that will finally emerge.

Discussion

What is clear from the discussion of the three curriculum reform moments in South Africa is an increasing emphasis on the prioritization of knowledge in the curriculum – a concern specifically with academic disciplines, their structuring and curriculum entailments. Although it is not possible to claim whether the prioritization is commonly agreed upon or understood, in formal argument (i.e. in official review reports) the social justice implications of access to disciplinary and specialized forms of knowledge has been foregrounded. The consideration of the three reform moments also shows a change in the relationship between the what and the how of teaching and learning. In other words there has been some shift in thinking about the distinction between curriculum and pedagogy. In concluding this chapter and thinking about the current curriculum debates in South Africa there are two points that I want to make in relation to this latter distinction between curriculum and pedagogy.

The first point concerns the issue of control over pedagogy. The approach taken in Curriculum 2005 and in the NCS was to attempt to control pedagogy *through* curriculum. Pedagogy, as it has been constituted in curriculum reform in South Africa, has been treated as an outcome of curriculum, in other words, pedagogy is 'legislated' through curriculum. Teachers are *instructed* through curriculum prescription (again Tables 10.1 and 10.2 provide good examples, as do the Learning Programme Guidelines of the National Curriculum Statement) to deploy particular pedagogic forms in their classrooms. This is understandable when one considers it as a response to the tyranny of 'fundamental pedagogics' in schools under apartheid. Alexander provides a broader explanation, relevant to current times as well, which is more generally about control over the vagaries of the classroom:

> Pedagogy was the ultimate prize for any government wishing to secure a level of control of the educational process as close to absolute as – given the stubbornness of the human spirit and the wayward chemistry of classrooms – is feasible.
>
> (Alexander 2001: 142)

However, what Curriculum 2005 produced with its eschewal of the 'traditional' in favour of a 'constructivist' pedagogy was an alienation of teachers from their own practice (Jansen and Christie 1999; Taylor and Vinjevold 1999). The NCS did little to address this distance between teachers' practice and the ideal practice proffered in policy.

If we conceive of pedagogy as an independent social form, which has a history, consisting of sedimented practices over time (as in the German tradition of Didaktik), then simply changing pedagogic practice by fiat through curriculum stipulation is misguided.[1] One cannot eclipse pedagogy through curriculum stipulations, even though the reasons why one might want to do this are compelling, as Alexander (2001) points out. Neither on the other hand should a curriculum be obscured by pedagogy – either a real or imagined pedagogy – as occurred in the case of Curriculum 2005. As Hamilton (1999: 145) puts it, our analysis and conceptions of pedagogy should be built on 'the lived experience of practitioners, an awareness of the historicity of practice, and an anticipation of the life-worlds of future practitioners (cf. "what should they become")'. A consideration of how particular constructions of *curriculum* can shift pedagogy also needs to be considered.

The second issue relating to the conflation of curriculum and pedagogy refers to the more general point about boundaries raised earlier. In pedagogy, the everyday is always a 'portal to the esoteric' (Dowling 1998). In curriculum, however, the necessity of the incorporation and stipulation of everyday knowledge varies with subjects and their relation to everyday/workplace practices. In the more specialized subjects, such as mathematics and science for example, the dominance of everyday knowledge has the potential to obscure, confuse or dilute conceptual specification. In the case of Curriculum 2005, and to a lesser extent the NCS, everyday knowledge infused the curriculum. Everyday knowledge as a portal to the specialized knowledge of the school became confused with the specialized knowledge itself. What was produced was a dilution of what was to be learnt by how to learn it. This is a case of a particular theory of learning (constructivism), being transformed into a set of 'pedagogic techniques', which bled into the structuring of the curriculum so that knowledge, knowers and knowing all became blended into one (as we see in Tables 10.1 and 10.2).

The Bernsteinian framework, which underpinned the second and third reform moments, draws attention to knowledge boundaries. In his enduring interest in social justice and knowledge, Bernstein outlines the rights that must be institutionalized to meet the conditions of an effective democracy (2000: xx). He describes one of the rights as 'enhancement', which concerns boundaries and the right to experience boundaries. These boundaries are tension points which open up the possibility for condensing the past and opening up possible futures. In other words, it is not possible for students to think things as they aren't, to imagine alternatives, unless they have access to the non-local, non-everyday, context-independent knowledge that allows this. So for Bernstein, 'Enhancement entails a discipline'. The latter has two meanings – access to disciplinary knowledge; and the 'labour of acquisition' (Davis 2005). The intrusion of the Bernsteinian framework in the reform efforts and the attention it drew to issues of the organization of knowledge in the curriculum and its social consequences reconfigured the knowledge–knower relationship, reasserting the boundary between knowledges and between knowledge and the knower. In a Durkheimian sense, it is not the knower or knowing that makes the knowledge, but primarily knowledge that shapes the knower.

Yates provides a definition of pedagogy as that which 'can include attention to the person and subjectivity, and the world and culture, and even policy and institutions, but seems to put the emphasis particularly on the interpersonal instructional (or facilitative) act' (2009: 20). Bernstein (1999) extends this definition by establishing the authority of the transmitter in the pedagogic relation. The relation is intrinsically asymmetrical and teacher and acquirer are always unequal as it is the transmitter who holds the criteria for what is to be learnt and who controls the rules for evaluating whether those criteria have been acquired. He also ties the definition to curriculum in asserting the 'what' that is to be transmitted: '... there is a purposeful intention to initiate, modify, develop or change knowledge, conduct or practice by someone or something which already possesses, or has access to, the necessary resources and the means of evaluating the acquisition' (Bernstein 1999: 267). But he is clear: 'Curriculum defines what counts as valid knowledge, pedagogy defines what counts as valid transmission of knowledge' (Bernstein 1975: 85). What this chapter has tried to show is that confusion between curriculum and pedagogy, or conflation of the two, has led to problems in the implementing of that curriculum. The various reform efforts have thus far largely missed this distinction in thinking about curriculum, pedagogy and the failure to improve the possibilities education offers students in the majority of schools in South Africa.

If any act of curriculum construction is to decide what knowledge is of most worth to its citizens, then a consideration of knowledge *and* knower is crucial. And the structuring of a curriculum in relation to what students can and should do at what point (selection and sequence) entails a theory of knowing. Different curricula deal with these categories differently – making all three explicit and coherent, emphasizing one to the exclusion of others, or holding the three in tension. Separating out curriculum and pedagogy allows for the possibility of making principled decisions around what belongs where and how we might achieve our educational aspirations. It may also enhance clarity around the possibilities for stipulation in terms of knowledge, knowers and knowing, and how we might meaningfully achieve educational change in a society with an enduring fractured social milieu, with a very particular history and a fragile knowledge project.

Note

1   For example, in the case of Curriculum 2005 where there was an attempt to insert a 'constructivist' notion of pedagogy, where student discovery was prioritized and where knowledge was treated as open and negotiable, in a system where the authority of the teacher and her knowledge had for years been paramount in the social relations in the classroom, premised on class, ethnic and historical bases (see Chick 1996), as well as relating to the extent to which teachers had been given an opportunity to 'internalise the grammar of the subject' in question (Muller 1989), i.e. the nature of their training and qualification.

References

Alexander, R. (2001) *Culture and Pedagogy: international comparisons in primary education*, Oxford: Blackwell.

Allais, S. (2006) 'Problems with qualification reform in senior secondary education in South Africa', in M. Young and J. Gamble (eds), *Knowledge, Curriculum and Qualifications for South African Further Education*, Cape Town: HSRC Press.

Allais, S. and Taylor, N. (2007) 'A nation in denial', paper presented at the Kenton Education Conference, Kwa-Zulu Natal, October 2007.

Bernstein, B. (1975) *Class, Codes and Control, Volume 2: applied studies towards a sociology of language*, London: Routledge & Kegan Paul.

Bernstein, B. (1990) *Class, Codes and Control, Volume 4: the structuring of pedagogic discourse*, London: Routledge.

Bernstein, B. (1999) 'Pedagogy, identity and the construction of a theory of symbolic control: Basil Bernstein questioned by Joseph Solomon', *British Journal of Sociology of Education*, 20: 265–279.

Bernstein, B. (2000) *Pedagogy, Symbolic Control and Identity: theory, research and critique,* revised edition, Oxford: Rowman & Littlefield.

Chick, J. K. (1996) 'Safe-talk: collusion in apartheid education', in H. Coleman (ed.) *Society and the Language Classroom,* Cambridge: Cambridge University Press.

Chisholm, L. (2005) 'The making of South Africa's National Curriculum Statement', *Journal of Curriculum Studies,* 37, 2: 193–208.

Chisholm, L., Hoadley, U. and wa Kivilu, M. (2005) *Educator Workload in South Africa. Final report prepared for the Education Labour Relations Council,* Pretoria: Child, Youth & Family Development, Human Sciences Research Council.

Cross, M., Mungadi, R. and Rouhani, S. (2002) 'From policy to practice: curriculum reform in South African education', *Comparative Education,* 38, 2: 171–187.

Davis, Z. (1996) 'The problem-centred approach and the production of the vanishing pedagogue', paper presented at the Kenton-at-Wilgespruit conference, Johannesburg, October 1996.

Davis, Z. (2005) 'Pleasure and pedagogic discourse: a case study of a problem-centred pedagogic modality', unpublished PhD dissertation, University of Cape Town.

Donnelly, K. (2005) *Benchmarking Australian Primary School Curricula.* Canberra: Australian Government: Department of Education, Science and Training.

Dowling, P. (1995) 'Discipline and mathematise: the myth of relevance in education', *Perspectives in Education,* 16, 2: 209–226.

Dowling, P. (1998) *The Sociology of Mathematics Education: mathematical myths/pedagogic texts,* London: Falmer.

Enslin, P. (1984) 'The role of fundamental pedagogics in the formulation of educational policy in South Africa' in P. Kallaway (ed.) *Apartheid and Education: the education of black South Africans,* Johannesburg: Ravan Press.

Ensor, M.P. (1999) 'A study of the recontextualizing of pedagogic practices from a South African pre-service mathematics teacher education course by seven secondary mathematics teachers', *Collected Original Resources in Education,* 24, 3.

Ensor, P. (1997) 'School mathematics, everyday life and the NQF: a case of non-equivalence?', *Pythagorus,* 41: 36–44.

Fataar, A. (2006) 'Policy networks in recalibrated political terrain: the case of school curriculum policy and politics in South Africa', *Journal of Education Policy,* 21, 6: 641–659.

Hamilton, D. (1999) 'The pedagogic paradox (or why no didactics in England?)', *Pedagogy, Culture and Society,* 7, 1: 135–152.

Harley, K. and Parker, B. (1999) 'Integrating differences: implications of an outcomes-based National Qualifications Framework for the roles and competencies of teachers', in J. Jansen and P. Christie (eds.) *Changing Curriculum: studies on outcomes-based education in South Africa,* Cape Town: Juta.

Harley, K. and Wedekind, V. (2003) 'A time for discipline: disciplinary displacement and mythological truths', *Journal of Education,* 31: 25–46.

Jansen, J.D. (1999) 'Why outcomes-based education will fail: an elaboration', in J.D. Jansen and P. Christie (eds) *Changing Curriculum: studies on outcomes-based education in South Africa,* Cape Town: Juta.

Jansen, J.D. (2001) 'Explaining non-change in education reform after apartheid: political symbolism and the problem of policy implementation', in Y. Sayed and J.D. Jansen (eds) *Implementing Education Policies: the South African experience,* Cape Town: University of Cape Town Press.

Jansen, J.D. and Christie, P. (1999) *Changing Curriculum: studies on outcomes-based education in South Africa,* Cape Town: Juta.

Kraak, A. (1999) 'Competing education and training policy discourses: a "systemic" versus "unit standards" framework', in J.D Jansen and P. Christie (eds.) *Changing Curriculum: studies on outcomes-based education in South Africa*, Cape Town: Juta.

Moore, R. (2004) 'The problem of knowledge', *Education and Society*, Cambridge: Polity Press.

Morrow, W. (2001) 'Scriptures and practices', *Perspectives in Education*, 19, 1: 87–106.

Motshekga, A. (2009) 'We've signed OBE's death certificate: statement by Minister of Basic Education, Angie Motshekga, on curriculum review process', National Assembly 5 November 2009. Online. Available HTTP: http://www.politicsweb.co.za/politicsweb/view/politicsweb/en/page71656?oid=150055&sn=Detail (accessed 3 May 2010).

Muller, J. (1989) '"Out of their minds": an analysis of discourse in two South African science classrooms', in D. Roger and Bull, P. (eds.) *Conversation: an interdisciplinary approach*, Clevedon/Philadelphia, PA: Multilingual Matters.

Muller, J. (2000) *Reclaiming Knowledge: social theory, curriculum and education policy*, London: RoutledgeFalmer.

Muller, J. and Taylor, N. (1995) 'Knowledges sacred and profane: schooling and everyday life', *Social Epistemology*, 9, 3: 257–275.

NEPI (1992) *Curriculum*, Cape Town: Oxford University Press.

South African Department of Education (1995) *Curriculum Framework for General and Further Education Document*, Pretoria: South African Department of Education.

South African Department of Education (1997) *Curriculum 2005: Lifelong Learning for the 21st Century*, Pretoria: South African Department of Education.

South African Department of Education (2000a) *A South African Curriculum for the Twenty First Century: report of the Review Committee on Curriculum 2005*, presented to the Minister of Education, Professor Kader Asmal, Pretoria: South African Department of Education.

South African Department of Education (2000b) *Curriculum 2005: Towards a theoretical framework*, Pretoria: South African Department of Education.

South African Department of Education (2009) *Report of the Task Team for the Review of the Implementation of the National Curriculum Statement*, Pretoria: South African Department of Education.

Taylor, N. and Vinjevold, P. (1999) *Getting Learning Right*, Johannesburg: Joint Education Trust.

Van der Berg, S. and Louw, M. (2008) 'Lessons learnt from SACMEQII: South African student performance in regional context', in G.C Bloch, L. Chisholm, B. Fleisch and M. Mabizela (eds) *Education and Investment Choices for Vulnerable Children in South Africa*, Johannesburg: Wits University Press.

Yates, L. (2009) 'From curriculum to pedagogy and back again: knowledge, the person and the changing world', *Pedagogy, Culture and Society*, 17, 1: 17–28.

Young, M. (2002) 'Educational reform in South Africa (1990–2000): an international perspective', in A. Kraak, and M. Young (eds) *Education in Retrospect: policy and implementation since 1990*, Cape Town: HSRC Press.

Young, M. (2007) 'What is schooling for?', in H. Daniels, H. Lauder and J. Porter (eds) *The Routledge Companion to Education*, London: Routledge.

11 Making Nothing Happen

Affective Life Under Audit

Peter Taubman

If it can't be measured, it doesn't exist.

(Spellings 2007)

And the one thing we're saying that isn't going to work is doing nothing.

(Duncan 2010a: 12)

For poetry makes nothing happen: it survives
In the valley of its making where executives
Would never want to tamper, flows on south
From ranches of isolation and the busy griefs,
Raw towns that we believe and die in; it survives,
A way of happening, a mouth.

(Auden 1940)

If it can't be measured it doesn't exist; it is nothing. And the one thing that doesn't work is doing nothing. Contrary to these views, expressed by President Bush's and President Obama's Secretaries of Education and which inform so much of what passes for educational reform today, this chapter looks at what it might mean to make nothing happen, to find in that happening what Auden referred to as a mouth, or the words that might issue from and bring us out of the 'isolation and the busy griefs', the raw places so many educators in the United States now inhabit in the age of audit and the Race to the Top. This chapter considers what happens when teachers are overwhelmed, shocked, and numbed in an educational order that renders any alternative, linguistic or otherwise, as dangerously regressive or fungible within its own coordinates. It explores professional melancholia, the affective state that results when public discursive forms cannot convey the inchoate, inaudible losses that one's profession has sustained. But the chapter also offers the possibility of finding within that melancholia and accompanying loss of speech an immanent utopianism. Quite simply, my intention in this chapter is to talk about what it might mean to survive in the new educational order.

The chapter begins with an overview of the current situation and a discussion of possible reasons for the absence of any real alternative. I move on to discuss how working in this new educational order affects the psychic lives of teachers and educators. Finally, I shall suggest that surrendering to the professional weariness, melancholia and alienation, to the 'isolation and busy griefs' provoked by the new educational order, may itself provide alternatives, may make nothing happen.

Part One: The Current State

> We have lost the great ideas, the Utopias, we have lost all faith, everything that creates meaning. Incapable of faith, hopeless to the utmost degree, we roam across a toxic waste dump in extreme peril; everyone of those incomprehensible shards, these odds and ends of junk and detritus, menaces us, constantly hurts and maims us and sooner or later, inevitably kills us.
>
> (Richter 1995: 171–172)

> Basic optimism is the inheritance that bonds the varied philosophies and institutional arrangements of American education.
>
> (Francis Keppel quoted in Ritchie 1977: 477)

Where to start? Perhaps putting side by side two quotes, one by the father of free market capitalism, Milton Friedman, and one by the current US Secretary of Education, Arne Duncan, will provide a sense of where things stand and where they are headed.

After the devastation of Hurricane Katrina and shortly before he died, Friedman wrote an op-ed in the *Wall Street Journal* in which he stated that New Orleans schools were failing 'because the schools are owned and operated by the government. Is there any doubt', he asked, 'that the private market would provide schooling for children … faster and better than the state?' (2005: A20). The statement was consistent with Friedman's belief that 'public schools are an island of socialism in a free market sea' (1980: 154) and need to be privatized as quickly as possible. This past January, almost five years after Katrina, Arne Duncan stated on 'Washington Watch with Roland Martin' that '[t]he best thing that happened to the education system in New Orleans was Hurricane Katrina. That education system was a disaster. And it took Hurricane Katrina to wake up the community to say that we have to do better' (quoted in Tapper 2010). Duncan later apologized for his remark but he, along with President Obama, media pundits, politicians, mainstream educational organizations, conservative, neoliberal and self-styled progressive think-tanks, a great many deans of education, and the popular media – actually it seems everyone but historian Diane Ravitch who has, since 2007 been leaping off the bandwagon of accountability that she helped build – seem to believe that the best way to cure the apparent educational crisis is to subject the whole system of public education to the neoliberal logics and practices of the corporate world, which paradoxically dooms the system to failures and corruption. Of course, the so-called educational reformers respond to the failure of the system, brought on by the reforms, with an intensified program of downsizing, surveillance, privatization, generically packaged curriculum and methods, and strict management guidelines as well as demands for increased productivity.

There is little doubt that we in the USA are witnessing the most extensive transformation in education since the rise of public education in the nineteenth century (see Taubman 2009). Touted as educational reform and occurring under the twin banners of standards and accountability, the transformation has, over the last decade, materially affected every aspect of schooling, teaching, and teacher education in the United States. The most palpable aspect of the transformation has been No Child Left Behind and the focus on high-stakes testing, which everyone seems now to criticize. But high-stakes testing in K–12 schools has been only the most prominent aspect of a transformation that now reaches into higher education, threatens the existence of public education, and defines all of us in terms of our potential contribution to the global marketplace.

So profound is the transformation that the terms in which and under which teaching and teacher education may now be discussed appear set and non-negotiable. These terms, such as 'best practices', 'performance outcomes', 'value added', 'rubrics', 'data-driven decision making', 'learning environments', emanate from within neoliberal economic policies, corporate business practices, neoconservative social agendas, and the learning sciences, the latter having solidified the dominance of psychology in our understanding of teaching and education. The fact that leading educational organizations have embraced this transformation suggests how even progressive impulses and aspirations have been appropriated, re-formed and aligned with educational policies and practices that were once seen as inimical to those very impulses and aspirations.

In *Teaching by Numbers: Deconstructing the Discourse of Standards and Accountability in Education* (Taubman 2009), I argued that a confluence of forces contributed to the transformation. I shall very briefly summarize five of these. First, since the early 1980s there has been an acceptance and then a celebration of neoliberal economic policies, which, as Thomas Friedman put it in *The World Is Flat: A Brief History of the Twenty-first Century* (2006), allow us to think of the world as a single market. Neoliberalism, and I am simplifying things considerably here, posits the market as the final determinant of all values. It has been described as a doctrine that pursues policies of de-regulation, privatization and spending cuts, breaks unions, unravels social nets and renders the individual as an autonomous entrepreneur responsible for his or her self-progress and position. The consequence of such a doctrine for education was that starting in the early 1980s business interests turned their attention to education as a potentially enormously profitable market, which today is valued in the hundreds of billions of dollars. It is the swamping of that 'island of socialism' by the free market that Diane Ravitch has over the last three years warned about when she writes that public education is in danger of disappearing. 'At the present time', she writes in her latest book, *The Death and Life of the Great American School System*, 'public education is in peril. Efforts to reform public education are, ironically … endangering its very survival' (2010: 242). It is the penetration of the market into education and the triumph of neoliberal economic policies and the logics of the marketplace that have resulted in, among so many other things, students being configured as consumers, the cutbacks in state funding for public higher education with the accompanying rise in tuition, and the recent drive to make the BA a three-year program because, as

Robert Zemsky, a guru for many in higher education, stated in an article in the *Chronicle of Higher Education*, it would allow students to 'get to the labor market faster and more expeditiously' (2009).

The second phenomenon driving the transformation concerned the growing interest among state governors in the 1980s and 1990s in education. In those decades several states, such as North Carolina and Arkansas, developed policies and initiated programs to address what was increasingly construed as, or according to some scholars manufactured as, an educational crisis. The upshot of the interest at the state level was that several committees and organizations were formed, the majority of whose members were from the business sector. These groups, particularly the National Governors Association's various task forces on education, issued policy statements about the failure of schools, and the need for higher standards and greater accountability. During these decades the standards movement took off, but increasingly policy statements on education resembled the statements on education issued by the Business Roundtable and the Chamber of Commerce. Thus policy at the state level took on the language of the corporate sector and linked education to national economic success, championed standards and accountability, and raised the threat that if we didn't improve our schools, we would lose our economic standing in the world. All this mind you at a moment when worker productivity was rising as wages, even with health benefits factored in, flattened out (Harvey 2005).

The third factor that has driven the transformation we are witnessing has to do with the enormous advances in technology coupled with the spread of what British anthropologists in the 1980s started calling audit culture (see Ong and Collier 2005; Power 1994; 1997; 2003; Strathern 2000). Audit culture refers to the importation into public sectors such as education of various terms and practices once confined to the worlds of finance, accounting, and business. As Power describes it, in audit culture questions of quality are replaced or subsumed by the logics and objectives of management. Audit serves as a form of meta-regulation. Institutions become auditable by rendering themselves in terms of quantifiable performance objectives and by developing a system for defining and monitoring performance. The National Council for the Accreditation of Teacher Education, to take one of the most obvious examples in teacher education, is primarily interested in ascertaining if there is a data aggregation system in place at the unit level which monitors how well the data at the program level is aggregated and disaggregated. In K–12 schools today one hears more about data than about the content of curriculum. One result of audit practices as these are instituted in higher education can be seen in the recent move of various graduate and undergraduate programs to outsource to India the grading of papers (June 2010). If you can provide explicit enough rubrics anyone can grade the papers. Or, to take another example, in 2008 a for-profit teacher education outfit promised the University of Toledo's school of education a boost in enrollment numbers if it agreed to implement an on-line program which has 'coaches' do the grading using rubrics and delivering instruction that uses performance outcomes rather than textbooks. At the last moment UT rejected the program, but is has been implemented in teacher education programs in Arkansas and

Texas (Baines and Chiarelott 2010). As Thomas Friedman wrote in *The World is Flat*, if you standardize the work, chop it up finely enough, and define your performance outcomes, it can be outsourced (2006: 86, 15). Perhaps audit culture is best captured in a phrase used by the previous Secretary of Education, Margaret Spellings and echoed by the new Secretary Arne Duncan: 'If it can't be measured, it doesn't exist.' A representative from NCATE, – the National Council for Accreditation of Teacher Education, the most prominent body in charge of accrediting teacher education programs – recently told the head of a program in the School of Education at Brooklyn College, 'We are not interested in syllabi; we want numbers' (Reed: 2010).

The craze for numbers that allow for particular kinds of comparisons, those between or among entities that can be easily quantified, has accelerated in recent years, so much so that, as Gary Wolf (2010) points out, we have begun to use numbers as a way to track our own self-improvement toward a pre-determined goal or one that is unknown. The danger in such self-tracking is not its self-surveillance, but rather the reduction of who one is into a quantified and quantifiable self. The assumption, at least according to Wolf, is that if we have the sensitively calibrated instrument, the solutions to problems lie in tracking behaviors that are measurable according to a set standard. This is exactly what has happened in education, where numerical data now determines employability, school survival, financial success, and what it means to be educated.

The fourth factor that made the transformation possible had to do with the triumph of the learning sciences. It is beyond the scope of this chapter to present this in detail (for further analysis see Taubman 2009). Suffice it to say that the influence of cognitive science and a residual behaviorism provided a language for educators that rendered knowledge in terms of information, the curriculum in terms of meta-cognitive skills, and learning in terms of a change in the organism as demonstrated by observable behavioral change. As teaching became linked to learning in a causal narrative and learning was rendered demonstrable on tests or discrete standardized assessments, teachers were positioned as solely responsible for student learning and learning was reduced to performance on tests and to students' abilities to engage in de-contextualized meta-cognitive strategies. We can note the influence of the learning sciences in the behavioral approaches to teacher training, which increasingly focus on observable behaviors that teachers can learn in order to produce the expected results. So, for example, in the online version of the recent *New York Times* magazine article entitled 'Building a Better Teacher', all the video clips of what is considered good teaching focus on behavior management strategies. There is nothing about curriculum.

The fifth and final factor that made the transformation possible concerns the vulnerabilities of educators. We are a fairly vulnerable group. For more than a century we have been the scapegoat for social, economic and political problems. One can read the complaints of businessmen in the 1920s about how poorly educated the workforce is or read the editorials from the 1950s about how Johnny can't read, and they all sound much like the warnings issued today about the crisis in education (see Rothstein 1998). But one can also read today about those lone, heroic educators who have saved a mind or rescued an entire class of generally impoverished students of color from ignorance and despair. On the one hand we are held responsible for the rotten state of the nation, and on the other hand we are, told how we can shape a mind and save the nation. It's a terrible sado-masochistic ritual we engage in and the result is that we are softened up to buy the promises that some new educational reform will finally give us the status we deserve or create that perfect class we all long for.

That is a very brief summary of the main points in *Teaching by Numbers*. I finished the book in 2007 and at the time was cautiously optimistic that a new administration would at least interrupt the educational reforms I'd been chronicling and experiencing. With Obama's election the transformation of education at every level has progressed much more quickly than anyone might have anticipated. In part the success of the Obama/Duncan educational vision rests on the availability of Race to the Top funds at a moment when schools have experienced severe financial cutbacks. Race to the Top promises billions of dollars to those states that agree to a series of reforms in K–12 education that link teacher pay to student performance, close down schools deemed to be failing, increase the number of charter schools, and, through a data tracking system, hold all teachers and schools of education accountable for low achieving students.

But in order to 'reform' education at the pace the new administration has set, a particular narrative had to be in place. Today that narrative, accompanied by a range of audit practices, is firmly established, although it requires relentless repetition. The narrative consists of twelve claims – a kind of corporate twelve-step program. All the claims are put forward as uncontestable:

First claim: *There is a crisis in education.*

Pretty much everyone now in the USA believes there is a crisis in public education. As proof they refer to reports of falling test scores, poor test performance relative to other countries' students, skyrocketing dropout rates, stories of incompetent and abusive teachers, and a general perception that schools, particularly urban schools, are violent, in shambles, and do terrible things particularly to kids of color. In addition, as Arne Duncan put it, 'Many if not most of the nation's 1,450 schools, colleges, and departments of education are doing a mediocre job of preparing teachers for the realities the 21st century' (2009d). The crisis appears so severe, many commentators worry that the fate of the country is at stake. As *New York Times'* liberal columnist Bob Herbert wrote a few months ago, 'America's greatest national security crisis is the crisis in its schools' (2010: A19). All the research that was done for example by Richard Rothstein (1998; 2004), David Berliner (Berliner and Biddle 1995), Pauline Lipman (2005) and the late Gerald Bracey (2004, 2006), which complicates or challenges such a claim is blithely ignored. So too is the logical extension of such a claim. If indeed our schools constitute our greatest national security crisis, one would think that schools would receive the funding the military does, that teachers would be treated with the respect our fighting forces are, and that education, like the military, would be taken as an inherent good, such that education was held as accountable as a military that has won one war in the last half century, which saw several wars.

Second claim: The USA's ailing economy, loss of a competitive edge in the global marketplace and continued racial and class divides, result from the failure of our schools.

Here is Arne Duncan: 'Our schools are perpetuating poverty and are perpetuating social failure' (2009b). 'Reform', he has said, 'is all about jobs. We have to educate our way to a better economy' (2009a). In such a narrative young people are articulated as potential or virtual labor, which is yet to be materialized but which must be channeled into future promises of work. Unemployment and dwindling jobs only mean that students must do better to realize their productive capacity or entrepreneurial potential, both of which now define their subjectivity.

The reason our economy is in trouble has nothing to do with political and economic policies, the war, or corporate malfeasance in a de-regulated marketplace, but rather with lousy schools. If blaming schools for the state of the economy does not appear an outrageous claim, it is interesting to note that when the economy boomed in the 1990s and early 2000s or when worker productivity sky rocketed in the 1980s and 90s, no one patted teachers on the back, or when Japan went into recession in the 1990s, no one took back their comments that we should be emulating the Japanese system of education. The standard retort to such comments is that, while they may be true, no one would argue that 'schools have nothing at all to do with a nation's economic health … [because] good schools are important for a nation's future economic, civic, social and cultural development' (Ravitch 2010: 28). The problem with this response is that, unlike the critique, which explicitly holds schools responsible for the nation's economic and social future, it offers an empty generalization, which explains neither how schools are important – perhaps as some have argued they reproduce class divisions – nor what if any their relationship is to economic success. Ireland, which has one of the most educated citizenry in the West – it is one reason why so many companies chose to re-locate there – has an economy that according to the International Monetary Fund is the worst in Europe, and will, according to the Economic and Social Research Institute, have an unemployment rate of 17 per cent next year.

Third claim: We know schools are failing because students are not learning, as evidenced by their test scores and the data.

Here is the first switch point in the narrative. With little if any serious critique or challenge, although some lip service is given to authentic assessment, learning is matter-of-factly equated with test scores. It is more than likely that as budgets are cut further schools will rely even more on tests, which are less expensive and less time consuming than other forms of assessment. But why are students not learning or performing well on exams?

Fourth claim: Since all students can learn, the reason they don't is that there are bad teachers and administrators and a lack of high standards and accountability.

Students are not succeeding because they are not learning and they are not learning because teachers are failing to teach them. Here is Duncan again: '[T]he single biggest influence on student academic growth is the quality of the teacher standing in front of the classroom – not socioeconomic status, not family background, but the quality of the teacher' (2009d). Or as Joel Klein, chancellor of NYC public schools puts it, 'The root cause of test-score disparities is not poverty or family circumstances, but subpar teachers and principals' (quoted in Hernandez 2009). Given this apparently clear link between the economy, student/school failure, and bad teaching, what is to be done?

Fifth claim: We need a revolution.

The new narrative calls for a revolution, frames the issues in terms of civil rights, and positions those in favor of the policies as educational reformers and those who oppose them as obstructionists, mired in the past. 'I believe,' said Duncan to a cheering audience at Teachers College, 'education is the civil rights issue of our generation' (2009d). 'We need a revolution in education,' urges Duncan (2010a). The obstructionists are those teacher unions, which as Thomas Toch said in *US News and World Report* 'are driving out good teachers, coddling bad ones and putting bureaucracy in the way of quality education' (1996: 1).

The sixth and perhaps the key claim in the narrative, the second switch point, if you will, involves equating the 'revolution' and 'the greatest civil rights issue of our generation' with putting a qualified teacher, now defined as one who can raise test scores, in every classroom.

Not equal resources and not equal educational opportunities, but a qualified teacher in every classroom. These teachers are, as Michelle Obama (2009) has repeatedly stated, the key to the success of our economy. They are also, as almost all mainstream educators, such as Linda Darling-Hammond (2006), now claim, the most significant factor in student learning. So, what has happened here? The enormous inequities we have in wealth, housing, health, and education, the problems of racism and sexism we face, the fact that schools are more segregated today than at any time since the 1950s, the reality that we are in a state of war and the profound consequences of this for our society – all these are re-coded in terms of a revolution that will put a qualified teacher in every classroom and close the racial gap on test scores. Progressive educational projects are transformed by translating them into rationales for greater accountability and by reconfiguring pressing social and political issues as the responsibility of teachers, who can only meet that responsibility by surrendering to disciplinary technologies and audit practices, such as those required by NCATE or No Child Left Behind (NCLB) or state and local educational regulatory agencies. Once the causal chain has been established, tying the health of our economy, and the progress of civil rights to student learning, i.e. test scores, and learning is tied to the quality of teachers and administrators, the next step logically follows.

Seventh claim: True educational reform consists of holding teachers accountable for student success, as measured by test scores and using 'world class standards', rubrics, tests and data aggregation systems to track value added and the teacher's effect on student learning.

As Duncan has stated, 'The biggest problem with NCLB is that it doesn't encourage high learning standards' (2009c). Not, mind you, opportunity to learn standards, but performance standards which can be measured. Duncan, like so many other educators in the USA today, believes in the magical power of data. 'Data gives us the roadmap to reform. It tells us where we are, where we need to go, and who is most at risk' (2009a). 'A robust data system can track student achievement and teacher effectiveness' (2009b). 'Data doesn't lie', claims Duncan (2009a).

Eighth claim: Given that teachers are responsible for student performance, given that we can measure that performance, and given that we are armed now with data, that doesn't lie, teachers who have no or weak impact on students' learning must be let go.

The March 2010 issue of *Newsweek* said it all. In the center of the cover appeared the title of the lead article by Evan Thomas and Pat Wingert: 'The Key to Saving American Education.' Behind it a blackboard on which was written, over and over: 'We must fire bad teachers.' In the lead story in the August 2009 issue of *The New Yorker*, we read 'By now, most serious studies on education reform have concluded that the critical variable when it comes to kids succeeding in school isn't money spent on buildings or books but, rather, the quality of teacher … But, in New York and elsewhere, holding teachers accountable for how well they teach has proved to be a frontier that cannot be crossed' (Brill 2009: 33). Who is to blame for those incompetents?

Ninth claim: Teachers are incompetent because schools of education have not fulfilled their responsibility of ensuring that their graduates will get their students to learn.

We have a broken teacher education system', Arne Duncan tells audiences (2009e: 3). Arthur Levine, ex-president of Teacher's College, Columbia University and Lee Schulman echo the view. 'Graduates are insufficiently prepared for the classroom', warns Levine (2006: 1), and Schulman has claimed the state of teacher education is 'chaotic' (2005: 7). In the *Newsweek* article mentioned above, Thomas and Wingert informed readers, 'Teaching can be taught to some degree but not the way many graduate schools of education do it, with a lot of insipid or marginally relevant theorizing and pedagogy' (2010: 25). David Steiner, the new Commissioner of Education in New York, has claimed that education schools devote 'too much class time to abstract notions about the role of school in democracy and the view that schools exist to perpetuate a social hierarchy' (quoted in Foderaro 2010). With several other educators, most prominently Arne Duncan, Steiner argues that too much theory has ruined teacher education. I always find it interesting that schools of education are blamed for poor teachers and thus student performance. I am waiting for business schools to be blamed for the current economic crisis or medical schools to be blamed for rising rates of diabetes in the country or seminaries' to be held responsible for the church's sexual abuse scandals.

Tenth claim: To ensure teacher education programs produce qualified teachers, they must be subjected to audit practices that track how their student teachers and their graduates are impacting their students' learning.

If such data is not forthcoming or if the data system in place is weak, or if it reveals that there is little or no impact, those programs should be shut down.

The chain is almost complete. Schools of education and unions are responsible for incompetent teachers who are responsible for students not learning, which, in turn, is responsible for the USA's economic, racial and political problems.

Eleventh claim: Given that public schools and schools of education are performing so poorly, not only should we lift caps on charter schools, so we can have more successful schools like KIPP (Knowledge is Power Program), but we must open up alternative certification routes, such as Teach for America.

As *Atlantic Monthly* reporter Amanda Ripley writes in 'What Makes a Great Teacher': 'If school systems hired, trained, and rewarded teachers according to the principles Teach for America has identified, then teachers would not need to work so hard. They would be operating in a system designed ... for success' (2010: 66).

Twelfth claim: If the US educational system does not constantly improve, i.e. embrace the revolution, it will lose the global race in a flat world.

After all, as Arne Duncan asks, 'What's the alternative? Sit back and accept the status quo? Do nothing?' (quoted in Clark 2010: 23). In these budget strapped time, high schools, colleges, teacher preparation programs must do more with less and prove they are worthy of the financial crumbs tossed to them.

So that is a very short summary of the situation, which is pretty bleak, but of course, not for everyone. This revolution constitutes a windfall of billions of dollars in profits for various corporations, particularly those selling packaged curriculum, like Mark Tucker's America's Choice, or data systems like Dell, or exam and exam guide manufacturers, like ACT Inc or ETS Inc.

What is so difficult to bear is how deeply this narrative has penetrated, how it has eroded public control and the public sphere, how it informs and shapes practices that shrink teacher autonomy in the name of empowerment, and how in the guise of altruism, it sadistically punishes students, schools and communities. Perhaps worst of all, it renders any approach or idea or feeling that is not consistent with its own programs as out of date, obstructionist or incoherent.

As the transformation subjects all educational phenomena to digitization, mathematization, and the logics, practices and drives of the marketplace, as it replaces older identities with entrepreneurial, commercial and self-enhancing, yet to be realized but always receding potentialities for improvement and employability, any alternative appears outdated and doomed. If there is an outside to the new educational order, it is the space created by that very order, the space of irrational enjoyment, one where crazed teachers, violent students, and corrupt administrators perform for the insatiable appetite of a media that turns teachers into clowns, incompetents, deviants, or romanticized, heroic loners.

All those older forms of critique and resistance that might have challenged or provided alternatives to the new educational order, for example, histories and philosophies of education, which could historicize the transformation and critique its assumptions, are disappearing from teacher education programs.

One self-announced alternative to the new order takes the form of what the AERA Panel on studying teacher education (Cochran-Smith and Zeichner 2005) referred to as the social justice agenda, but those in the USA who promote this agenda often seem myopically focused on the politics of identity, such that only a handful of teacher educators or curriculum theorists who champion social justice address how the transformation in education is affecting teachers, students, schools and communities at the micro level, shaping new entrepreneurial masculinities and femininities, and hollowing out and constructing new identities whose allure is based on their purported transcendence of race, class, gender and sexuality and on the promised excitement of choice and the freedom to fashion oneself in ever changing forms. For example, in the May/June 2010 issue of *JTE: Journal of Teacher Education*, the theme of which was 'social justice and teacher education', the focus was almost exclusively on race, whiteness, culturally relevant pedagogy, and structures of privilege. Never mentioned, let alone analyzed, were the penetration of education by the marketplace, what the consequences are for our understanding of citizenship, democracy, new identities, and education or how the social justice agenda itself has been appropriated by mainstream educational organizations, such NCATE, that appear wholly committed to audit practices and the quantification of educational experience while championing culturally relevant pedagogies.

So immediately questions present themselves. How can we live through this nightmare? What if anything can life under the sign of audit teach us? How do we survive the alienation, restlessness, the grim isolation? What does it mean to live in the space between what is no longer and what is not yet? Is such a space not a melancholic one? Let me now turn to these questions.

Part Two: Making Nothing Happen

> [M]elancholia is a paradoxical kind of utopian thinking.
>
> (Cranfield 2006)

> Melancholy is a form of resistance.
>
> (W.G. Sebald quoted in Santner 2006: 45)

> The nonconventional, veiled language of the melancholic can bring about a sensitivity to that which can barely be heard.
>
> (Salvio 2007: 15)

We educators live today increasingly in a world of answers: right and wrong answers on tests, answers that can be easily rendered as numerical data, the answers of purportedly research-based best practices that quickly become scripted lesson plans or of rubrics used to rationalize writing and drain it of its wild magic or of performance outcomes that further reduce answers to demonstrable behaviors. We are informed that curriculum, the artistry of creating conditions where individuals can study themselves and the world coming to form in the disciplines, is really about cognitive skills, strategies and higher order thinking. CEOs, business tycoons and billionaires assure us they know how to run schools and what is best for students. Media pundits never tire of telling us how incompetent we are, how students are worse than they used to be, how if we just adopted models imported from the business world we would solve the economic and racial problems for which we are, amazingly enough, held responsible. The mysteries of science and the humanities, the ineffable questions they raise and that animate them have been numericized. To ask questions today, to entertain the possibility that, as Freud (1995/1937: 248) said, teaching is an impossible profession, is to risk marginalization and even loss of a job. To slow down is to move backwards and to move backwards is to die. Thus does intellectual life appear a shadow of itself in the new educational order. As Milan Kundera often stated, the totalitarian world is the world of answers. 'The stupidity of people', he wrote 'comes from having an answer for everything. People prefer to judge rather than to understand, to answer rather than to ask' (quoted in Jaanus 1996: 231). Is it any wonder so many educators feel alienated from their own field?

These days when I drop below the surface of the incessant talk about performance outcomes, data, and standards, when I disengage from the whirlwind of mandates, accreditation agencies, bulletins from American Association of Colleges for Teacher Education (AACTE), and demands to tell us what to do, tell us how this can be used in the classroom, I feel sad, irritable, bored and profoundly disconnected from the field of education. I know there are various dissident groups one can form or join, little pockets where educators try to talk a different language, but my own despair at the situation has led me to wonder if these affects, themselves, might provide a different way of thinking, and perhaps even lead to another question, one that responds to the demand to do something by making nothing happen.

In an article entitled 'Evaluating the Audit Explosion' written in 2003, Michael Power described the 'auditee':

> The auditee is undoubtedly a complex being simultaneously *devious and depressed*; she is skilled at games of compliance but *exhausted* and *cynical* about them too; she is *nervous* about the empty certificates of comfort that get produced, but she colludes in amplifying audit mandates in local settings; … she loathes the time wasted in rituals of inspection but accepts that *this probably is what 'we deserve'*; … she knows the past was far from being a golden age but despairs of the iron cage of auditing; she knows the public accountability and stakeholder dialogue are good things but wonders why, after all her years of training, she is not trusted as an expert anymore.
>
> (Power 2003: 199–200)

If, as so many educators now seem to believe, it is nothing if it can't be measured, then much of the auditee's life in education fades into a silent nothingness outside the reality of numbers. The psychic results are palpable. Depressed, weary, anxious, longing for a past that never was and falling into passive-aggressive behavior and self-loathing, auditees in schools of education and in public school sound a good deal like the melancholic Freud described in his essay 'Mourning and Melancholia'.

The melancholic, Freud wrote, 'represents his ego as worthless, incapable of achievement and morally despicable; he reproaches himself, vilifies himself and expects to be cast out and punished' (1995/1937: 249). The melancholic withdraws libido from the external world, using it, on an unconscious level, to keep alive through identification, the idea, person, ideal or object that has been lost.

In his essay Freud suggested individuals respond in one of two ways to 'the loss of a loved person, or to the loss of some abstraction which has taken the place of one, such as one's country, liberty, an ideal, and so on' (1995/1937: 243). They respond with either mourning or melancholia. If the lost object was properly mourned, that is if there were social rituals or opportunities or appropriate language for the mourning process to unfold and the bereaved took advantage of them, then he or she would be able to mourn successfully and move on with his or her life. 'We can't live in the past', the successful mourner says. 'We must move into the future and let the past go.'

On the other hand if the sufferer cannot mourn or refuses to, he or she may incorporate the lost object into the psyche and there, unleash against the sufferer's own ego the ambivalent feelings once directed toward the lost object. For Freud melancholia resulted.

Numerous scholars and theorists have re-worked Freud's concept of melancholia to make ethical claims. In his *Creaturely Life: Rilke, Benjamin, Sebald*, Eric Santner (2006), glosses these claims as follows:

> On the one hand there is the claim made by the partisans of the 'ethical turn' in deconstruction that melancholy is the only affective posture that can maintain fidelity to those losses that the reigning ideological formation would like to disavow. Whereas mourning, which culminates in a reattachment of libido to new objects of desire (or idealization) proves to be an ultimately adaptive strategy to the governing reality principle and the demand to ;get on with life,' melancholy retards adaptation, attaches itself to loss; it says no! to life without the object (or ideal) and thereby – so it is claimed – holds open the possibility of alternate frameworks of what counts as reality...
>
> On the other hand, we find the competing claim that melancholy is really a mode of defense that ... conflat[es] an impossible possession (or structural lack) with a determinate loss.
>
> (Santner 2006: 89–90)

And thus leads to compliance with the dominant ideology.

Those theorists who exemplify the first claim include Kelly Oliver (2004), who argues that social melancholia results from the loss of a valued self in a society that oppresses women and minorities, and Judith Butler (1990), who has argued that melancholy both reveals and can keep alive an attachment to a lost same-sex love object.

Both Slavoj Zizek and Giogio Agamben are among those theorists associated with the second claim. They argue that the lost object, to which the melancholic remains attached, was in fact 'lacking from the very beginning'. 'Its emergence', they claim 'coincides with its lack' (Zizek 2000: 660). It is as if Zizek and Agamben were theoretically riffing on the Portuguese word *saudades*, which refers to the feeling of missing that which never was. Both these writers play with this 'that which never was' and suggest that the melancholic stages a kind of self-deception, in which a never-possessed lost object is construed as lost so it can be possessed.

As Eric Santner explains, 'according to this view, melancholy proves to be the ultimate adaptive strategy' because it converts 'an impossible possession or, more important, a fundamental impasse … into a contingent or local loss … one that does not fundamentally call into question the coordinates of reality' (2006: 91). The melancholic then is incapable of an ethical act.

Such a view would construe the melancholic teacher under the sign of audit as unconsciously preserving ideals that never really existed, ideals, for example, such as the movement for racial integration or economic equality. In bemoaning their loss in half-articulated concern, puzzlement and worry that the schools are segregated or that there are never enough resources as opposed to the old days, the melancholic leaves unexamined both the actual movement for racial integration and economic justice, its failures and flaws, and the racial and class deadlock at the heart of urban public schooling. Or to take another example, one on the edges of education, there are several older, white retired teachers with whom I come into contact. They send me photos or emails about the good old days, when there was only one phone in the house, when families played board games together or there were picnics and the Dodgers were in Brooklyn. The photos they send are always filled with white people. My point is that the melancholia these retired teachers often seem to exude is not just for a time that never was, but acts as a defense against more serious racial and class deadlocks in our society. It also, as I'll suggest in a moment, contains fragment of an immanent utopianism.

Eric Santner tries to chart a middle course between these two opposite claims about melancholia, those that argue for its ethical potential and those who see it as a defensive reactionary posture, by arguing for the study of stranded objects, objects which no longer, but once did, receive our desires. These 'stranded objects' consist of 'traces of another, unconscious reality that haunts one's conscious reality like a revenant being' (Santner 2006: 152–153).

According to Santner:

> they would be traces of knowledge denied, of deeds left undone, … of moments when it might have been impossible to ask a question or to resist, but one didn't ask and one didn't resist. These were moments when a chance for solidarity with (or later mourning for) the victims was offered but was left untouched. For [us], it is, I am suggesting, a matter of seizing those chances now, of constructing an alternative legacy out of the archive that bears witness to what could have been but was not.
>
> (Santner 2006: 152–153)

I have briefly touched on these various approaches to melancholy, because each has something of importance to offer our understanding of melancholic life in the new educational order. I find compelling the idea that attachment to the lost object even if it is imagined, might still harbor aspirations for something other than what is. The idea of stranded objects offers a way to remain open to the historical landscape, to attend to overlooked, half-murmured ideas and feelings, older, failed educational experiments, bits and pieces of approaches to education that may still survive but are out of view.

None of these theories of melancholia, however, offer a way to understand melancholia's relationship to the absence of structures, rituals, discursive openings, linguistic opportunities, or communal modes of expressivity that could put into words the half-spoken, barely sensed, and quickly forgotten affects, the angry ravings, the complaints without an addressee, the confused sense of failing and inadequacy, the weary resignation, and the misdirected jibes, passive-aggressive behaviors and collapsed compliance we associate with life in the new educational order. To approach that relationship, I want to turn to the work of Paula Salvio who has done so much to explore the relationship between melancholia and education, particularly in her book, *Anne Sexton: Teacher of Weird Abundance* (2007).

For Salvio, melancholia results from a forced attachment to the lost object. It is forced in that the absence of available language, rituals or expressive modalities casts the melancholic's inchoate affective responses beyond the pale. Salvio suggests that the losses of the melancholic are 'not deemed grievable by our culture and therefore cannot be spoken aloud' (2007: 26).

> The melancholic temperament ... is marked by a loss of address that gives way to an unbounded state in which a person appears to abandon her position as subject, for she has no addressable Other – that is there is no one to listen to her plaints, no one who recognizes the grievances as worthy of attention.
>
> (Salvio 2007: 21)

For Salvio, melancholy holds the promise of resistance to oppressive ideological formations, not because the melancholic remains committed to the lost object or lost cause, but because the inability to find within available structures of expression a way to make herself heard, constitutes a rebuff to the prevailing ideology and an implicit critique of it. Salvio reads melancholia as a

> lyric lament that holds nascent political texts that are fused with possibility precisely because melancholia has the capacity to expose the limits of representation and representability – that is the nonconventional, veiled language of the melancholic can bring about a sensitivity to what can barely be heard.
>
> (Salvio 2007: 13)

It is in this sense that Salvio argues the melancholic proceeds from an attitude of revolt. So what is the significance of this for our understanding of professional melancholia in the new educational order and the way it makes nothing happen?

My first response to this question is to say that the libidinal disinvestment in all educational approaches, positions, discourses, offers an opportunity for a detached or disinterested observation of the extant field. Such a withdrawal is not intentional. It is the very result of the oppressiveness of the new order, but it does involve a de-cathecting of not only the policy statements and mandates constitutive of educational reform but also all the various approaches, particularly those that advocate action. Such distance opens before us a field of figures, objects, discourses, to which we feel no allegiance. If we follow Santner, we might speculate that such a position allows us to survey, catch glimpses of what might be the stranded objects littering the desolate wasteland of audit culture. We become melancholic scavengers. Might such scavenging not open up the possibility of what Ernst Boch labeled immanent utopianism?

Human geographer Ben Anderson in an article entitled 'A principle of hope: Recorded music, listening practices and the immanence of utopia' suggests Bloch's immanent utopianism refuses closure. In such a view 'the utopian' involves 'an attunement to the immanent transcendence of the world in its becoming' (2002: 224). Such immanent utopianism does not posit utopia as a vision which exposes the walls of our own prison. Nor does it offer an ideal to which we can aspire. Nor does it offer a set content. It exists in what is, but only as an 'as yet'. It relies on affects understood as moving beyond the possession of any one individual into the collective, but affects, as we have seen, only partially articulated. Such utopianism points always to an 'as yet to be'.

> [T]hrough the immanent utopianism of Bloch ... each event enacts a promise of something better: a longing ... for something else ... [which] is felt momentarily only as a trace ... [T]he utopian is carried in the not-yet of ephemeral phenomena that swerve, and spiral, in and out of the non-conscious background of thought and life. ... Bloch's concept inevitably attunes attention to the presence of absence.
>
> (Anderson 2002: 223)

This presence of absence is equivalent to what I have been calling the happening of nothing. I would venture that the Blochian immanent utopianism Anderson describes, lingers in those transitory inarticulate feelings arising when or telling us that we know something does not have to be as it is, that right there on the horizon other possibilities or potentialities mass, waiting. We can sense this in the melancholia of those white teachers yearning for a time that never was. What feelings tremble behind such nostalgia, what pieces of communal experiences, of failed working class solidarities, what desires for intimacy and what shames and humiliations haunt these dreams?

The world of the melancholic under audit is a world bereft, bereft of the very affects, ideas, imaginings, concepts that cannot yet be articulated. They are not waiting silently, waiting for us to read the words always already printed on them. They remain only so many potentialities. The world of the melancholic under audit is then bereft of nothing. But to make that nothing happen requires finding language, first tentatively certainly with no concern initially for making sense or calling for action. Any move in that direction will be caught on surveillance tape and lead to arrest in performance outcomes or programs for altering the world. Any language must come down from the 'valley of its making/..../..../ From ranches of isolation and the busy griefs,/Raw towns that we believe and die in; it survives,/A way of happening, a mouth' (W.H Auden: 'In Memory of W.B. Yeats'). We do not have the words yet, we melancholics under the sign of audit. We stumble, meet the reproving eyes of colleagues who chide us for not bringing forth policy, the skeptical looks of students who want to know what to do on Monday, the hard stares of the activists who urge us to do something. We are in the presence of nothing happening.

References

Anderson, B. (2002) 'A Principle of Hope: Recorded Music. Listening Practices and the Immanence of Utopia', *Geografiska Annaler. Series B. Human Geography*, 84, 3/4: 211–227.

Auden, W.H. (1940) 'In Memory of William Butler Yeats', in *Another Time*, Random House, New York.

Baines and Chiarelott (2010) 'Public/Private Partnership: A Trojan Horse for Higher Education', unpublished paper.

Berliner, D. and Biddle, B. (1995) *The Manufactured Crisis: Myths, Fraud, and the Attack on America's Public Schools*, Reading, MA: Perseus Books.

Bracey, G. (2004) *Setting the Record Straight: Responses to Misconceptions about Public Education in the U.S.*, 2nd edn, Portsmouth, NH: Heinemann.

Bracey, G. (2006) *Reading Educational Research: How to Avoid Getting Educationally Snookered*, Portsmouth, NH: Heinemann.

Brill, M. (2009) 'The Rubber Room: The Battle over New York's Worst Teachers', *The New Yorker*, 31 August, 30–36.

Butler, J. (1990) *Gender Trouble: Feminism and the Subversion of Identity*, New York: Routledge.

Clark, K. (2010) 'Can School Reform Ever Really Work?', *U.S. News and World Report*, 147, 1: 23.

Cochran-Smith, M. and Zeichner, K. (eds) (2005) *Studying Teacher Education: The Report of the AERA Panel on Teacher Education*, New York: Routledge.

Cranfield, B. (2006) 'Kathy Slade and the Infinite Sadness of Utopian Melancholy', text from a talk given on 22 April at the Tracey Lawrence Gallery. Online. Available HTTP: <http://www.kathyslade.com/texts/melancholy.php> (accessed 11 August 2010).

Darling-Hammond, L. (2006) 'Securing the Right to Learn: Policy, Practice for Powerful Teaching and Learning', *Educational Researcher*, 35, 7: 13–25.

Duncan, A. (2009a) 'Secretary Arne Duncan Addresses Fourth Annual IES Research Conference', 8 June. Online. Available HTTP: <http://www2.ed.gov/news/speeches/2009/06/06082009.html> (accessed 11 August 2010).

Duncan, A. (2009b) 'Secretary Arne Duncan's Remarks at the 2009 Governors Education Symposium', 14 June. Online. Available HTTP: <http://www2.ed.gov/news/speeches/2009/06/06142009.html> (accessed 11 August 2010).

Duncan, A. (2009c) 'Speech at University of Virginia', 9 October. Online. Available HTTP: <http://www2.ed.gov/news/speeches/2009/10/10092009.html> (accessed 11 August 2010).

Duncan, A. (2009d) 'Teacher Preparation: Reforming the Uncertain Profession. Remarks of Secretary Arne Duncan at Teachers College, Columbia University', 22 October. Online. Available HTTP: <www.ed.gove/news/speeches/2009/10/1022009.html> (accessed 11 August 2010).

Duncan, A. (2009e) 'Elevating the Teaching Profession', *American Educator*, 33, 4: 3–5.

Duncan, A. (2010a) 'U.S. Secretary of Education Press Conference Call on Education Reform Blueprint'. Online. Available HTTP: <http://www.ed.gov/blog/wpcontent/uploads/2010/03/transcript-20100315.doc> (accessed 11 August 2010).

Duncan, A. (2010b) 'The Quiet Revolution: Secretary Arne Duncan's Remarks at the National Press Club', 27 July. Online. Available HTTP: <www.ed.gov/news/speeches/quiet-revolution-secretary-arne-duncans-remarks-national-press-club> (accessed 11 August 2010).

Foderaro, L. (2010) 'Alternate Path for Teachers Gains Ground', *New York Times*, 18 April. Online. Available HTTP: <http://www.nytimes.com/2010/04/19/education/19regents.html> (accessed 11 August 2010).

Freud, S. (1995/1937) 'Analysis Terminable and Interminable', in J. Strachey (ed.) *Standard Edition*, volume 23, London: Hogarth Press.

Freud, S. (1995/1917) 'Mourning and Melancholia' in J. Strachey (ed.) *Standard Edition*, volume 14, London: Hogarth Press.

Friedman, M. (1980) *Free to Choose: A Personal Statement*, New York: Harcourt, Janovich.

Friedman, M. (2005) 'The Promise of Vouchers', *The Wall Street Journal*, 5 Dec: A20.

Friedman, T. (2006) *The World Is Flat: A Brief History of the Twenty-first Century*, New York: Farrar, Straus & Giroux.

Harvey, D. (2005) *A Brief History of Neoliberalism*, Oxford: Oxford University Press.

Herbert, B. (2010) 'A Serious Proposal', *The New York Times*, 12 January: A19.

Hernandez, J. (2009) 'Study Cites Dire Economic Impact of Poor Schools', *The New York Times*, 22 April. Online. Available HTTP: <http://www.nytimes.com/2009/04/23/nyregion/23klein.html> (accessed 11 August 2010).

Jaanus, M. (1996) 'Kundera and Lacan: Drive, Desire, and Oneiric Narration', in W. Apollon and R. Feldstein (eds) *Lacan, Politics, Aesthetics*, New York: SUNY Press.

June, A. (2010) 'Some Papers Are Uploaded to Bangalore to Be Graded', *The Chronicle of Higher Education*, LVI, 30: A1 and A10.

Levine, A. (2006). *Educating School Teachers: Executive Summary*, Washington, DC: Education Schools Project. Online. Available HTTP: <http://www.edschools.org/pdf/Educating_Teachers_Exec_Summ.pdf> (accessed 11 August 2010).

Lipman, P. (2005) 'Educational Ethnography and the Politics of Globalization, War and Resistance', paper presented at the 26th Annual Ethnography in Education Research Forum, Center for Urban Ethnography, Graduate School of Education, University of Pennsylvania, 25 February.

Obama, M. (2009) 'Michelle Obama: Teachers are Key to a Successful Economy. U.S. News and World Report'. Online. Available HTTP: <http://politics.usnews.com/opinion/articles/2009/10/15/michelle-obama-teachers-are-key-to-a-successful-economy.html> (accessed 11 August 2010).

Oliver, K. (2004) *The Colonization of Psychic Space: A Psychoanalytic Social Theory of Oppression*, Minneapolis, MN: University of Minnesota Press.

Ong, A. and Collier, S. (eds) (2005) *Global Assemblages: Technology, Politics and Ethics as Anthropological Problems*, Malden, MA: Blackwell.

Power, M. (1994) *The Audit Explosion*, London: Demos Press.

Power, M. (1997) *The Audit Society: Rituals of Verification*, New York: Oxford University Press.

Power, M. (2003) 'Evaluating the Audit Explosion', *Law and Policy*, 25, 3: 185–202.

Ravitch, D. (2007) 'Challenges to Teacher Education', address to AACTE, 25 February.

Ravitch, D. (2010) *The Death and Life of the Great American School System: How Testing and Choice are Undermining Education*, New York: Basic Books.

Reed, W. (2010) Personal communication.

Richter, G. (1995) *The Daily Practice of Painting: Writings, 1962–1993* trans. David Britt, Cambridge, MA: MIT Press.

Ripley, A. (2010) 'That Makes a Great Teacher?', *The Atlantic*, 305, 1: 58–66.

Ritchie, J. (1977) 'The Magic Feather: Education and the Power of Positive Thinking', *Teachers College Record*, 78, 4: 477–486.

Rothstein, R. (1998) *The Way We Were? The Myths and Realities of America's Student Achievement*, New York: Century Foundation Press.

Rothstein, R. (2004) *Class and Schools: Using Social, Economic, and Educational Reform to Close the Black–White Achievement Gap*, New York: Teachers College Press.

Salvio, P. (2007) *Anne Sexton: Teacher of Weird Abundance*, Albany, NY: SUNY Press.

Santner, E. (2006) *On Creaturely Life: Rilke, Benjamin, Sebald*, Chicago, IL: University of Chicago Press.

Schulman, L. (2005) 'Forum Questions: Teacher Effectiveness', *Stanford Educator: Stanford University School of Education Newsletter*, 7. Online. Available HTTP: <http://www.digitaldivide.net/news/view.php?HeadlineID=956> (accessed 11 August 2010).

Spellings, M. (2007) 'Secretary Spellings Delivers Remarks at Boston Higher Education Summit'. Online. Available HTTP:<http://www.ed.gov/news/pressreleases/2007/05/05222007.html> (accessed 11 August 2010).

Strathern, M. (ed.) (2000) *Audit Cultures: Anthropological Studies in Accountability, Ethics and the Academy*, London: Routledge.

Tapper, J. (2010) 'Duncan: Katrina Was The "Best Thing" for New Orleans School System, Political Punch, ABC news blog. Online. Available HTTP: <http://blogs.abcnews.com/politicalpunch/2010/01/duncan-katrina-was-the-best-thing-for-new-orleans-schools.html> (accessed 11 August 2010).

Taubman, P. (2009). *Teaching by Numbers: Deconstructing the Discourse of Standards and Accountability in Education*, New York: Routledge.

Thomas, E. and Wingert, P. (2010) 'The Key to Saving American Education', *Newsweek*, 15 March: 24–27.

Toch, T., Bennefield, R., Hawkins, D. and Loeb, D. (1996) 'Why Teachers Don't Teach', *U.S. News and World Report*, Online. Available HTTP: <http://www.usnews.com/usnews/culture/articles/960226/archive_034011_3.htm> (accessed 11 August 2010).

Wolf, G. (2010) 'The Data-Driven Life', *New York Times Magazine*, 2 May.

Zemsky, R. (2009) 'Will Higher Education Ever Change as It Should?', *The Chronicle of Higher Education*, 3 August. Online. Available HTTP: <chronicle.com/article/Will-Higher-Education-Ever/47536/> (accessed 19 January 2010).

Zizek, S. (2000) 'Melancholy and the Act', *Critical Inquiry*, 26. 4: 657–681.

Part IV

Curriculum Responses to Politics and Vulnerabilities

12   Images of the 'Other' in school Textbooks and Islamic Reading Material in Pakistan

Tariq Rahman

Introduction

The function of the curriculum, as Michael W. Apple famously puts it, is to 'explicate the manifest and latent or coded reflections of modes of material production, ideological values, class relations, and structures of social power – racial and sexual as well as politico-economic – on the state of consciousness of people in a precise historical or socio-economic situation' (Apple 1979: 1–2). The most obvious way of affecting the consciousness of people is through textbooks. Though only one of the several ways of exercising control over the mind they are easy to use since they are disseminated through the education system and affect people at impressionable ages.

But textbooks are only one of many influences on a person's world view. How significant the influence may be depends on many variables – teachers, peer group pressure, family and friends, childhood experiences, exposure to discourses other than textbooks – and cannot be easily determined. What can be determined, however, is the intention of the writers of textbooks; the policy guidelines of those who get the textbooks written; and the values which the educational authorities responsible for writing and disseminating textbooks in educational systems support.

In general these values belong to the 'in-group', i.e. they are values and perceptions which support one's own group: nation, ethnic group, religious group, ideological group, etc. This necessitates the creation of an 'out-group' or 'Other' which must be held in opposition to the self. The 'Other' is generally created on the basis of selective data and in this process of creation it is transformed. It may either be romanticized or demonized. Edward Said in his book *Orientalism* (1978) tells us how the European scholars of the Orient created an image of the 'Other' which made it the 'Other' of the Occident. Said further postulates that this justified the conquest of the Orient in order to 'civilize' it.

This chapter intends to look at the way the 'Other' is represented in Pakistani textbooks and religious printed material which is in circulation both in the religious seminaries and outside them. The specific focus is on social studies and history textbooks – the subject of Pakistan studies has both history and social studies – used from class 8 to 10 in government schools. In addition to that the printed literature of the Islamic militants is described for the first time by this writer.

Review of Literature

The Pakistani ruling elite used Islam and Urdu to resist the challenge posed by fissiparous ethnicity – Bengali, Sindhi, Pashtun, Baluchi, Siraiki (see Rahman 1996) – and textbooks were changed from the very beginning for that purpose.

Moreover, a conspiracy theory of Pakistan's history, explaining the birth of Pakistan in terms of British–Hindu conspiracy against the Muslims, was created. Under General Ziaul Haq's Islamization campaign (1977–88), the Islamic indoctrination became even more pronounced. Pervez Hoodbhoy and A.H. Nayyar, both academics and social activists, made the point that the concept of the 'ideology of Pakistan', was incorporated in many texts. The 'Other', which has always been India, was now also the Pakistani – or foreigner – who denied this ideology. Summing up the changes in the textbooks, Hoodbhoy and Nayyar said:

> In Pakistan, because of the adoption of an exclusionist national ideology, there are no constraints on the free expression of communal hatred. Thus, the Hindu is portrayed as monolithically cunning and treacherous, obsessively seeking to settle old scores with his erstwhile masters. This Hindu is responsible for the breakup of Pakistan.
>
> (Hoodbhoy and Nayyar 1985: 175)

A number of other researchers have carried out even more detailed and in-depth studies of the images of the Indian non-Muslims (Hindus) in Pakistani textbooks. K.K. Aziz, the famous Pakistani historian, studied 66 textbooks on social studies, Pakistan studies and history in use from class I to BA level. Among other things, he points out that these textbooks glorify war and create hatred for India (Aziz 1993: 192–193). Rubina Saigol (1995), a sociologist, has analyzed all the myths which help the state to maintain a high level of militarization and aggressive nationalism. In this case too the 'Other' is India. This is not to say that in India such an exercise in brain-washing has not been carried out. It certainly has been, as Krishna Kumar explains in his insightful book *Prejudice and Pride* (2001). Kumar examines the contrary historical narratives of India as well as Pakistan and concludes that 'there is little reason to expect that the state policy in either India or Pakistan will remedy this situation in the foreseeable future' (Kumar 2001: 244).

As for religious material in print, this is of two types: the traditional Urdu writings refuting the beliefs of rival sects, Western philosophies and heresies which are called '*munazara* literature' (Rahman 2008) and the '*Jihadi*' or militant literature which presents the views associated with radical Islamists, especially the Al-Qaeda (PIPS 2010). Both types of works are described, in this case for the first time by this author as far as Pakistan is concerned, in the last section.

Objectives

This paper attempts to analyze:

1   The textbooks introduced in government schools after 2002 and in use at present.
2   Textbooks and supplementary reading material available both to the public and the religious seminaries (*madrassas*) – with reference to the following questions:
      a   Do they refer to the non-Muslims or do they ignore them even in contexts where their contribution should have been acknowledged or their rule recognized?
      b   If they do refer to the non-Muslims, do they do it in a positive, neutral or negative manner?
      c   How do they refer to ideologies, philosophies, values, points of view etc owing their origin to, or coming from, the 'Other' – specifically from India and the West?
3   The literature of the Islamic militants with a view to finding out how much of it is produced and what are its major themes.

Methodology

Textbooks of Urdu-medium government schools from class 8 to 10 were studied item by item with reference to the above three objectives. Textbooks used from 1999 to 2002, which were studied in the same way earlier, are given in the appendix, in order to determine what changes have occurred since that date in Pakistani textbooks (for that study see Rahman 2002a). Supplementary reading material available to madrassa students was also studied with the same objectives in mind. For an earlier study, *Language, Ideology and Power* (Rahman 2002), the present researcher gave a questionnaire to 1,500 students in order to determine, among other things, their attitude towards Christians, Hindus and Ahmedis (declared a non-Muslim religious community since 1974 in Pakistan). The responses to these questions are also brought together here.

The literature of the Islamic militants was also examined in passing in order to determine what images of the 'Other' – in this case Western people as well as the ruling elite in Muslim countries – it contains.

Educational Background of Pakistan

Before analyzing the textbooks of Pakistani schools, let us give a brief synopsis of the essential facts of the educational scenario in Pakistan. Briefly, in 2007–08 – the latest figures available are for this date – the overall literacy rate (age 10 and above) was 56 per cent (69 per cent for males and 44 per cent for females). School attendance for the same period and age group was 58 per cent (71 per cent for males and 46 per cent for females) (GOP 2009: 158). The country has three major types of educational institutions: the government vernacular-medium

Table 12.1   Numbers of schools in Pakistan

Level	Number	Students	Teachers
Primary	158,023	117,366,169	437,106
Middle	41,326	5,400,435	320,609
Secondary	13,108	1,795,444	66,522

Source: GOP (2009: 158).

schools (i.e. Urdu- and Sindhi-medium); English-medium schools (private elitist; state-influenced public schools and cadet colleges; and non-elitist private English-medium schools); religious seminaries (madrassas of the two major sects of Islam Sunni and Shia and within the Sunnis of sub-sects such as Deobandis, Barelvis, All-i-Hadith and the Jamat-i-Islami).

The number of government vernacular-medium schools in the country is given in Table 12.1. The exact number of English-medium schools is not known but a census of private schools in 2006 gave the figure of 227,791 for the total number of educational institutions. Out of these 64.6 per cent used Urdu, 10.4 per cent English, 15.5 per cent Sindhi and 9.5 per cent other languages such as Pashto, Balochi and Arabic as media of instruction (GOP 2006: 37). English-medium schools are of varying quality and are spread all over the cities and towns of the whole country (Census Private 2001: 12; Rahman 2002: 303–307; 2004).

There are over 12,000 madrassas with between 1.5 to 1.7 million students (GOP 2006: 24). Most of them are Sunni – the major sect of Islam in Pakistan – but some are of the Shia sect too.

As textbooks are not the only formative influences on students, let us also add the effects of four more variables: peer group, teachers, family and exposure to extra-curricular discourses. Interaction with students shows them to be as given in Table 12.2.

The Objective of Textbook Board Books

The Government of Pakistan lays down certain objectives for the teaching of various subjects. These are often ideological. They use Islam as a marker of identity to define the boundaries of the self. The 'Other' is, by definition, non-Muslim. However, this notion of Islam is so tempered with nationalism as to exclude Indian Hindus rather than non-Muslims who are friendly with Pakistan. Here is an abstract from the objectives laid down in different instructional books from the Ministry of Education:

- To inculcate the unflinching love for Islam and Pakistan, strong sense of national cohesion, and state integrity.
- To promote understanding of socio-economic and socio-cultural aspects of Pakistani society, the Ideology of Pakistan and struggle for freedom.

(GOP 2002a)

Table 12.2   Influences other than textbooks on students

	Peer group	Teachers	Family	Extra-curricular discourses
Urdu-medium schools	Anti-India, anti-Hindu, anti-Israel, anti-Semitic, anti-America. Impressed by the West.	Anti-India, anti-Hindu, anti-Israel, anti-Semitic. Likely to be impressed by the West but also against it.	Likely to be the same as (2)	Pakistan TV/ Radio, Urdu newspapers, Islamic literature.
Sindhi-medium Schools	Ambivalent towards Hindus. Anti-Israel, anti-America. Ambivalent towards the West but impressed too.	Same as (1). Likely to be Sindhi nationalists and anti-Punjabi too.	Same as (2)	Pakistan TV/ radio, Sindhi newspapers/ magazines.
English-medium elitist	Contemptuous and dismissive of Pakistan's indigenous culture. Pro-West. Ambivalent towards the West.	Mostly anti-India. Ambivalent towards the West. Anti-Israel	Same as (2)	Cable TV, English films, English music, English newspapers/ magazines/ comic books/ cartoons.
English-medium (Cadet colleges)	Anti-India, anti-Hindu, anti-Israel. Ambivalent towards the West	Same as (1)	Same as (2)	Cable TV at home but not in boarding school. English newspapers/ Urdu magazines.
English-medium (non-elitist)	Anti-India, anti-Hindu, anti-Israel, anti-Semitic.	Same as (1)	Same as (2)	PTV, Urdu newspapers/ magazines.
Madrassas	Anti-Hindu, anti-India, anti-Israel, anti-Semitic, anti-West	Same as (1)	Pre-modern. Folk religion and superstition.	Religious books/sermons. Talks by religious figures. Munazara literature and militant literature.

Source: Conversation, interaction, observation and loosely structured interviews.

- History of Pakistan
- To evaluate the Islamization effort by various Governments in perspective of an Islamic ideological state.
- To inculcate among students the qualities of *Khudi*, self-reliance, tolerance, research, sacrifice, *Jihad*, martyrdom, modesty and the behaviour patterns of national character.

(GOP 2002b)

These objectives appear to counteract the ostensibly secularization trend of General Musharraf's government. Indeed, they are quite similar to the objective of the Islamization trend of the Zia regime. In short, the use of Islam to define the self and to mark out the 'Other' has not changed. Because of this Pakistani students exposed to the textbook Board books tend to be intolerant of Hindus, Christians and non-Muslim minorities. The opinions of students about these communities prove this – see Table 12.3.

As the survey reveals, the students who tend to be least tolerant of the 'Other' – in this case Hindus, Christians and Ahmedis – are the madrassa students. Those who are most tolerant are from Sindhi-medium institutions and from the elitist English-medium ones. In the latter two cases there are alternative discourses which influence the students' opinions. In the case of the Sindhi-medium students, although they do study Textbook Board books, there is the alternative discourse offered by the Sindhi nationalist press. This opposes most of the opinions, including the anti-India bias, which the central government cultivates. Moreover, the Sindhis still cherish the poetry and values of the Islamic mystics who advocated harmony between creeds. Even more important, perhaps, is the fact that Sindh is the only place in Pakistan with pockets of Hindus. These factors make Sindhi students more tolerant of the religious 'Other' than either Punjabis, Pathans or Mohajirs.

Table 12.3   Tolerance of the 'Other'

1. What should Pakistan's priorities be? Give equal rights to Ahmedis in Pakistan?

				English-medium		
	Madrassas ($n = 131$)	Sindhi-medium ($n = 132$)	Urdu-medium ($n = 520$)	Elitist ($n = 97$)	Cadet colleges ($n = 86$)	Non-elitist ($n = 119$)
Agree	06.87	58.33	44.04	53.61	33.72	47.90
Disagree	81.68	18.18	33.85	22.68	39.54	28.57
Don't care	11.45	23.48	22.12	23.71	26.74	23.53
2. Give equal rights to Hindus and Christians in Pakistan?						
Agree	11.45	65.15	56.73	57.73	41.86	51.26
Disagree	71.76	18.18	23.65	20.62	36.05	27.73
Don't care	16.79	16.67	19.62	21.65	22.09	21.01

Source: Survey of 1,500 students carried out through a questionnaire in 1999–2000. For details see Rahman (2002: Appendix 14.7).

As for the students of the English-medium schools, they are also exposed to discourses originating in, or influenced by, the West. They also do not study Textbook Board books. Thus they too are tolerant of the religious 'Other'.

Analysis of the Punjab Textbook Board School Textbooks

In a previous study of all language and literature Textbook Board books from class 1 to class 10 the present author counted ideology-carrying items. They were divided under three main headings: Pakistani nationalism, Islam and the military. Under the first heading were all items – prose lessons, poems, exercises etc – about the Pakistan movement, nationalist heroes, messages on national integration, Pakistani identity, ideology of Pakistan etc. Under the second were items relating to religious personages, beliefs and movements. Under the last were articles about war, Pakistan's wars with India, war heroes, glorification of the military etc. The percentage of the number of ideological items in the textbooks is given for each province in Appendices B, C, D and E. Table 12.4 gives the consolidated data for the textbooks of different languages.

As Arabic, Pashto and Persian are optional languages and Sindhi is studied only in Sindh, Urdu emerges as the main ideology-carrying language. It influences all, except madrassa students as even English-medium school students have to study this language.

The books in use until 2002 have been analysed by the present author and a sample of the kind of assertions they make are given in the appendix. The two textbooks being used nowadays are being described for the first time.

These are *Mu'ashrati Ulum* (social studies) for class 8 (Punjab Textbook Board 2002a) and *Muta l'a Pakistan* (Pakistan studies) for classes 9 and 10 (Punjab Textbook Board 2002b). Both books were approved by the Curriculum Wing of the Federal Ministry of Education. The second was approved in 2002 according to a government letter (Letter No. F-11-2/2002-SS) while the first carries no date but was also approved during the Musharraf regime.

Let us now consider the social studies book for class 8. This has thirteen lessons out of which four – over a quarter – are on the movement for the creation of

Table 12.4   Language-wise ideological contents of language textbooks expressed as percentages of total items

Language	Content (percentage)
Arabic	66
Urdu	40
Pashto	43
Persian	32
Sindhi	29
English	8

Source: Physical counting of all items in the textbooks of all provinces in 1998. For details see Rahman (2002: 519–22).

Pakistan during the first half of the twentieth century. While the tone of all these historical writings is far less anti-Hindu and anti-British than the earlier textbooks, there are anti-India and anti-British remarks in it.

The second book is on Pakistan studies which has always been used as a propagandist reinforcing the narrative of the Pakistani ruling establishment. Although this is true of about half of the lessons in this book, there is less actual verbal abuse of India and the Hindus though there are biased remarks against both.

In short, while the textbooks presently in use in most of the government Urdu-medium schools in Pakistan remain biased and polemical, they are less crudely so than the texts used before the events of 9/11 and the attack on the Indian parliament in December 2001 after which the previous aggressive policies were ostensibly reversed by General Musharraf as mentioned above.

Analysis of Extra-Curricular Reading Material in the Madrassas and Society

While the school textbooks described above probably contributed to the shift in public discourse towards the religious right from the 1980s onwards, the informal printed material to be described in this section created space for fundamentalist and even militant interpretations of Islam. Since the war between militant groups – loosely called the Tehrik-e-Taliban Pakistan and the Punjabi Taliban – and the Pakistani state is going on in Pakistan, it is necessary that attention is paid to the kind of literature which is available as alternative or supplementary reading material to the public both within the madrassa system and outside it.

All madrassas teach some modified form of the Dars-i-Nizami which is an eighteenth-century curriculum in Arabic put together by Mulla Qutb al-Din Sihalvi (Robinson 2002: 43–55; Sufi 1941: 68–75). These Arabic books do not emphasize *jihad* nor do they refute the Sunni sub-sects which appeared during the nineteenth century in India (Rahman 2004: 80–83). However, they also teach their students the beliefs of their sub-sect or *maslak* as it is called. In doing so the emphasis is to refute the beliefs of other sects, sub-sects and contemporary philosophies considered heretical by the *ulema* (Islamic scholars). These texts for refutation of heterodox, unacceptable or heretical doctrines may be called *Radd*-texts (the word *Radd* means refutation in Urdu) or *munazara* (disputation) texts since they incorporate many of the features of oral debates. These texts are in Urdu rather than Arabic or Persian. This means that they are internalized by the students rather than only memorized as the Arabic and Persian texts are. While such texts are part of all religious teaching all over the world, they have acquired a new role in Pakistan because religious forces feel they have an agenda, and ability, to govern and reform society. Thus the refutation taught in these books has the potential to become an agenda for revolution in the name of good governance and Islam.

This kind of literature has been studied in more detail by the present author elsewhere but only a brief summary will be given here (for details see Rahman 2008: 197–220). They may be sub-divided into two categories: those which refute the West and those which refute other sects and sub-sects.

Most books focus on philosophy and economics, and refute Western ideas of individualism, freedom and secularism. This entails either a complete rejection of women's rights, individual freedom, intellectual freedom and even democracy or a position of dissatisfaction with the way they are practised in the West. Other books refute the economic systems associated with the West (for examples see Nadvi n.d.; Usmani 1997).

Pakistan is predominantly Sunni and the few Shia madrassas keep a low profile though there are militant Shia organizations which fight Sunni militants. Sunni books refuting Shia doctrines are galore. Among them the *Hidayat ul Shi'a* by Maulana Mohammad Qasim Nanautvi (1833–77), the pioneer of the Darul Uloom at Deoband (Metcalf 1982), is the most well known. The level of scholarship is higher than other books on such subjects.

Other books refute the doctrines of Sunni sub-sects. These are Deobandis, Barelvis and Ahl-i-Hadith. The Barelvis, followers of Ahmed Raza Khan of Bareilly (1856–1921) (Sanyal 1996) practise what may be called folk Islam (low church) in which rituals, worship of the graves of saints and reverence for the Prophet of Islam has a central significance. The Deobandis, on the other hand, are strict in their interpretation of monotheism so that the intercession of saints is disallowed, while the Ahl-e-Hadith, influences by Abdul Wahab of Saudi Arabia (1703–92) are even stricter than the Deobandis in their condemnation of the saint-ridden, folk Islam of the common people (Ahmed 1994).

Apart from these, the *ulema* refute what they call heresies. In the context of Pakistan these are the doctrines of the Ahmedis (Qadianis or Mirzais), as they are called (Friedmann 1989). They are considered non-Muslims because they do not believe in the finality of Prophet Muhammad. Certain other doctrines, such as that of Ghulam Ahmed Pervaiz, are also refuted. Indeed, most schools of thought refute each other so that even the doctrines of Syed Abul Ala Mawdudi (1903–79), who created the revivalist Islamic party the Jamat-i-Islami, have been refuted (as *Fitna-e-Maudoodiat* i.e. the heresy of Maudoodi) (Zikria 1975; Lahori 1997).

Militant Literature

Apart from the literature mentioned above, which has been in circulation for over a hundred years as the *Administration Reports* of the British era testify, a lot of new literature advocating armed conflict with the government is in circulation. This was analyzed by Zafarullah Khan, a Pakistani social activist, and published by the Pakistan Institute of Peace Studies (PIPS 2010). He collected hundreds of samples of newspapers, pamphlets and magazines from outside mosques, bus stands and train stations. As a rough estimate there are 51 militant newspapers (including all periodicals) with a circulation of 813,000 (PIPS 2010: 107–108).

Briefly, South Asian folk Islam emphasized the reverence of saints (*Sufis*) which manifested itself in seeking their intercession, visits to shrines and emphasis upon cleaning oneself spiritually – something the Barelvis uphold in doctrine even now. During the colonial era, Muslim modernist reformists challenged folk Islam and gave a rationalistic and reformed version of Islam which appealed to Western-educated people. Riffat Hassan, one of the modernist Muslims, calls their interpretation 'forward-looking, life-affirming' philosophy in consonance with enlightenment ideas and progress (Hassan 2009: 184). However, the fundamentalists and the militants reject both the saint-ridden folk Islam as well as the modernists.

They either draw upon the hardline philosophies of Deobandi, Ahl-i-Hadith and Saudi Wahabi Islam or the even more radical interpretations of the fundamentalists and the radicals. The Pakistani Islamist thinker, Syed Abul Ala Mawdudi (1903–79), is one of those who contributed to revivalist Islam by trying to bring Islam into both national and international politics. This implied struggle against the Westernized rulers of the Muslim world for the establishment of an Islamic state and the struggle against unbelief globally despite tactical alliances with the United States against the greater evil of Soviet atheism (Armstrong 2000: 236–239; Nasr 1996). Among the most influential thinkers who shared some of these beliefs were Syed Qutab of Egypt (1906–66) (Haddad 1983). The genealogical line does not run straight on from the Muslim Brotherhood to the Al-Qaeda vision of global war against Western people who are labelled 'crusaders' and Muslim leaders who are seen as their collaborators. However, the radical Islamists of today give *jihad* the kind of centrality given to it by the fundamentalists mentioned above. The theoreticians of the militant Islamists draw upon the work of the jurist Taqi al-Din ibn Taymiyya (1263–1328), who, they claim justified the killing of Muslims if they sheltered or supported infidels. That this is probably a misunderstanding of Ibn-e-Taymiyya may be the view of scholars (Hassan 2010: 359), but militant literature does justify armed struggle against Muslim leaders who collaborate with the West. In this struggle even suicide bombing – otherwise not allowed in any sect of Islam – is considered justified mostly with reference to the Palestinian struggle against Israel (Cook and Allison 2008: 32–33). The phenomenon has caused havoc in Pakistan where the Pakistani Taliban, who espouse some of the ideals of Al-Qaeda, are fighting a war for survival and the ascendance of their ideology. It has also spread to 32 countries (counting interceptions) through the Al-Qaeda (Burke 2003) which has used the media competently in order to further its global aims (Schweitzer 2006: 141–142).

The story of the strengthening of the religious extremists (all dubbed Taliban) has been narrated, among others, by Ahmed Rashid (2008), Imtiaz Gul (2009) and Amir Mir (2009). Militant literature first appeared during the 1980s in order to mobilize public opinion in favour of the war against the Soviet Union. By 1989 the number of such publications was over a hundred and the number is still growing despite the ban against some organizations. As these groups were used by the army and the Inter Services Intelligence (ISI) to fight in Kashmir against India, publications like *Jihad-e-Kashmir* was circulated in 46 countries before 9/11 and its publication only in Rawalpindi was 52,000 copies (PIPS 2010: 47).

A number of militant organizations – Jaish-e-Mohammad, the Jamat ud Dawa, the Harkatul Mujahideen, the Jamat ul Furqan – keep publishing periodicals (under new names if banned). The Jamat-e-Islami has 22 publications (PIPS 2010: 71–72) and sectarian groups also publish vitriolic material against each other. These are different from the *munazara* literature which is much older in that it is not given to advancing arguments in the traditional manner of a debate.

Rather, there is more condemnation and call for action against the 'Other'. The literature includes leaflets, pamphlets and letters meant for circulation at night (*shab namas*). Madrassas also produce this kind of ephemeral material meant to deal with a given situation such as the attack on the Red Mosque in Islamabad in July 2007. The Deobandis are important because they publish a lot of this kind of literature (PIPS 2010: 69–71).

Conclusion

The images of the 'Other' in Pakistani textbooks portray Hindus, Christians and Western people in negative terms. The state-controlled Textbook Boards focus on creating nationalistic opinion against India so as to create a garrison state mentality among the citizens. Such a mentality makes it easier for the state to spend more funds on the military than might have been possible otherwise. However, because the 'Other' is often defined in both nationalistic and religious terms, such image construction creates grounds for further Islamic radicalization among the youth.

As for the images of the 'Other' in religious literature, the extra-curricular *munazara* literature is not necessarily anti-India. It is, however, anti-West at both the deep, theoretical level as well as the emotive level. They do, however, refute other interpretations of Islam. They are also conducive towards producing religious antagonism towards other sects and sub-sects of Islam. However, the militant Islamist discourses mentioned above are not only against the West (especially America) but also against Israel and the Jews as well as the Hindus and India. They are also against the ruling elites of most Muslim countries which are condemned as being stooges of the West and very corrupt.

While the state can and should change its textbooks, and should also expose students to discussions created in other cultures, the madrassas will lose their appeal only if the state invests massively in welfare and education. This will prevent the very poor from sending their children to the madrassas which provide social security and education to people whom the state neglects. Such changes are both difficult and costly but they are absolutely necessary if Pakistani children are to be taught to co-exist peacefully with the other people of the world.

Appendix

Table 12.5   Images of the 'Other' in English textbooks of the pre-2002 era

Class-6	There are sentences like 'I am a Muslim. I am a Pakistani'. However, no adverse comment against Hindus or Christians appears in the book.
Class-7	No adverse comments on any religious group. Girls are clad in scarves which cover the hair (*dopattas*).
Class-8	No adverse comments. No negative image.
Class-9	A statement: 'Islam was a dominant force in Spain for about eight hundred years' (p. 84), implicitly glorifies Muslim rule over Christian Spain.
Class-10	An essay on Tariq Bin Ziad, the conqueror of Spain, justifies his conquest.
Conclusion:	English textbooks generally do not portray the 'Other' adversely but Islamic rule over the West is justified.

Table 12.6   Images of the 'Other' in Urdu textbooks of the pre-2002 era

Class-6	An Urdu couplet which in English translation reads as follows: 'The Himalaya remembers their (the Muslims') deeds. Gibraltar still carries their stamp on it' (p.24). In an essay on the 1965 Pakistan–India war: 'clever and manipulative enemy' (for India) (p. 68).
Class-7	In praise of the poet Akbar Ilahabadi: 'He was against Western culture in India'. Anti-Hindu remarks: 'In those days the extremist Hindus had launched a movement against Urdu since they considered it the Muslims' language' (p. 137).
Class-8	With reference to the partition in 1947: 'The Hindus and Sikhs killed Muslims whenever they were in a minority. They burnt their houses and forced them to migrate to Pakistan' (p.46). About an Indian pilot: 'In the other world he had to burn; here too he died by fire'.
Class-9	Romanticizing Muslim rule over India: 'The Muslims ruled South Asia for about a thousand years. They treated their Hindu subjects with justice. However, the Hindus would revolt at the least opportunity' (p.11). The conspiratorial Hindus had a large share in harming Tipu Sultan and Siraj Ud Dowlah. When the English consolidated their rule, the Hindus openly sided with them – because both hated the Muslims – Hindus are ready to change for their advantage – they made a plan to enslave the Muslims permanently' (p.12).
Conclusion	Urdu textbooks portray the Hindus, and to a lesser degree the colonial British, very negatively. The Hindus are accused of being cunning, deceptive and scheming and are accused of hating the Muslims. Both the British and the Hindus are supposed to have conspired together to deprive the Muslims of their rights.

Table 12.7   Images of the 'Other' in social studies textbooks of the pre-2002 era

Class-7 (English version)	'The people of Africa requested the Muslims to invade their lands to save them from the tyranny of their Christian rulers who extorted taxes from them' (p.21). This essay refers to the Muslim conquest of foreign lands with pride (p.22).
Class-8	'As a result of Hindu–British collusion, Muslims were subjected to great hardships – they could not be cowed down by the atrocities committed on them by the British and the Hindus' (p.73). 'Both the communities [British and Hindus] conspired against the Muslims to turn them into a poor, helpless and ineffective minority' (p.74). On the crusades: 'They [Christians] wanted to average themselves on Muslims – the Christians took to their traditional tactics of conspiring against the ruler' (p.27). On colonialism: 'European nations have been working during the past three centuries, through conspiracies or naked aggression to subjugate the countries of the Muslims world' (p.43).
	Anti-Hindu remarks: 'The Quaid-i-Azam saw through the machinations of the Hindus' (p.51). 'The ignoble behaviour of the Hindus forced the Muslims to rally to the Muslims League Flag to get their demands conceded – the Hindus had treated the Muslims cruelly and shamefully during their rule' (p.82).
Class-9 and 10	In Bengal Haji Shariat Ullah and Tito Mir started the struggle to free the Muslims from the slavery of the English and the Hindus (p.13).
Conclusion:	Social studies textbooks strongly reinforce the conspiracy theory that the Hindus and the colonial British wanted to suppress the Muslims and keep them in perpetual slavery. They romanticize and glorify Muslim rule over Hindus and Western people.

Table 12.8   Ideological contents of language textbooks expressed as percentages of total number of lessons (Urdu, English and Pashto)

	Urdu	English	Pashto
Class I	20	Nil	22
Class II	36	7	39
Class III	50	20	44
Class IV	50	27	66
Class V	54	Nil	37
Class VI	50	6	46
Class VII	44	17	50
Class VIII	50	26	36
Class IX	33+	16	Not taught
Class X	33+	4	Not taught

Source: NWFP data from 1998–99.

Notes:
English starts from class VI under the old system and in class I under the new one. Not all schools have adopted the new system.
+ Same book for IX and X

Table 12.9   Ideological contents of language textbooks expressed as percentages of total number of lessons (Urdu, English and Arabic)

	Urdu	English	Arabic
Class I	6		Not taught
Class II	18		Not taught
Class III	31		Not taught
Class IV	43		Not taught
Class V	38		Not taught
Class VI	49	7	50#
Class VII	52	11	70
Class VIII	48	8	81
Class IX	33+	32	50
Class X	33+	33	80

Source: Punjab and Islamabad data of 1998–1999.

Notes:
Arabic books are compulsory for all non-elitist government schools in Pakistan in class VI–VIII.
+ Same book for IX and X.

Table 12.10 Ideological contents of language textbooks expressed as percentages of total number of lessons (Urdu, English and Sindhi)

	Urdu	English	Sindhi
Class I	32	Nil	19
Class II	41	Nil	42
Class III	38	Nil	36
Class IV	46	Nil	33
Class V	49	Nil	26
Class VI	49	Nil	34
Class VII	93	Nil	36
Class VIII	53	20	26
Class IX	47+	35	21
Class X	47+	4	21

Source: Sindh data of 1998–99.

Note:
+ Same book for IX and X.

Table 12.11 Ideological contents of language textbooks expressed as percentages of total number of lessons (Urdu, English and Persian)

	Urdu	English	Persian*	
Class I	28		Not taught	
Class II	30		Not taught	
Class III	32		Not taught	
Class IV	47		Not taught	
Class V	47		Not taught	
Class VI	58	3	16	14
Class VII	46	Nil	50	47
Class VIII	48	4	46	35
Class IX	25+	23	28	28+
Class X	25+	14	28	28+

Source: Balochistan data 1998–99.

Notes:
* Figures on the right are for books prescribed in the NWFP. Figures on the left are for Balochistan. The new textbooks of the Punjab Board are the same as those of the NWFP Board.
+ Same book for IX and X.

References

Original Sources

(a) Textbook Board books

Punjab Textbook Board (2002) *English: Class-6*, Lahore: Punjab Textbook Board. [82,000 copies]

Punjab Textbook Board (2002) *English: Class-7*, Lahore: Punjab Textbook Board. [180,000 copies]

Punjab Textbook Board (2002) *English: Class-8*, Lahore: Punjab Textbook Board. [82,000 copies]

Punjab Textbook Board (1996) *English: Class-9*, Lahore: Punjab Textbook Board. [number not indicated]

Punjab Textbook Board (1996) *English: Class-10*, Lahore: Punjab Textbook Board. [number not indicated]

Punjab Textbook Board (2002) *Social Studies for Class-VII*, Lahore: Punjab Textbook Board. [number not indicated]

Punjab Textbook Board (2002) *Social Studies for Class-VIII*, Lahore: Punjab Textbook Board. [number not indicated]

Punjab Textbook Board (2000) *Pakistan Studies 9 and 10*, Lahore: Punjab Textbook Board. [number not indicated]

Punjab Textbook Board (2002) *Urdu Barae Jamat Sisham*, Lahore: Punjab Textbook Board. [number not indicated]

Punjab Textbook Board (2002) *Urdu Barae Jamat Haftam*, Lahore: Punjab Textbook Board. [number not indicated]

Punjab Textbook Board (2002) *Urdu Barae Jamat Hashtam*, Lahore: Punjab Textbook Board. [number not indicated]

Punjab Textbook Board (1987) *Muraqqa-e-Urdu 9th to 10th*, Lahore: Punjab Textbook Board. [number not indicated]

Punjab Textbook Board (2002a) *Mu'ashrati Ulum (Social Studies) for class 8*, Lahore: Punjab Textbook Board.

Punjab Textbook Board (2002b) *Muta I'a Pakistan (Pakistan Studies) for classes 9 and 10*, Lahore: Punjab Textbook Board.

(b) Islamic reading material

Lahori, A.A. (1997) *Haq Parast ulama Ki Maudoodiat Se Narazgi ke Asbab*, Lahore: Anjuman Khuddam-ul-Islam. [Refutes Maudoodi.]

Nadvi, S.A.H.A. (n.d.) *Muslim Mamalik Mein Islamiat our Maghribiat Ki Kash Makash* Karachi: Majlis-e-Nashriat-e-Islam. [Historical and philosophical book about the conflict between Islam and Westernization in the Muslim world.]

Qasim, M. (n.d.) *Hidayat ul Shi'a*, Multan: Taleefat -e-Ashrafiya. [Refutes Shia doctrines.]

Usmani, M.R. (1997) *Europe Ke Teen Mu 'ashi Nizam*, Karachi: Idara-ul-Mu' arif [Refutes capitalism, socialism and feudalism.]

Zikria, M. (1975) *Fitna-e-Maudoodiat*, Lahore: Maktaba ul Qasim. [Refutes the doctrines of Abul Ala Maudoodi.]

Secondary Sources

Ahmed, Q. (1994) *The Wahabi Movement in India*, New Delhi: Manohar.

Apple, M.W. (1979, 2nd edn 1990) *Ideology and Curriculum*, New York: Routledge.

Armstrong, K. (2000) *The Battle for GOD: A History of Fundamentalism*, New York: Random House.

Aziz, K.K. (1993) *The Murder of History in Pakistan*, Lahore: Vanguard Press.

Burke, J. (2003) *Al-Qaeda: Casting of Shadow of Terror*, London: I.B. Tauris.

Census Private (2001) *Census of Private Educational Institutions 1999–2000*, Islamabad: Federal Bureau of Statistics.

Cook, D. and Allison, O. (2007) *Understanding and Addressing Suicide Attacks*, London: Praeger Security International; republished (2008) New Delhi: The Faith and Politics of Martyrdom Operations Pentagon Press.

Friedmann, Y. (1989) *Prophecy Continuous. Aspects of Ahmadi Religious Thought and its Medieval Background*, Berkeley, CA: University of California Press.

GOP (2002a) *National Curriculum: Social Studies for Class VI–VIII*, Islambad: Government of Pakistan, Ministry of Education.

GOP (2002b) *National Curriculum. History of Pakistan for Classes IX–X* Islamabad: Government of Pakistan, Ministry of Education.

GOP (2006) *National Education Census Pakistan 2006*, Islamabad: Government of Pakistan, Ministry of Education, Federal Bureau of Statistics.

GOP (2009) *Economic Survey of Pakistan 2008–09*, Islamabad: Government of Pakistan, Economic Advisory Wing, Finance Division.

Gul, I. (2009) *The Al-Qaeda Connection: The Taliban and Terror in Pakistan's Tribal Areas*, New Delhi: Penguin Viking.

Haddad, Y. (1983) 'Sayyid Qutb: Ideologue of Islamic Revival', in J. Esposito (ed.) *Voices of Resurgent Islam*, Oxford, New York: Oxford University Press.

Hassan, M. (2010) 'Modern Interpretations and Misinterpretations of a Medieval Scholar. Apprehending the political thought of ibn Taymiyya', in Y. Rapoport and S. Ahmed (eds) *Ibn Taymiyya and His Times*, Karachi: Oxford University Press.

Hassan, R. (2009) 'Islamic Modernist and Reformist Discourse in South Asia', in S.T. Hunter (ed.) *Reformist Voices of Islam Mediating Islam and Modernity*, New Delhi: M.E Sharpe; also published New York: Pentagon Press.

Hoodbhoy, P. and Nayyar, A.H. (1985) 'Rewriting the History of Pakistan', in A. Khan (ed.) *Islam, Politics and the State*, London: Zed Press.

Kumar, K. (2001) *Prejudice and Pride. School histories of the freedom struggle in India and Pakistan*, New Delhi: Penguin Books India.

Metcalf, B.D. (1982, reprinted 1989) *Islamic Revival in British India: Deoband, 1860–1900*, Karachi: Royal Book Company.

Mir, A. (2009) *Talibanization of Pakistan from 9/11 to 26/11*, New Delhi: Pentagon Security International.

Nasr, S.V.R. (1996) *Mawdudi and the Making of Islamic Revivalism*, New York: Oxford University Press.

PIPS (2010) *Understanding the Militants' Media. Outreach and Impact*, Islamabad: Pakistan Institute for Peace Studies.

Rahman, T. (1996) *Language and Politics in Pakistan*, Karachi: Oxford University Press.

Rahman, T. (2002) *Language, Ideology and Power: Language-Learning among the Muslims of Pakistan and North India*, Karachi, Oxford University Press.

Rahman, T. (2002a) 'Images of the Other in Pakistan Textbooks', *Pakistan Perspectives*, 7, 2: 33–49.

Rahman, T. (2004) *Denizens of Alien Worlds. A study of education, inequality and polarization in Pakistan,* Karachi: Oxford University Press.

Rahman, T. (2008) 'Munazarah Literature in Urdu. An extra-curricular educational input in Pakistan's religious education', *Islamic Studies,* 47, 2: 197–220.

Rashid, A. (2008) *Descent into Chaos. How the war against Islamic extremism is being lost in Pakistan, Afghanistan and Central Asia,* New York: Allen Lane.

Robinson, F. (2002) *The Ulema of Farangi Mahal and Islamic Culture in South Asia,* Lahore: Ferozesons.

Said, E. (1978) *Orientalism.* London and Henley: Routledge and Kegan Paul.

Saigol, R. (1995) *Knowledge and Identity. Articulation of gender in educational discourse in pakistan,* Lahore: ASR Publications.

Sanyal, U. (1996) *Devotional Islam and Politics in British India. Ahmad Riza Khan Barelwi and his movement, 1870–1920,* Delhi: Oxford University Press.

Schweitzer, Y. (2006) 'Al-Qaeda and the Global Epidemic of Suicide Attacks', in A. Pedahzur (ed.) *Root Causes of Suicide Terrorism. The globalization of martyrdom,* Oxford: Routledge.

Sufi, G.M.D. (1941, republished 1977) *Al-Minhaj. Being the evolution of curriculum in the Muslim educational institutions of India,* Delhi: Idarah-i-Adabiyat-i-Dilhi

13 In Search of Identity

Competing Models in Russia's Civic Education

Anatoli Rapoport

The political nature of curriculum determines the scale, depth and intensity of curricular reforms in the first decades of the twenty-first century. Driven by ideologies, national, regional, or even local, curriculum represents the intersection of socially constructed meanings, emotional aspirations, and power (McLaren 1989). Like every programmatic reflective text, curriculum is highly ambiguous. It should demonstrate a traditionalistic consistency to preserve social cohesiveness; and it should normally pave the way to new societal, political, and ideological goals. Therefore, curricular reform is a euphemism that obscures (or reveals) tectonic shifts in a society where those shifts are a reaction to external or internal challenges.

Since the disintegration of the Soviet Union in 1991, two such challenges, among others, have influenced curricular reform in the Russian Federation. With the re-emergence of an independent Russia, a new state, ideologically and politically, emerged and distanced itself from the former Soviet Union by positioning itself as a new republic adherent to the democratic development. Nation-building and identity construction were among major governmental political concerns. Thus, nation-building rationale dictated the context, conditions, and priorities of education reforms that were launched immediately after 1991, particularly a reform in civic education. However, it is worth noting that the nation-state is no longer the sole repository of citizenship. If we accept a nation's imaginary status (Anderson 1991; Zajda 2009), why would we assume that a nation-state or the national citizenship model is less vulnerable or less susceptible to changes? The term nation-building presents an interesting example of syntactic dichotomy: on the one hand, the nation-building process, as the term implies, aims at building a nation; on the other, due to its ideological nature, nation-building is an endless process whose ultimate goal, a nation, never takes a final shape. That is why history, or rather mythology, from which political leaders usually draw inspiration, is so carefully monitored and constructed to make sure that 'a continuous process of redefinition, revision, reinterpretation, and rewriting of historical narratives' (Zajda 2009: 4) is under control. Russia, which recently has experienced contradictory reforms in civic education, is not an exception here.

The second challenge that the Russian Federation faced was globalization, which deeply influenced the school reform development: it unexpectedly generated new discourses and discovered a never-seen-before multiplicity of truth. Debates about globalization, curriculum, and pedagogy magnified through the metaphorically constructed reality, revealed the centrality of properly negotiated terms and meanings as well as the importance of culture, both political and imaginary-traditional, or the lack thereof in our understanding of citizenship. Globalization has profoundly influenced the very notion of citizenship and citizenship education rationales by not only infusing a more distinct global perspective but also by challenging the core principles of citizenship as an idiosyncratically nation or nation-state related concept. The routine of permanency particularly for the citizens of the 'unbreakable' Soviet Union, turned into the chaos 'of the centrifugal proliferation of interpretation and genres' overnight (Matus and McCarthy 2003). Suddenly, people discovered that the world was no longer monochromic, and even more disturbing was the fact that it had never been monochromic. Therefore, survival in this new era required people to acquire new knowledge, to learn and to practice new skills, and to carefully re-examine their values. The most challenging curricular task in this new environment was to develop the ability to deconstruct previously unquestioned assumptions (Smith 2003) in order to reconstruct and eventually to renegotiate newly contextualized meanings.

During its short post-Soviet history since 1991, Russia witnessed two competing curricular models, namely liberal and traditional, which followed one another, and mirrored two distinct social and economic developmental models during the last decade of the twentieth century and the first decade of the twenty-first century. Both models are Russia's response to the two major challenges that I have mentioned earlier: construction of the new identity and globalization. The choices are highly reflective and demonstrative of the type of citizens that the ruling elite intended to educate. Due to specific features of the contemporary political system and the state of democratic development in the Russian Federation, it seems problematic to argue that curricular reforms, including those in citizenship education, are dictated by the needs of society. Rather, the changes in civic education in the last decade appear to have been determined by ideological intents. This, in a broader perspective, once again, poses a question of the role of schooling and curricula in social and political reforms, particularly at the most decisive moments of a nation's history. Thus, civic education that is particularly susceptible to even miniscule shifts in ideological and political paradigms, found itself at the very intersection of organic needs of society and individual political ambitions.

Very few aspects of civic education have recently drawn so much attention by government officials and practical educators as patriotic education. The state program *Patriotic Education of the Citizens of the Russian Federation for Years 2001–2005* (Gosudarstvennaya programma 2001) adopted by the government in 2001, was soon followed by the development of a new conception of patriotic education in 2003 (Kontseptsiya 2003). A new state program for the years 2006–2010 (Gosudarstvennaya programma 2005) passed by the Russian government in 2005 was aimed at providing a smooth transition from the outdated program to a newer one and adjustments of patriotic education to new conditions in Russia. This alone demonstrates special government attention to patriotic education of Russian citizens. Together with numerous local educational programs in Russia's regions, this campaign presents one of the most intensive patriotic education campaigns in

Russian history. This obviously heightened official attention to patriotic education starkly contrasts with the more liberal model of civic education of the 1990s. Observers noted that the educational reform of the early 1990s to humanize, democratize, and decentralize schools in Russia, drastically changed its direction (Ioffe 2006) and now the new model aims at the promotion and restoration of some of the Soviet features, including 'centralized control, curricular rigidity and political-ideological functions' (Karpov and Lisovskaya 2005: 23). They argue that restoration of military education and focus on patriotic education are vivid signs of stylistic re-Sovietization.

This chapter will demonstrate that the focus on patriotic metaphoric narrative, the infusion of patriotic discourse in civic curriculum and the revitalization of the Soviet-style military rationale are attempts to expeditiously solve the problem of new civic identity and, at the same time, are a traditionalistic counter-reaction to radical political processes on Russia's borders ('colored revolutions' in Georgia, Ukraine, and Kyrgyzstan). Historical prerequisites of patriotic education in Russia and recent tendencies in political discourses as they are articulated through official texts will be analyzed. The chapter concludes that patriotic, military, and to some extent nationalistic components have become dominant in contemporary civic curriculum in Russia. It also argues that patriotism that is conceptualized through a traditionalist framework does not leave much room for critical thinking and decision-making techniques that are central to democratic citizenship education.

Patriotism and Patriotic Education in the Soviet Union: Brief Overview

'Patriotism plays the role of the most reactionary ideology, whose function is to justify imperialist bestiality and to deaden the class consciousness of the proletariat, by setting impassable boundaries to its struggle for liberation' stated the *Soviet Encyclopedia of State and Law* in 1925 (Barghoorn 1956: 12). The Bolshevik attitude to patriotism was conditioned by the Marxist dictum that the proletariat does not have a homeland. This vulgar cosmopolitanism was based on the idea that the proletariat is exploited everywhere and, therefore, cannot be attached to any state or locality. 'Whoever in this war [World War I] accepts defense of the fatherland becomes an accomplice of his "own" national bourgeoisie' wrote Lenin in winter of 1917 (Lenin 1917/1964: 254). However, following the same logic, after the Bolsheviks seized power, patriotism gradually became introduced into the paradigm of new values in the form of Soviet or socialist patriotism.

The new concept of Soviet patriotism became particularly popular among ideologues in the late 1920s and early 1930s when the Soviet officials realized the futility of attempting to ignite the world proletarian revolution. The Stalin government and local authorities skillfully used the mobilizing effect of patriotic campaigns to successfully conduct domestic and international policies: manipulations with Soviet patriotism assisted in recruiting thousands of volunteers for gigantic industrialization projects. At the same time, it allowed condemnation of political opponents during the staged government-orchestrated political trials. It is symptomatic that the official educational journal *Sovetskaya Pedagogika* (*Soviet*

Education Science) published a number of articles about patriotic education in its first issues in 1937 (Shchyogolev 2007).

Changes in the centralized national school curriculum also reflected the emergence of patriotism as one of the central ideological concepts. Historians agree that Soviet patriotism was a proxy of Russian nationalism (Laqueur 1998). Many political figures and heroes from Russian history, who had previously been erased, were rehabilitated; Russian History became a mandatory course in all schools of the multiethnic Soviet Union, and Arabic or Latin alphabets that were traditionally used by many non-Slavic languages were substituted by Cyrillic. At the same time, most innovations that had been characteristic of the new Soviet school in the 1920s (Counts 1957; Dewey 1929; Nearing 1926) were terminated. Curricular reforms in the early 1930s were conducted along with the adoption of an updated and renewed version of the State Patriotism policy (Rapoport 2009; Yekelchyk 2002) that originated in the first half of the nineteenth century in Imperial Russia. In 1833, Count Sergei Uvarov, the new Minister of Education in Nicolas I's government, coined the tripartite formula of *autocracy, orthodoxy, nationality* which became an ideological doctrine that dominated the reign of Nicolas I and later Alexander III and Nicolas II (Riasanovsky 1967). This formula provided a rationale for the Russian Idea which is seen by some as purely a Russian messianic imperative that holds a range of discourses and narratives, in which Russian collective identity has been contested, constructed, and reproduced for centuries (Bouveng 2008). Ironically, only 27 years after condemning patriotism as 'reactionary ideology that … justifies imperialist bestiality' (Barghoorn 1956: 12), Soviet patriotism was defined as 'the marvelous fusion of the progressive national traditions of the peoples with the common vital interests of all the toilers of the USSR' (Matyushkin quoted in Barghoorn 1956: 9). This definition of 1952 best reveals the true nature and origin of Soviet patriotism. The party leaders created and used Soviet patriotism for the purpose of ideological, political, and social changes to maintain the status quo by conducting various well-planned propagandistic campaigns under the motto of patriotism that solely served their short- or long-term needs.

Despite the hardly-masked Slavophile and Russia-centered focus of patriotic education, a specific feature of Soviet patriotism and patriotic education in the Soviet Union was the concentration on the military component in patriotic discourses rather than nationalistic. The nation-building as well as social identity construction rationales appeared secondary to the military rationale that dominated patriotic discourses and took a lion's share of civic curriculum. The reason was in the fact that unlike patriotic sentiments elsewhere, Soviet patriotism discourses were more ideologically determined rather than nationally or ethnically (Vaillant 2005). Questionable nationality policies and the status of a nation with an unpredicted history left very little room for the Soviet-era mythology to support patriotic sentiments. Therefore, suitable major historic events, such as the participation and the victory of the Soviet Union in World War II, which is officially called in Russia the Great Patriotic War, or the flight of the first cosmonaut Yuri Gagarin, were usually used in the Soviet Union as a framework for civic and patriotic education. Another challenge of Soviet patriotism was its limited time functionality: due to its heavily political and ideological content, Soviet patriotism meant unquestionable love of the Soviet Union that was founded in December 1922. As for its predecessor, the Russian Empire, Soviet citizens were supposed to be more selective in the display of their patriotic sentiments.

Theoretically and practically, patriotic education was always perceived in the Soviet Union as military–patriotic education. Very often these two terms were used interchangeably. This fusion was achieved through an uncritical analysis of military operations conducted by the Soviet Union in the courses of History or Literature, compulsory military training in high school, and numerous extra-curricular activities that included national military games, meetings with war veterans and acting military, festivals of military songs, etc. (Bodrova 2008; Shchyogolev 2007; Sredin 1988; Zajda 2007). Hence, the Soviet Union's patriotic education paradigm was primarily concentrated on instilling political phraseology and on militarizing citizen consciousness. Thus, the 'love of one's Socialist Motherland' was translated in practical educational discourses into curricular and extra-curricular activities whose objectives were: (a) to construct and develop Soviet civic identity, (b) to teach unequivocal commitment to the Communist Party and ruling regime, and (c) to mobilize and train warriors who will unquestionably follow military orders.

Civic and Patriotic Education in Contemporary Russia: Two Models

The disintegration of the Soviet Union in 1991 and the demise of the one-party and one-state-ideology system marked a new stage in Russia's history and led to new radical changes in education. In these circumstances, civic education came to the forefront of reforms. New tasks to educate free democratically-minded citizens of a new democratic society resulted in significant changes in civic curriculum (Eklof and Dneprov 1993; Froumin 2004; 2005). It should be noted that Russian educational tradition maintains that the process of education consists of two separate but interdependent components: academic education (*obucheniye*) and moral or character education (*vospitaniye*). Civic education was an integral part of both components: it was normally provided through a number of academic courses (e.g. History, Study of Society, Literature) and through the system of extracurricular activities that were a part of *vospitaniye*. After 1991, a number of new courses in civic education were developed and added to civic academic curriculum (Froumin 2004; Vaillant 2005). New interactive methods of teaching became increasingly popular among educators. Extracurricular work became less political and more creative. More and more innovative schools that were called laboratory schools appeared all over Russia. The new openness helped Russia's education to become more susceptible to global changes. Attention was directed to instill 'common human values'. It was a time of close cooperation with civic educators from Europe and the United States. The priorities of civic education were to educate a democratic, knowledgeable citizen who will be concerned about the well-being of the country and the world and who will work to continue the democratic development of Russia. Patriotism, as it followed from the school reform documents, was interpreted as aspiration to build a democratic Russia that will be successfully integrated in the new global system.

Despite the enthusiasm and creativity of many teachers, the problems and unresolved issues, some of them very specific, continued to accumulate. One such specific problem was the teaching of History: old Soviet textbooks were no longer used, new textbooks were not published. Many teachers were disoriented in the tide of new and mostly sensational information that inundated TV and printed media (Lisovskaya and Karpov 1999; Zajda 1994; 2007). For many educators, who were primarily trained in Soviet teacher-training colleges, it was very difficult to change their teaching style (Polozhevets, Schechter, and Perelmuter 1997). That was particularly true for social science teachers, who were trained as '(Communist) Party policy forerunners'. Slow political and social progress, a deep crisis in economy, and predictably frail support of painful reforms led to changes in the ruling elite in the late 1990s. A new developmental model was based on a more traditionalistic conservative approach where populist patriotic rhetoric played a critical role.

It is not at all surprising that the intensification of patriotic rhetoric on a governmental level, as well as on government-controlled television and in media, led to a surge of patriotism and patriotic education related texts in mainstream educational journals. Interpreted through the terms that spanned across the whole political and ideological spectrum from almost extreme left to extreme right, the conceptualization of patriotism reflected the existing dichotomy deeply enrooted in Russian culture and mentality (Arkhipenkova 2004). However, despite few attempts to address various aspects of patriotism from critical-analytical standpoints (Bolshakov 2004; Galkin 2005; Grigoryev 2005; Ioffe 2006), mainstream political, sociological and educational journals focused on such traditional for Russia aspects of patriotism as love to one's fatherland, pride in one's fatherland, devotion, sometimes sacred, to one's fatherland, and commitment to serve its interests (Bykov 2006a; 2006b; Ivanova 2003; Lutovinov 2006; Mikryukov 2007; Pulyayev and Shelyapin 2001). Patriotism is a traditional Russian moral value that instills the patriotic idea of 'a spiritual unity of a person and the Russian society', contended Pulyayev and Shelyapin (2001: 71) who specifically pointed at the incompatibility of patriotism and nationalism or cosmopolitanism. That was a remarkable note considering traditional negative attitudes to constantly vilified cosmopolitanism and a hardly concealed similarity between state-supported patriotism and growing nationalism.

Ivanova (2003) argued that state patriotism plays the most important consolidating role in a society. When the state is the object of patriotic sentiments and the people are subjects, patriotism is 'an expression of subjects' pride for the Fatherland, their active participation in consolidation and strengthening the state and statehood for the purpose of efficient functioning of social institutions, development of the society and individuals' (2003: 295). Thus, state patriotism, Ivanova concluded, can become the leading consolidating idea of the official policy. Patriotism as a developmental process goes through three stages (Mikryukov 2007): love of one's family and relatives, love of one's 'little Motherland' (which is euphemistically used for the birthplace), and love of one's Fatherland and society. Analyzing relations between patriotism and citizenship in the framework of civic-patriotic education, Lutovinov (2006) asserted that compared with the vague, blurred, and badly defined concept of citizenship, patriotism is a clear and theoretically better developed construct that represents a unity of spirituality, civic maturity, and social activity. These qualities motivate the individual to serve the fatherland. He then made a very symptomatic statement that patriotism, not citizenship, should be a leading component of civic-patriotic education because 'overestimation of citizenship that assumes depatriotization of education of citizens, is a deformation unacceptable for the state, society as well as for the individual whose ultimate predestination is to serve their Fatherland' (2006: 54).

It is important to understand that the program of patriotic education in Russia was planned as a ubiquitous national campaign that encompasses all spheres traditionally responsible for moral and ideological development of the Russian society. What impelled the Russian government to launch this campaign? Why now? The official documents, such as the state programs *Patriotic Education of Citizens of the Russian Federation'* (Gosudarstvennaya Programma 2001), or *Conception of Patriotic Education of Citizens of the Russian Federation* (Kontseptsiya 2003) briefly explain that 'economic disintegration, social differentiation of the society, devaluation of spiritual (moral) values negatively effected public consciousness … Apathy, selfishness, individualism, cynicism, unmotivated aggressiveness, disrespect to the state and social institutions have become widespread phenomena in public consciousness. State and military services tend to be less prestigious' (Gosudarstvennaya Programma 2001). All these, the program states, are the results of elusive 'events of the recent time'. Blame for the 'present state' (a usual euphemistic substitute for 'bad' or 'inappropriate') of patriotism and patriotic education is usually attributed to: (1) deheroization of Russian history, (2) humiliation of Russian national dignity, (3) prioritizing universal human values over national values (Ivanova 2003), (4) neglect of military training (Bykov 2006a; Lesnyak 2005; Lutovinov 2006), and (5) deideologization of the Russian youth (Karpelman 2002). Those who are familiar with the content of Russian political discourses are very well aware that the ideologically loaded grandiloquent constructs, such as deheroization, deideologization, or universal human values, are metaphors or coded 'stigmas' of a very concrete period of Russian history, namely the end of the 1980s and 1990s or in other words, the post-Soviet period when a liberal-democratic model was being implemented in politics and education. If properly contextualized and decoded, deheroization would mean a process of demythologization of Russian and Soviet history, a painful process of rationalizing historic events. Deideologization, in turn, stands for the attempts to find and to instill in the society paradigms of interpersonal and inter-institutional relations that would be based on common sense devoid of Communist rhetoric. Hence, what we witness here is an attempt to use patriotic sentiments substituted by the policy of State Patriotism against the feeble liberal reforms of the 1990s.

The intensification of patriotic education is also explained by ethnic and civic identity crises in Russian society (Blum 2006; Pulyayev and Shelyapin 2001; Vaillant 2005). Traditionally, people in the Soviet Union or in Russia self-identify ethnically rather than civically. When Leonid Brezhnev bombastically declared in 1972 that a new ethno-political community 'Soviet people' was created, it was perceived by the majority of the population, Russian and non-Russian alike, as usual official propaganda, produced in abundance in Brezhnev's Soviet Union. The term 'Soviet', as a civic identifier, obviously existed and was frequently used in the Soviet Union; however, it almost never substituted for an ethnic self-identifier of Russians or representatives of any other ethnic groups. The democratic model that was used in the 1990s proved impotent to quickly form a new civic identity. It would be naïve to expect otherwise considering the problems that Russia faced in the 1990s. Often media and officials of various ranks pointed at the crisis of self-identity among Russians as one of the major threats to the moral health and stability of the society. Statistical data demonstrated the relative success of the traditionalist-patriotic approach. According to the poll conducted by Levada Center, 80 percent of the population of Russia always or in most cases identified themselves as Russians in 1994, by 2003 this number had increased to 90 percent (Levada 2005). It remains problematic for English speakers to comprehend this problem, because the English language does not differentiate between the two distinct concepts of *Russkiy*, that is to say a Russian as (self-)identified by ethnic origin, versus *Rossiyanin*, Russian by civic-formal attribution or a Russian Federation citizen, but not necessarily ethnically Russian. However, it should be noted that the propagandistic patriotic campaign, particularly on state-controlled TV channels and in media, was based on the principles of so-called loyal or blind patriotism (Merry 2009; Staub 1997), when Russia was counter-opposed to the West. Obviously, the mobilizing effect of patriotic discourses in mass-media and in school curriculum produced a prompt unifying effect. However, it remains to be determined whether this effect is positive or negative in the long run.

Another reason for launching the patriotic campaign was the impact of global political and economic processes, particularly the fear that the effect of so-called 'Colored Revolutions' (the Rose Revolution in 2003 in Georgia, the Orange Revolution in 2004 in Ukraine, and the Tulip Revolution in 2005 in Kyrgyzstan) will transcend the borders of the Russian Federation. Politically, the reasons for and the development of all Colored Revolutions are ambiguous; however they resulted in preventing or ending authoritarian regimes in their countries (Forbrig and Demeš 2007; Tucker 2007). The intensification of patriotic campaigns in Russia in response to the Colored Revolutions brings a historical parallel with the similar actions of Nicolas I who was afraid to 'catch a French disease', his definition of the French Revolution, and whose new policy of State Patriotism was a direct reaction to European revolutionary movements.

The official institutionalized approach to patriotism and patriotic education is best presented in the *Conception of Patriotic Education of the Citizens of Russian Federation*, adopted by the government in 2003 (Kontseptsiya 2003). The document that claims to 'reflect the whole complex of officially acknowledged ideas' about patriotic education, unequivocally defines patriotism as 'love to one's Motherland, commitment to one's Fatherland, strong desire to serve its interests, and readiness to defend it, even if it requires self-sacrifice' (2003: 2). According to the Conception, patriotism is a specific type of self-realization and social behavior of citizens that are determined by the protection of the unity and sovereignty of Russia, its national security, stable development, duty, and responsibility. By the latter the authors understand the priority of public and state interests over individual and personal interests. The specific features of patriotism in Russia identified by the Conception – togetherness, integrality, obedience to the laws, need of collectiveness – remarkably resonate with the basic principles of the famous Russian triad of *autocracy, orthodoxy, nationality* that constituted the quintessence of the policy of State Patriotism in the second quarter of the nineteenth century during the reign of Nicolas I. In general, the emphasis on the overall subordination to state interests at the expense of individual interests is idiosyncratic to the concept of patriotism as well as the idea of patriotic education, which is interpreted as a 'set of systematic and goal-oriented activities of state bodies and institutions as well as public organizations aimed at forming and inculcating in citizens heightened patriotic consciousness …, readiness to carry out one's civic duty, and constitutional obligations to defend the interests of the Motherland' (2003: 4). The document specifically accentuates a military component in patriotic education, declaring military education an inseparable part of patriotic education. It is symptomatic that the Conception, which is presented as a traditionalist type of narrative that internalizes uncritical loyalty to the nation and the state, still twice mentions 'civil society' as one of the beneficiaries of proper patriotic education outcomes. Although the text does not clarify how the development of civil society can benefit from a hyper-centralized and ideologically conservative system of patriotic education, the very reference to it is indicative of possible shifts, however insignificant they might be, in the rationale of value-related education among traditionalists in Russia.

The state program *Patriotic Education of Citizens of the Russian Federation for Years 2006–2010* (Gosudarstvennaya Programma 2005) is based on the ideas and goals set out in the Conception of Patriotic Education of 2003 and, in terms of methods and approaches, is the continuation of the previously passed and similarly entitled program for years 2001–2005. Although symbolic in nature (the state-funded budget portion of the five-year program was less than $20 million), the program is very eloquent in categorizing and indicating the general ideological development direction in Russia and patriotic education in particular. Claiming that the ultimate goal of patriotic education is the revival of Russia's greatness and prominence, the program postulates state activities that would enhance patriotic education including such elements as: an increase of military components in all areas of education, more careful attention to history textbooks, influence on electronic and printed media, and assuming more control over children's organizations. In reality, the tasks outlined by the program have been long under way. Examples are plentiful: from secretly supported puppet youth organizations, such as the infamous *Nashi* movement, to multiple orchestrated campaigns in mass media against Russia's neighbors that create a sensation of a world conspiracy against Russia.

The most recent example is the campaign to put history education under strict government control. At a meeting with educators in June 2007 President Vladimir Putin labeled the texts about World War II that included criticism of the political or military actions of the USSR 'inadmissible and even insulting for our people's interpretation of history' (Sokolov 2007). He also blamed those who used international grants to create history textbooks and requested the writing of new textbooks. This initiative was immediately supported by the Russian parliament whose Speaker announced that a new bill would require official state registration of history textbooks. This means that the government will carefully verify and control all textual content. Besides, the number of history textbooks that teachers can use in classrooms will be limited and only a few state-endorsed publishers will be allowed to publish approved textbooks. The history revision campaign logically continued in May 2009 when the new Russian President Dmitry Medvedyev signed an executive order that established a presidential commission 'to oppose attempts to falsify history to the detriment of Russia's history' (Novosyolova 2009). These examples once again demonstrate the key role of control over history teaching in 'repositioning competing and ideologically driven discourses of historical narratives and processes' (Zajda 2009: 4).

In discussing the rationale and motivations behind the ongoing amplification of official activities in patriotic education and the infusion of additional patriotic discourses in civic curriculum, observers often refer to poll results that demonstrate an increasing interest in patriotic education among the population of Russia. In 2004, 89 percent of respondents agreed that it was necessary to devote greater attention to patriotic education (Blum 2006). A more recent poll in November 2006 indicated that 93 percent of respondents agreed that schools and colleges should engage in the patriotic education of youth (VTsIOM 2006). However compelling these numbers are, they should be viewed with skepticism and caution. The survey conducted in February 2007 by the same state-run All-Russia Central Institute of Public Opinion (VTsIOM) indicated that only 12 percent of the respondents would advise the state to conduct patriotic education in educational establishments of various levels (VTsIOM 2007). Ironically, less than 5 percent of respondents would recommend the state to conduct the activities that are pinnacles in the state program of patriotic education. Despite the fact that 30 percent of respondents said that various formal events are important for patriotic education, only 3–4 percent admitted participating in those events while 86 percent reported that neither they nor members of their families ever participated in any of such events.

Patriotic Education or Military-Patriotic Education?

The most conspicuous feature of the contemporary patriotic education campaign is probably its military spirit. Ironically, the adjective 'military' is used only three times in the text of the Program of 2006–2010 compared with 22 times in the text of the Program of 2001–2005 (both texts are almost similar in length). Nonetheless, whether the word 'military' is formally mentioned or not, the term 'patriotic education' by itself is a code phrase that implies military education, military training, and military preparation. Thus, it is not surprising that all or almost all materials about patriotic education or the implementation of the newly adopted program include information about the military or examples of military training. By 2006, there were 1,350 youth military clubs with membership of more than 300,000. Russian military established cooperation with 1,130 military-patriotic clubs and organizations; there were 452 summer military camps in all regions of Russia (Surzhko 2006). There are literally hundreds and hundreds of regular propagandistic campaigns conducted at national, regional, and local levels. The list of examples of militarization of consciousness is long and almost emulates, stylistically and operationally, activities and programs from patriotic education curricula of the Soviet period (Sredin 1988; Vyrshchikov 1990). This striking resemblance to the Soviet period curricula explains why everyone in Russia perceives patriotic education as a rationale with a dominating military agenda. The term that was commonly used in the Soviet Union for patriotic education was 'military-patriotic education'. Therefore, the military rationale of the patriotic education campaign does not need to be explicitly explained or clarified: the mutually shared codes 'patriotism' or 'patriotic education' are normally 'correctly' decoded by educators. The centuries-long tradition of 'military/patriotic' symbiotic unity also explains the fact that almost 75 percent of respondents related patriotic education to military games or military clubs and camps (VTsIOM 2007).

Final Thoughts

The question every nation faces regarding civic education is essentially what kind of citizen the society needs. This question is rhetorical because every society needs citizens who act for the progress of the society. But who defines progress? A recent survey conducted among civic educators in various parts of Russia demonstrated that the majority selected patriotism as the most important civic concept. Rights and freedoms were ranked second, rule of law sixth, freedom was ranked tenth, and democracy, which received only a fifth of the votes given to patriotism, was ranked twelfth (Ioffe 2006; 2009). These data together with the Levada Center research presented earlier in this chapter (Levada 2005) and the results of other surveys (Russian Center for Citizenship Education 2008) evidence that the developers of the patriotic campaigns almost achieved the desired results. But are these the results that the democratic reforms of the early 1990s intended to achieve? The ubiquitous patriotic campaign that was supposed to be a part of civic curriculum but in reality substituted the civic curriculum (Semko 2007) was planned as a response to the challenges of globalization and Russian civic and ethnic identity construction. Ironically, the two concepts that were rarely identified by surveyed social science teachers were self-identification and globalization (Ioffe 2009).

Curriculum, as a political text, reflects societal political intent only in societies where there are mechanisms that guarantee the influence of rank-and-file members of those societies on school reform. Proper democratic procedures provide opportunities for all interested members of a society to voice their opinions and to reflect their concerns in curricula. In the societies where citizens are disengaged from decision making, curricular policies, particularly in such sensitive area as civic education, turn into campaigns that serve the interests of those in power, rather than work for the overall development of society. Rather than using the challenges of globalization to deconstruct, reinterpret, and eventually renegotiate old assumptions through civic curriculum, Russian officials substituted public debates of real controversies by traditionalistic metaphors and symbols that only postponed but did not resolve real problems of identity and socialization. Patriotic and military emphases in educational discourses contextualized through the Soviet era codes and symbols are not simply a stylistic move to a conservative stage of educational reform in Russia (Karpov and Lisovskaya 2005) but rather a sign of a deeper involvement of the state, not citizens, in civic education processes to shape, control, and eventually sustain the chosen ideological framework. The current development of patriotic education in Russia is the continuation of the long-standing tradition to silence critical reconceptualization of civic constructs through the means of education. Furthermore, the re-institutionalization of the State Patriotism policy is no longer symbolic, but a real departure from the liberal democratic changes of the 1990s that contradicts the stated objectives of educational reform and might eventually hamper the development of a democratic school system in Russia and slow down the creation of Russia's civil society.

References

Anderson, B. (1991) *Imagined Communities*, London: Verso Books.

Arkhipenkova, N.S. (2004) 'O mentalitete natsional'noi kul'tury' (On the mentality of national culture), in S.N. Poltorak (ed.), *Istoricheskaya Psihologiya, Psihometriya, Sotsial'naya Psihologiya: Obshcheye i Razlichiya* (Historic psychology, psychometrics, social psychology: commonalities and differences), St. Petersburg.

Barghoorn, F.C. (1956) *Soviet Russian Nationalism,* New York: Oxford University Press.

Blum, D.W. (2006) 'Official patriotism in Russia; its essence and implications', *PONARS Policy Memo*, 46. Online. Available HTTP: <http://www.csis.org/media/csis/pubs/pm_0420.pdf> (accessed 12 May 2008).

Bodrova, E.V. (2008) 'Voyenno-patrioticheskoye vospitaniye v gody Velikoy Otechestvennoy voiny' (Military-patriotic education during the Great Patriotic war), *Prepodavaniye Istorii i Obshchestvovedeniya v Shkole*, 5: 3–9.

Bolshakov, V.P. (2004) 'Problemnost' patriotizma kak tsennosti sovremennoi rossiiskoy kul'tury' (Problematic character of patriotism as a value of contemporary Russian culture), in: *MirovayaPpolitika i Ideinye Paradigmy Epohi* (World politics and ideological paradigms of the epoch), St. Petersburg: State University of Culture and Arts.

Bouveng, R. (2008) 'Revamping the Russian national idea: Contemporary Russian messianism', paper presented at an Interdisciplinary Post-Graduate Conference, University of Oxford, 6–7 June. Online. Available HTTP <http://www.mod-langs.ox.ac.uk/russian/nationalism/postgradconference/Programme.htm> (accessed 10 May 2009).

Bykov, A. (2006a) 'Problemy patrioticheskogo vospitaniya' (Problems of patriotic education), *Pedagogika*, 2: 37–42.

Bykov, A. (2006b) 'Organizatsionno-pedagogicheskiye voprosy patrioticheskogo vospitaniya v shkole' (Organizational and methodological problems of patriotic education in school), *Vospitaniye Shkol'nikov*, 6: 5–11.

Counts, G.S. (1957) *The Challenge of Soviet Education*, New York: McGraw-Hill.

Dewey, J. (1929) *Impressions of Soviet Russia and the Revolutionary World Mexico–China–Turkey*, New York: New Republic.

Eklof, B. and Dneprov, E. (1993) *Democracy in the Russian School: the reform movement in education since 1984*, Boulder, CO: Westview Press.

Forbrig, J. and Demeš, P. (2007) *Reclaiming Democracy: civil society and electoral change in Central and Eastern Europe,* Washington, DC: The German Marshall Fund.

Froumin, I. (2004) 'Citizenship education and ethnic issues in Russia', in J.A. Banks (ed.) *Diversity and Citizenship Education: global perspectives,* San Francisco, CA: Jossey-Bass.

Froumin, I. (2005) 'Democratizing the Russian school: achievements and setbacks', in B. Eklof, L.E. Holmes, and V. Kaplan (eds) *Educational Reform in Post-Soviet Russia: legacies and prospects,* London: Frank Cass.

Galkin, S. (2005) 'Patriotizm glazami psihologa' (Patriotism from the point of view of a psychologist). Online. Available HTTP: <http://pedsovet.org/forum/lofiversion/index.php/t332.html> (accessed June 2008).

Gosudarstvennaya Programma Patrioticheskoye Vospitaniye Grazhdan Rossiyskoi Federatsii na 2001–2005 Gody (State program of patriotic education of the citizens of the Russian Federation for years 2001–2005) (2001) *Krasnaya Zvezda,* 2 March 2001.

Gosudarstvennaya Programma Patrioticheskoye Vospitaniye Grazhdan Rossiyskoi Federatsii na 2006–2010 Gody (State program of patriotic education of the citizens of the Russian Federation for years 2006–2010) (2005) *Vospitaniye Shkol'nikov,* 4: 2–7.

Grigoryev, D. (2005) 'Patriotizm velikodushiya' (Patriotism of generosity), *Narodnoye Obrazovaniye,* 4: 75–80.

Ioffe, A. (2006). 'Sovremennye vyzovy i riski razvitiya grazhdanskogo obrazovaniya v Rossii' (Contemporary risks and challenges of civic education in Russia), *Istoriya i obshchestvoznaniye v shkole,* 9: 19–24.

Ioffe, A. (2009) 'Aktivnye i interaktivnye metody prepodavaniya v grazhdanskom obrazovanii' (Active and interactive teaching methods in civic education). Online. Available HTTP: <http://www.apkpro.ru/content/view/1868/360> (accessed 17 January 2010).

Ivanova, S.Y. (2003) 'Gosudarstvennyi patriotism –al'ternativa ideologii natsionalizma i kosmopolitizma' (State patriotism – an alternative to the ideologies of nationalism and cosmopolitanism), *Sotsial'no-Gummanitarnye Znaniya,* 3, 293–302.

Karpelman, E.L. (2002) 'O patrioticheskom vospitanii molodyozhi' (On patriotic education of the young), *Novaya i Noveishaya Istoriya,* 5: 102–106.

Karpov, V. and Lisovskaya, E. (2005) 'Educational change in the time of social revolution: The case of post-communist Russia in comparative perspective' in B. Eklof, L.E. Holmes and V. Kaplan (eds) *Educational Reform in Post-Soviet Russia: legacies and prospects,* London: Frank Cass.

Kontseptsiya Patrioticheskogo Vospitaniya Grazhdan Rossiiskoi Federatsii (Conception of patriotic education of the citizens of the Russian Federation) (2003) Online. Available HTTP: <http://www.ed.gov.ru/junior/rub/patriot/konzept/konzept.doc> (accessed May 2008).

Laqueur, W. (1998) *Black Hundred: the rise of extreme right in Russia,* New York: Harper Collins.

Lenin, V.I. (1917/1964) *Collected works. Volume 23,* Moscow: Progress.

Lesnyak, V.I. (2005) 'Tchelyabinskiy patrioticheskiy forum' (Tchelyabinsk patriotic forum), *Pedagogika,* 7: 119–124.

Levada, Y. (2005) '"Homo Sovieticus" limits of self-identification', *Russia in Global Affairs,* 2. Online. Available HTTP <http://eng.globalaffairs.ru/numbers/11/907.html> (accessed May 2008).

Lisovskaya, E. and Karpov, V. (1999) 'New ideologies in postcommunist Russian textbooks', *Comparative Education Review,* 43: 4: 522–543.

Lutovinov, V.I. (2006) 'Grazhdansko-patrioticheskoye vospitaniye segodnya' (Civic-patriotic education today), *Pedagogika,* 5: 53–59.

Matus, C. and McCarthy, C. (2003) 'The triumph of multiplicity and the carnival of difference: curriculum dilemmas in the age of postcolonialism and globalization', in W. Pinar (ed.) *International Handbook of Curriculum Research*, London: Lawrence Erlbaum Associates.

McLaren, P. (1989) *Life in Schools: an introduction to critical pedagogy in the foundations of education*, New York: Longman.

Merry, M. (2009) 'Patriotism, history, and the legitimate aim of American education', *Educational Philosophy and Theory*, 41, 4: 378–398.

Mikryukov, V. (2007) 'Patriotism: k opredeleniyu ponyatiya' (Patriotism: about the definition of the concept), *Vospitaniye Shkol'nikov*, 5: 2–8.

Nearing, S. (1926) *Education in Soviet Russia*, New York: International Publishers.

Novosyolova, E. (2009) 'Pravda o voine i mire' (The truth of war and peace), *Rossiyskaya Gazeta*, No. 4913 (89), 20 May 2009.

Polozhevets, P., Schechter, S. and Perelmuter, R. (1997) 'Civic education and the future of democracy in Russia', *The International Journal of Social Education*, 12, 2: 84–100.

Pulyayev, V.T. and Shelyapin, N.V. (2001) 'Sotsial'nye tsennosti v sisteme rossiyskoi natsional'no-gosudarstvennoi ideologii' (Social values in the system of Russian national-state ideology), *Sotsial'no-Gumanitarnye Znaniya*, 5: 69–79.

Rapoport, A. (2009) 'Patriotic education in Russia: stylistic move or the sign of substantive counter-reform?', *The Educational Forum*, 73, 1: 141–153.

Riasanovsky, N. (1967) *Nicholas I and Official Nationality in Russia, 1825–1855,* Berkeley, CA: University of California Press.

Russian Center for Citizenship Education (2008) *Ethnic Tensions in Modern Russia: Which Way to Go?* St. Petersburg: Russian Center for Citizenship Education – New Dartmouth Conference.

Semko, I. (2007) 'Civic education in Russia', *Adukatar*, 2, 12: 41–44.

Shchyogolev, A.A. (2007) 'Grazhdansko-patrioticheskoye vospitaniye shkol'nikov v SSSR v 1937–1945 gg' (Civic-patriotic education of school students in the USSR in 1937–1945), *Pedagogika*, 9: 76–85.

Smith, D.G. (2003) 'Curriculum and teaching face globalization', in W. Pinar (ed.) *International Handbook of Curriculum Research*, London: Lawrence Erlbaum Associates.

Sokolov, B. (2007) 'Darom prepodavatelyam' (Free for teachers). Online. Available HTTP: <http://grani.ru/Society/Science/m.124112.html> (accessed January 2008).

Sredin, G.V. (1988) *Osnovy Voyenno-PatrioticheskogoVvospitaniya* (Foundations of military-patriotic education), Moscow: Prosveshcheniye.

Staub, E. (1997) 'Blind versus constructive patriotism: moving from embeddedness in the group to critical loyalty and action', in D. Bar-Tal and E. Staub (eds) *Patriotism in the Lives of Individuals and Nations*, Chicago, IL: Nelson-Hall.

Surzhko, G. (2006) 'Patrioticheskoye obrazovaniye v Rossii: Tol'ko fakty' (Patriotic education in Russia: only facts), *Narodnoye Obrazovaniye*, 4: 34–35.

Tucker, J. (2007) 'Enough! Electoral fraud, collective action problems, and post-Communist colored revolutions', *Perspectives on Politics*, 5, 3: 535–551.

Vaillant, J.G. (2005) 'Civic education in a changing Russia', in B. Eklof, L.E. Holmes, and V. Kaplan (eds), *Educational Reform in Post-Soviet Russia: legacies and prospects,* London: Frank Cass.

VTsIOM (2006) 'Patriotizm istinnyi i mnimyi' (Pastriotism real and imaginary). VTsIOM Press-release 591, 5 December 2006. Online. Available HTTP: <http://www.wciom. com> (accessed June 2008).

VTsIOM (2007) 'Kak vospitat' patriota (How to raise a patriot), VTsIOM Press-release 636, 22 February 2007. Online. Available HTTP: <http://www.wciom.com> (accessed June 2008).

Vyrshchikov, A.N. (1990) *Voyenno-patrioticheskoue Vospitaniye: Teoriya i Praktika* (Military-patriotic education: theory and practice), Moscow: Pedagogika.

Yekelchyk, S. (2002) 'Stalinist patriotism as imperial discourse: reconciling the Ukrainian and Russian "heroic past", 1939–1945', *Kritika: Exploration in Russian and Eurasian History*, 3, 1: 51–80.

Zajda, J. (1994) *School curriculum reforms for the new values in post-communist Russia* (ERIC Document Reproduction Service No. ED368054).

Zajda, J. (2007) 'The new history school textbooks in the Russian Federation: 1992–2004', *Compare*, 37, 1: 291–306.

Zajda, J. (2009) 'Nation-building, identity, and citizenship education: Introduction', in J. Zajda, H. Daun, and L. Saha, (eds) *Nation-building, Identity and Citizenship Education: cross-cultural perspectives*, Dordrecht: Springer.

14 Configuration of Knowledge, Identity and Politics Through the Current History Curriculum in Israel

Eyal Naveh

Introduction

This chapter aims to explore the content, structure, explicit purpose and implied agenda of the history curriculum in the Israel national state system, as manifested in the curriculum that was formed during the first decade of the twenty-first century. The chapter will analyze the content of the current curriculum, and the relationship of this curriculum to the issues of nationalism, globalization, identity politics, and changes in hegemonic culture.

The major argument of this chapter is that despite the enormous changes in the last generation that indeed transformed the landscape of so many segments of the younger population in Israel, the curriculum is still very conservative in its content, purpose and implied agenda. Consequently, such a curriculum is becoming less and less meaningful and relevant to the life and experience of Israeli youngsters. The world that the official history curriculum aims to represent is moving away from the world that surrounds the students. Thus, the influence of the history curriculum on students' knowledge, identity, and political behavior is rather limited.

Moreover, there is a huge gap between the official aims of the history curriculum and its practical outcome. Most Israeli teachers cannot adhere to the curriculum requirements due to overcrowded classes, lack of time to cover the material, mediocrity among the teaching staff, and the incongruity between the textbooks on one hand, and the final examinations' requirements on the other. (The books try to develop critical thinking and historical empathy through diverse interpretations of historical narratives, and the examinations focus on facts, memorizing, and repetition.)

The curriculum reflects the national Zionist narrative, and focuses predominantly on Jewish experience in history. The rest of the world, particularly Christian Europe and the Arab Islamic world, served as 'Significant Other' to the formation of the Jewish–Israeli national identity. The Zionist movement emerged in Europe but the Zionist narrative claims that Jews are at odds with the European society, and can survive only if they leave Europe and move to their historical ancestral land. The population of the Middle East, however, is predominantly Arab and Moslem. Thus, the very creation of a Jewish state in the Middle East is in a way a paradoxical attempt, designed on the one hand to leave Europe, and on the other hand, to establish a European enclave in an Islamic area.

Such an attitude reflects the dilemma of how to reconcile between threat and exclusion on the one hand and acceptance and inclusion on the other. The Jews in Europe, and to a lesser extend in the Moslem world, were endangered by their hostile environment, because they were never accepted by the European or Moslem society. The movement of the Jews back to their national homeland and historical origin generated another threat since the Middle East is not going to accept or even legitimize a Jewish state in the area either. Thus the dilemma remains: how the curriculum can encourage an open-minded, reconciled, diverse and pluralistic consideration of Israel's place in the world, when it is persistently threatened. The movement from the abnormal existence in Europe in the past to the supposedly normal state of being as a sovereign nation in the world at present has not materialized yet. The creation of Israeli society and the formation of Israel as a Jewish state did not end the existential menace, and in many aspects even intensified it. Thus the hidden agenda of the curriculum cannot ignore this dilemma when it discusses the relationship between Israel and the rest of the world.

The history curriculum relates to three major geographic areas which construct three sites that constitute Jewish collective identity: the land of Israel, Christian Europe and the Arab Islamic world. Other locations in the world are hardly mentioned in the curriculum.

The land of Israel appears in the curriculum as the place where Jewish history started in the Biblical and the Second Temple period, when Jews lived on this land in ancient times, preceding all other inhabitants. Thus, the history curriculum stresses the normal, authentic, and 'organic' connection between the contemporary state of Israel and its ancient past.

Christian Europe appears in the curriculum as a place of exile, where Jews were never accepted, and never considered themselves as part of the area. Christians viewed Jews as heathen, profane and sinners but despite this sort of relationship, most Jews dwelled in the European continent till the mid-twentieth century. In modern times the emancipation officially changed the life of Jews in Europe, but also created problems for their continuing existence: when implemented, it led to the assimilation and ultimately disappearance of Judaism and Jews; when rejected, it brought about discrimination, anti-Semitism and ultimately destruction and continued suffering for Jews. Europe is both the place of creation of modern aspects of Judaism throughout the nineteenth and twentieth centuries, and the place that eradicated modern Judaism though spiritual and physical destruction (the Holocaust).

The Arab Islamic world was another place of Jewish exile, yet, unlike Christian Europe, the Jews were tolerated to a certain degree, being viewed as monotheistic misbelievers that nevertheless deserved legal protection. However, since the Islamic world remained pre-modern and traditional, modern Judaism has no origins in this world. For centuries, the land of Israel was part of this pre-modern Arab Islamic world and renamed Palestine. It was a desolate and barren area, essentially vacant of Jewish population and never appeared as a separate political or national entity.

Only with the creation of the Zionist movement at the late nineteenth century, did the Jews start to immigrate to the land of Israel/Palestine and develop again their autonomous society, quintessential culture and ultimately, their sovereign state. But the Middle East and the Arab Islamic world rejects the very legitimacy the state of Israel and therefore, the survival of Israel as a Jewish state still requires a continuing struggle against its enemies, until they accept its existence and acknowledge its right to live in peace in the region.

These elements appeared in the state's official history curriculum and in the major textbooks used by the public school system. Yet the public educational system in Israel is essentially a conglomerate of various systems. *The National State system* represents the official public state system of education, but in fact includes about 50 percent of the schools of Israel. It serves primarily the Hebrew-speaking, modern, Jewish-Israeli population that live in cities, villages and rural communities. This chapter will examine and analyze only this segment of the Israeli school system.

It should be mentioned, however, that in Israel there exist at least four other systems of education that work according to a different curriculum and use different textbooks: *The National Religious system* serves about 15 percent of Jews who consider themselves religious and live in cities, villages and many settlements in the occupied territories. *The Arab State system* serves more than 20 percent of the Arab Israelis who live in their own cities and villages or in their own enclaves in the mixed cities. (The instruction language of this system is Arabic.) *The Independent Education system* that exists outside the state control, serves the growing population of ultra-orthodox Jews. Although the state supports them financially, it cannot interfere in the curriculum of these institutions which are managed by the ultra-orthodox, mostly non-Zionist rabbinic institutions. They have a different historical narrative and no outsider has any access to the material taught in their schools. Finally, there are other, *semi-private systems* (external, adult, open, democratic, parochial, foreign, and bilingual), that emerged in recent years, financed mainly by parents, NGOs, or the students themselves. These practically separate systems are the outcome of a historical process, reflecting political compromises, demographical changes, and power struggles between various segments of Israeli society.

An Analysis of the Current History Curriculum and Textbooks

The current history curriculum is a compromise between the recommendations of official state committees and the availability of textbooks. Private publishers produce the books in the market and compete with each other, yet they need to pass through an official approval procedure by the Ministry of Education. Schools can choose the books from the list of approved books; however, there are some cases when students are using unapproved books that help them to pass the final exams. The structure of the school system, the nature of the final exams, the status of history inspectors and other ministry officials, and the shifting political control over the Ministry of Education, also have a significant impact on the material that is learned in history classes.

New instructions of history curriculum were published in 2006 and officially will endure till 2010–2012 when new books will replace the current ones. But until such replacement takes place, these instructions seem to be the best and most up-to-date source that characterizes the status of history as a discipline in the Israeli national state system of education.

According to the curriculum, students learn history only at the middle school and high school level, from the 7th grade to the 12th grade. In elementary schools they study social studies and focus on their community. They also study ancient history in combination with biblical studies. The students learn history in two stages: a chronological, introductory level during three years of middle school; and a thematic, in-depth level, during high school years that end in the final state exams.

An Analysis of the Middle School Curriculum and Textbooks

The curriculum is predominantly European. Out of the 45 topics of study, 29 topics (65 percent) focus on Europe. The picture become even more striking when viewed chronologically: out of the 29 European topics only nine topics cover the period from the middle ages up to the nineteenth century, and 21 topics (70 percent) deal with modern times (the last 200–250 years). Furthermore, 15 topics of modern Europe (75 percent of the modern and more than 50 percent of all European topics) cover the period from the eve of the First World War to the end of the Second World War, a period of roughly 40 years, from 1910 to 1950. Post-war Europe is viewed only through two indirect topics: the Cold War, and a General Global Transformation from 1950 to 1980.

The picture becomes more intricate when Jewish history is introduced. Out of the 45 topics, 24 topics (56 percent) focus on Jewish life and experience. The overlapping of European and Jewish history is very significant: out of the 29 topics that focus on Europe, 13 topics (more than 40 percent of European topics and more than 50 percent of Jewish topics) discus the relationship between Jewish life and experience and the European arena. The relationship between European history and Jewish history as appeared in the 13 common topics is significant: six topics discuss negative and problematic ties between Jewish life and the European society (46 percent), only two topics depict positive and hopeful relations (15 percent), and five (39 percent) reveal ambiguous and complicated links. Moreover, the first topic of the 13 views Christian Europe in the Middle Ages as the ultimate Jewish exile where Jews suffer persecution and discrimination. The last topic is about the Holocaust and the annihilation of European Jewry. Thus the overall framework of the European–Jewish encounter appears within a cognitive paradigm defined as 'from bad to worse'.

From a quantitative perspective, the status of the Islamic and Arab world in the history curriculum is totally different. Out of the 45 topics, only eight topics (18 percent) deal with Arab or Islamic society and culture, among them only two topics focus on Islamic world. Three out of the eight topics are about the pre-modern age; the other five come into sight in the twentieth century and in connection to European Imperialism: the disintegration of the Ottoman Empire, the Jewish Arab relations in the land of Israel and the Middle East. The curriculum ignores completely non-Arabic Islamic areas such as Iran, Pakistan, Indonesia, Malaysia, or central Asia.

The topics of Moslem/Arab history and Jewish history portray a mutual encounter. Out of the seven topics that discuss this encounter, four are negative, one is relatively positive (in comparison with the Christians), and three are ambiguous. Islam appears for the first time as another, though more benign, place of Jewish diaspora. Moslem or Arab history becomes visible in the curriculum only as a passive reaction to European, Jewish or Zionist history. Arabs and Moslems are hardly mentioned in modern times. They come into sight at the end of the curriculum as the enemy of Zionism and the Jewish state, as well as within the process of de-colonization in Asia and Africa that ended Jewish life in the Arab world. Like Europe, but in a different manner, the Arab Jewish encounter started in rivalry and ended in overt hostility.

Middle School Textbook Samples

When discussing the middle ages, the textbook stresses cultural interchange as the focus of study (Tabibian 2001: 5). When dealing with Islam and the Islamic empire, the textbook stresses the intercultural encounter between that empire and the Jews (Tabibian 2001: 33). Later, the textbook mentions that despite this benevolent Islamic treatment of the Jews, they were subject to all kind of humiliating restrictions (the Laws of Umar). However, 'in daily life these laws were hardly implemented and the rulers of the empire employed the Jews as bureaucrats, physicians, translators and merchants' (Tabibian 2001: 34).

On the Christian Jewish encounter in the middle ages, the textbook stresses the legal privileges of the Jews within the feudal society that were a source of strength as well as weakness (Tabibian 2001: 119). But following the chapter on Jewish interaction with the Christian society the textbook focuses on discrimination against the Jews by various means such as blood libel, official stigmatization and humiliation, forced expulsion and even violent riots (Tabibian 2001: 121–143). The Israeli textbooks depict the Crusades as a confrontation between Christians and Moslems in the land of Israel. Following the economic and religious reasons for the phenomenon, the books emphasize the riots that the Crusaders inflicted on Jewish communities in Europe on their way to the Holy Land which resulted in destruction of Ashkenazi centers in Germany. They also describe the massacre of Jews and Moslems in Jerusalem (Tabibian 2001: 146). Throughout the chapter the Crusaders appear as colonialists, alien to the area that ultimately led to their defeat and withdrawal after 200 years.

Jewish life in Moslem Spain appears as an example of tolerance and mutual respect. On the other hand, Jewish life in Christian Spain is characterized as an example of fanaticism, discrimination and ultimately eviction, forced conversion and intolerance. The Inquisition appears as tool of coercion and torture directed against Christian dissidents, many of them former Jews and Moslems (Tabibian 2001: 179).

The Ottoman Empire is seen as a place that gave Jews refuge and enabled them to develop their autonomous institutions and culture under Moslem control. The problem of the Empire appears in the Israeli textbooks as an example of the inherent weakness of the Moslem world. It could not be sustained as an integrated power, suffering both from European external pressure and from internal disintegration (Baruch 1998: 105). The textbooks describe a series of Western reforms that were intended to stop the Ottoman decline but failed (Baruch 1998: 109). Implicit in this argument is the notion that the Islam and Moslem population was inherently unable to accept changes, reforms and modernization.

The textbook on the nineteenth century is predominantly European and discusses the situation of the Jews primarily within the European context. The analysis of Jewish life is within the paradigm of modern emancipation, stressing the advantages and obstacles it created to the Jewish experience in Europe (Baruch 1998: chapters 1–10).

The textbook explains the historical development within the overall framework of nationalism. The European national sentiment that emerged in the context of modernity and enlightenment is turned into a sort of integral nationalism, based on exclusion and hostility toward the other (Baruch 1998: 116–119). These new modern theories nurtured European imperialism and supplied excuses for the atrocities Europe inflicted on the people of Asia and Africa (Baruch 1998: 119).

The chapter on modern anti-Semitism starts with the claim that 'Anti-Semitism was directed not only against the Jewish religion … but against the Jewish race. Since a person cannot change his blood and race, he cannot cease being Jew even if he will convert his religion' (Baruch 1998: 120). On this basis anti-Semitism is analyzed as a modern phenomenon, based on racist theories, and applicable to the various elements of modern Europe. The manifestations of anti-Semitism were drivers: hostile propaganda against the Jews, anti-Semitic political parties, government policy that considered the Jews as scapegoats, anti-Semitic literature such as the Protocols of the Elders of Zion, anti-Semitic trials such as the Dreyfus affair, and renewed pogroms and massacres against the Jews in the late nineteenth century, primarily in Russia (Baruch 1998: 121–127).

It seems that Jews had no future in Europe as a modern, autonomous as well as integrated collective entity. As a result a whole chapter is devoted to the various options aimed at solving the Jewish problem: (1) full assimilation that would result in the elimination of Jews from history; (2) an ultra-orthodox religious option, which would keep the Jews separate from the modern world; (3) immigration to the New World, which would end the European phase of Jewish history; (4) a revolutionary option which would supposedly end discrimination against Jews as part of a universal solution against any discrimination, injustice and racism (Baruch 1998: 128–133). The Jewish national option emerged thus as another option, designed to keep Jewish people as a significant collective in the modern world at the expense of leaving Europe and striving to build a separate sovereign Jewish society somewhere else. The rest of the chapters explore this option known as Zionism, thus making it an integral and inevitable remedy for the Jewish question and the Jewish problem of modern Europe. To the best of my knowledge, such an emphasis on the Zionist solution is directed to justifying the right of existence of the state of Israel as a modern national Jewish state.

Within the context of the twentieth century, Europe appears as a troublesome region. It suffers from weak democracies during the 1920s and 1930s, facing ominous totalitarian alternatives such as Communism, Fascism and ultimately,

Nazism. It reaches a point of physical, political and moral destruction with the Second World War. The most terrible event of mankind – the Jewish Holocaust – occurred on European soil. The people of Europe participated in this event as perpetrators, collaborators and bystanders, and thus reach the abyss of moral nihilism.

The Jewish Holocaust is analyzed in the textbook both as an extreme outcome of the modern anti-Semitism that characterized so many segments of European society, and as a phenomenon that transcended even the most radical manifestation of modern anti-Semitism. It has the components of an historical event but also as an existential crisis of humanity that transcended specific historical circumstances. Thus the chapter on the Holocaust ends with the paragraph that exemplified this duality toward the event:

> The holocaust of the Jewish people is a unique event in the history of mankind. Genocides occurred already in human history; however, they were never carried out in such a systematic and pre-planned method and in such a large scope as in the case of the scientific murder of the Jewish people. The Nazi ideology that marked the Jewish people as an object for annihilation emerged in the midst of European culture and employed science and technology to increase its efficiency. We need to learn and to remember what human beings are able to commit to other human beings, in order to be cautious and to warn against any phenomenon of hatred and racism between human beings.
>
> (Naveh 1999: 19)

Yet, with regard to Jewish existence in modern times, the rest of the textbook draws particular nationalist conclusions, rather than universal humanist conclusions from the Holocaust. The main point is that the state of Israel appeared as the ultimate answer to the Holocaust. Its creation and existence became the focal point of Jewish life, and manifested the inherent truth of Zionism as the most viable and enduring solution of Jewish existence (Naveh 1999: 149).

An Analysis of the High School Curriculum and Textbook Samples

The high school history curriculum derives from the final exams' requirement, which completely determines the level and scope of the studies. Mandatory history exams are divided into two sections; each exam takes place following a whole year of study. Those students who wish to take history as their major for the state exams will study selective topics for another year. Less than five percent of Israeli students take history as their major. The overwhelmed majority of the students (95 percent) study history in high school for two years (either 10th and 11th grade or 11th and 12th grade), thereby fulfilling the mandatory exam requirements. The small percentage of students that select history as their major indicates the unpopularity of the discipline. The exam is perceived by most youngsters as tedious, boring, superficial, unchallenging, and without any demand for creativity, originality or critical thinking. It is viewed by most students as detached from their experience, irrelevant to their life, something that they need to pass and forget the day after.

The following analysis will focus solely on the two mandatory sections that comprise the learning material of history for the majority of high school graduates. It is worth mentioning that for many of the students the real study of history are those topics of the exam, and for many of them it is the first (and probably the last) time that they engage in the study of history.

More than 75 percent of the curriculum deals with the first half of the twentieth century. Europe overall appears in this era as a place of imperialism and colonialism, weak democracies and totalitarian alternatives, the birthplace of two terrible wars that almost destroyed Western civilization. In this period Jews experienced troubled relations with Europe, were willing to integrate but encountered discrimination and anti-Semitism. Since the emphasis is on Zionist history and on the national Zionist community in Palestine, the national solution outside the European diaspora appears as the only solution for the Jews. The Nazi period, World War Two and the Holocaust is the largest topic both in scope and intensity; thus it substantiates the Zionist position that the fate of the Jew in Europe will lead to ultimate destruction.

Hence, Europe appears in the curriculum as a tragic 'modern Egypt'. It is the place where the vast majority of the Jewish people existed, cultivating their unique life as individuals and collectives, but ultimately had to leave in order to survive. The European phase of Jewish history ended either with the final solution of persecution and destruction in the Holocaust, or with the national solution of revival and independence in the Jewish state of Israel. When this 'double exodus' ended, the last 25 percent of the curriculum unties the bond between Europe and the Jews. Europe almost totally disappears from the curriculum except in the context of the Cold War. Jewish history turns into the history of Israel in connection to the Middle East, the ongoing wars against the Arab world, and the immigration of Jews from Arab countries to Israel.

The Arab world and Islam appear in the curriculum in various places, all of them connected to Jewish history. In the first part, a whole chapter with mandatory and comprehensive questions is devoted to Islamic countries and their Jewish population. Yet these countries appear as passive settings for the following active historical phenomena, such as the colonial policy and European control in North Africa and the Middle East; major changes of Jewish life in the Islamic countries; Zionist activities among Jews living in the Arab world; and changing attitudes of colonial and Moslem society towards the Jews in the 1930s.

In the section on building the Jewish national homeland in Palestine, the objectification of the Arab population is extremely apparent. Arabs appear as opponents to Zionism and to the British mandate, as perpetrators of the riots of 1921, 1929 and the 1936–39 Arab revolt. The curriculum focuses on the various attitudes of the Zionist movement and the Zionist community in Palestine toward the Arabic problem and the Arab inhabitants of the area.

In the second part of the curriculum, Arabs and Islam re-appear within the chapters that discuss the Jews in western, central, and southern Europe and north Africa during the Holocaust. It seems strange that students have a choice to focus on one European country, one north African country, and have a mandatory topic on the Jews of Tunisia under direct Nazi control. In my opinion this is a 'politically correct' gesture of the curriculum committee to Israeli Jews from oriental backgrounds, who claim to be under-represented in the state history curriculum.

The Arabs return to the curriculum in the chapter on the war of independence and the creation of the state of Israel. Obviously they are the ultimate enemy in various stages of the war. At the end of the war, the curriculum mentions the cease-fire and the formation of the Palestinian refugee problem. (This is the first time that the curriculum defines the Arabs as Palestinians.)

The last section of the curriculum discusses primarily the Middle East and the Arab world. As a subject of analysis, the Arab world appears within the discussion of trends of unification and separation among the Arab states, in relation to the Cold War, and the focus is on Egypt under Nasser, and on another Arab country chosen out of Syria, Lebanon and Jordan. In most cases the Arabs appear within the context of Israel's defense policy and the three wars that Israel fought against the Arab states: the Sinai Operation (1956), the Six Day War (1967), and the Yom Kippur War (1973). At the end of the section the focus is on Jewish immigrants from Islamic backgrounds, their difficult absorption, and their resistance towards being treated as second rate citizens by the veteran Ashkenazi Israelis.

High School Textbooks

The textbooks' first chapters of world history are actually European history. They cover topics such as the industrial revolution, liberalism, socialism, women's status, bourgeois culture, nationalism, and imperialism. The following chapters deal with the Jewish situation in the world, stressing demography, the challenge of emancipation and Jewish attempts to integrate as well as to keep their distinctiveness. Large segments of the discussion in these chapters are devoted to modern anti-Semitism in western and central Europe, and to Jewish hatred in Czarist Russia. The discussion ends with the assertion that 'at the discussed period Anti-Semite attitudes were central to a significant part of the population. But the actual outcome of these positions was hardly seen. Legal emancipation persisted … anti-Semitic movement remained peripheral, anti-Semitic ideas could not undermine the Jewish achievements' (Naveh 1999: 100).

In the Islamic world the Jews adopted either a traditional–national uniqueness, or a western orientation. According to the textbook this world tolerated Jewish existence but was never considered by the Jews as a place for assimilation. 'The Zionist movement remained small … and the Zionist idea appeared within a traditional framework … It seems that the national and secular nature of Zionism was incomprehensible till the eve of the First World War' (Naveh 1999: 113).

Following the Holocaust, the textbook emphasizes the international legitimacy of establishing a Jewish state, especially for the dislocated survivors from the European death camps. 'More than any other element the holocaust survivor put the issue of the land of Israel on the international agenda' (Inbar 2000: 11). Moreover, the textbooks show that anti-Semitism remained in Europe even after the Holocaust and found its violent manifestation in pogroms in Poland and other places in eastern Europe. It convinced many leaders that the national solution was inevitable. Those who opposed the creation of the Jewish state like the British

Mandate authorities who refused to let Jewish immigrants enter the country, or Arab countries and Palestinian leaders who resisted the very idea of establishing a Jewish state in the Middle East, obviously appear as instruments of evil that resisted historical inevitability and historical justice.

The UN resolution that endorsed the establishment of the state of Israel appears in the textbook as the culmination of a historical process and the ultimate success of the Zionist movement. This diplomatic success 'was based to a large extent on American support, the impact of the holocaust and the malfunction of the Arabs' (Inbar 2000: 114). But there is realization that the resolution was able to occur due to military operation against the Arab resistance. One of the textbooks that discuss the Jewish victory over the Palestinians argues that 'the adoption of an offensive initiative saved the Jewish community from defeat to the Arab of the land of Israel' (Inbar 2000: 122). The victory in the war of independence resulted from 'the weakness of the Arab armies – lacking general command and strategic co-ordination – and the improvisation skills, war spirit and right strategy of the Israeli army during the war' (Inbar 2000: 140).

Arab–Israeli relations during the 1950s, 1960s and 1970s are marked by the textbooks as continuous struggles between peace-seeking Israel and the Arab refusal to accept the very existence of the Jewish state. Every new Israeli victory implicitly proves the virtue of the Israeli position and its superiority over the Arab world. Thus the Israeli operation on 1956 is described as an inevitable step, necessary to stop Arab terrorist attacks. 'Israel's acts of retaliation did not stop the terror. Only by a large and impressive military operation did Israel succeeded in stopping the Arab terror' (Inbar 2000: 246). In a similar way, the 1967 war is described as 'the most successful war from a military aspect, the most problematic war from an international-political aspect, and most significant turning point in the history of the state of Israel' (Inbar 2000: 261).

A Content Analysis of the Curriculum Illustrations

The curriculum was produced as a booklet illustrated with thirteen pictures alongside the verbal information. Among them five pictures depict a European setting. Three of them depict distinct European events: the inauguration of the first train station in Germany in 1835 – representing progress and modernity (Israel, Ministry for Education 2006: 9); a French cartoon showing the cynical partition of Europe by reactionary kings in the Congress of Vienna – representing decadence and corruption (Israel, Ministry for Education 2006: 12); and leaders of the Bolshevik Revolution, Lenin, Stalin and Kalinin, next to a poster that ridicules the Revolution's enemies – representing failing hopes and the fading utopian European illusion (Israel, Ministry for Education 2006: 31).

The other two pictures depict the tragic and even catastrophic ties between Europe and the Jews. One picture portrays the humiliation of a German couple of mixed marriage (Jewish man and gentile woman) in Nazi Germany because they transgress the Nierenberg racial laws (Israel, Ministry for Education 2006: 34). The other picture shows the deportation of the Jews from the Krakow ghetto to an extermination camp in 1943 (Israel, Ministry for Education 2006: 68).

The final message that emerges form these pictures is that Europe is an origin of civilization and progress, albeit distorted and corrupted, which produced utopian illusions that turned into tragedies and the Jews bear the ultimate prize of the tragedy in the Holocaust.

The pictures on Zionism reinforce this message. One picture is a Zionist membership ticket of the second Zionist congress in 1898. It contrasts a weeping, bent traditional Jew of Europe with a proud, upright Jewish farmer tilling the soil in the land of Israel (Israel, Ministry for Education 2006: 15). Another picture is of the Zionist founder and visionary Theodore Herzle (Israel, Ministry for Education 2006: 18).

Four pictures portray the relationship between Jewish history and the Arab world. One depicts a miniature of the Cairo synagogue where precious archives of sacred Jewish books and ritual articles (the *Genizah*) were found in 1896 (Israel, Ministry for Education 2006: 26). The second picture shows a parade of Jewish school children in Tripoli (Libya) in support of the Zionist organization of the Jewish National Fund (Israel, Ministry for Education 2006: 64). The third picture depicts Prime Minister Golda Meier and defense minister Moshe Dayan meeting with Israeli reserve soldiers in the Golan Heights at the end the Yom Kippur War in 1973 (Israel, Ministry for Education 2006: 44). The last picture focuses on the peace ceremony between Israel and Jordan, showing King Hussein, Prime Minister Rabin and President Clinton (Israel, Ministry for Education 2006: 48).

According to the pictures, the Arab Islamic world represents a place where Jewish religion and tradition prevailed in a concealed form; yet also where a proud Zionist youth movement emerged and flourished. The Arabs embody the defeated enemies of Israel that, nevertheless, slowly and gradually will make peace with the Jewish state.

The most significant ingredient that symbolizes visually the message of history education in Israel, and consequently its attitude toward Europe and the Islamic Arab world, reveals itself in the cover pages of the curriculum. The front cover page portrays a large photo from 1935 of children from a Zionist school in Jerusalem celebrating *Tu-Bishvat* – a Jewish planting festival where school and youth movements plant new trees in the land of Israel to make the desolate country bloom (Israel, Ministry for Education 2006). On the back cover page two pictures stand side by side: one showing a group of Jewish, orthodox-looking youngsters from the city of Fez in Morocco on their way to Jerusalem to take part in a young Zionist leaders' course; the other depicting Holocaust survivors from Buchenwald concentration camp arriving to the shores of the newly born state of Israel (Israel, Ministry for Education 2006).

Hence, both Europe and the Arab world constituted places of exile where Jews were condemned either to traditional primitive lives (Arab countries) or physical annihilation (the European Holocaust). In order to enter history as active agents, they started a journey of exodus, leaving these places and reviving their new collective national existence in the land of Israel through active building and resettling of the country.

Concluding Remarks

The content and object of the history curriculum in Israel is still within a very noticeable national paradigm. The purpose is to construct both a humanistic and a national identity among the students, which hopefully will strengthen their ties with Zionism and the state of Israel as a Jewish national homeland and as a sovereign, unique state.

Yet enormous difference exists between the official goals of the curriculum, and the final outcome of the learning process. Due to the test-driven nature of the whole discipline, most teachers cannot adhere to the curriculum requirements of knowing the national historical heritage, reflecting on past human experience in relation to the present and future, developing a mature and multi-dimensional approach to historical events and encouraging critical thinking. At the end, the evaluation of the curriculum is measured according to student achievements by the average final exam grade. These measure-oriented requirements leave no time for in-depth analysis and reflection on the historical dilemma. Consequently, it stifles the purpose of developing an open-minded graduate, secure enough to cope with the challenges and complexities of their future world. The time pressure for comprehensive study of 'all' the exams' requirements produces a race to cover the material. Official pressure to focus on more 'practical' disciplines (such as mathematics or English) further obstructs the status of history education as well as other humanistic disciplines.

In middle schools only a few students learn the material until its end, and most of the modern period remains absent, because school reaches its culmination, and school officials claim that the material will be studied again in high school. Yet, this syndrome repeats itself in high school; there is a lack of time to cover the material, mediocrity among the teaching stuff and the irrelevance of the textbooks to examination requirements that focus on facts, memorizing, and repetition.

Reluctantly, but with no other choice, the Ministry of Education publishes three months before the final exams in history, a list of focused study topics relevant to the exams. Consequently, a whole industry of focused topics of study (booklets, DVDs, internet sites) replaces the official curriculum and the approved textbooks as the major study devices used to succeed in the test and to improve the average grade. Many teachers thus direct their teaching methods accordingly, bypass the textbooks altogether, ignore the goal of the curriculum and base their instruction on test-driven practical devices. The outcome is that most graduates of the national school system in Israel pass the examinations in history quite well but hardly know any history, hate the discipline and view it as boring and redundant.

Under such circumstances the national paradigm of history may lose some relevant meaning in the future. To a post-national, global younger generation, a more universal or integrated paradigm may well be developed in method and content. Such a potential paradigm may view other parts of the world population as potential partners to the Israeli identity, and not only as representing the significant other. However, the current hostile conflict between the state of Israel and the Arab Islamic world, as well as the ambiguous and tepid relationship between Israel and Europe, certainly obstruct such a development. These political circumstances reinforce the official national paradigm of history learning despite its anachronistic features and its lack of appeal to many young Israelis graduating from the current system of education.

References

Baruch, B.B. (1998) *The 19th Century*, Jerusalem: Tel Aviv Books.

Inbar, S. (2000) *Revival and State in Israel and the Nations 1945–1970*, Jerusalem: Lilach.

Israel, Ministry of Education (2006) *History Learning: Curriculum for the 7th–12th grade*, Jerusalem: Ministry of Education.

Naveh, E. (1999) *The 20th Century*, Jerusalem: Tel Aviv Books.

Tabibian, K. (2001) *Time of Horror and Hope, 1870–1970*, Jerusalem: Matach.

15 The Challenges of Writing 'First Draft History'

The Evolution of the 9/11 Attacks and their Aftermath in School Textbooks in the United States

Jeremy Stoddard, Diana Hess and Catherine Mason Hammer

We are fast approaching the tenth anniversary of the terrorist attacks on New York City and Washington, DC that occurred on September 11, 2001. While the long-term effects of those attacks are still unclear, there can be no doubt that they continue to influence the political ethos, decisions, and controversies in the United States and other nations. The wars in Afghanistan and Iraq have not ended, the Patriot Act is still in effect, and security at airports remains heightened. There are a plethora of 9/11-related court cases still being argued, and in Congress and the executive branch, there is sharp debate about what post-9/11 policies should be maintained and which should be changed.

But much has changed in the years since the attacks occurred. The United States has a new president, and a profound economic crisis has taken center stage in the minds of many citizens and political leaders. Recent opinion polls in the United States show that while terrorism is still considered a top issue for the government, the worsening economy and high unemployment rate are considered paramount. Specifically, in 2002, 83 percent of adults participating in a Pew poll said that 'defending the US against terrorism' should be a top government priority and 71 percent said 'strengthening the economy' should be in that category too. By 2009, 85 percent placed the economy in the top priority category, and 76 percent gave that billing to terrorism. What is notable here is that concern about terrorism is still high – it has not fallen off the political radar screen. Even though there has not been a major terrorist attack in the United States since 2001, the impact of 9/11 still reverberates throughout American society.

Because 9/11 was such a major event in US history, it would be reasonable to expect that it would quickly become part of official instantiations of American school curriculum, such as state and district adopted textbooks. And if the curriculum followed the political polls, this focus would have staying power. Did that occur? And more importantly, precisely what do textbooks say about terrorism, 9/11, and its effects? Given that these events are not very far in the past, it is quite possible that representations in textbooks published shortly after 2001 have not stood the test of time as new details and evidence emerge and events continue to unfold. Very little about 9/11 is 'settled,' especially policy questions about what should be done with respect to terrorism. Are textbooks presenting these controversies? Or are they following a more traditional pattern of treating the 'past' as settled business?

This chapter focuses on these questions by presenting findings from a study of how best-selling secondary social studies textbooks published in the United States in 2004/5 (the first to fully include 9/11 content) and their later editions published in 2009/10, deal with 9/11 and the war on terror. Examining the content of textbooks, and more precisely, how they change over time, is instructive for a variety of reasons, but chief among them is the well-documented way in which the school curriculum is an important site for contestation about which narratives should reign supreme in a society. This is not a new phenomenon in the United States, nor is it by any means unique to the United States. In fact, recent incidents in Japan, Russia, and China (e.g. Finn 2007; French 2004; Onishi 2007) seem to indicate that textbooks these days are structured even less by historians and the historical record and more by politics in the form of national history standards and the nationalistic narratives that appear in approved textbooks (Suh and Yurita 2010; Zajda 2003).

In the United States, there is no one set of national history standards that drives textbook structure, but textbook publishers tend to weigh some states' standards more heavily than others. States such as Florida, Texas, and California constitute the engine of the textbook market because of the vast number of textbooks that are purchased by schools in these states. This market power impacts the history that students in other states find represented in their textbooks (McKinley 2010a; 2010b). In the current debate over the approval of new Texas Essential Knowledge and Skills (TEKS) standards by the Texas State Board of Education, approved textbooks will focus more on the specifics of the 'conservative resurgence of the 1980s and 1990s, including Phyllis Schlafly, the Contract with America, the Heritage Foundation, the Moral Majority, and the National Rifle Association' (TEA 2010: 6) than the presidency of native Texan George W. Bush, the invasion of Iraq in 2003, or the status of those being held as enemy combatants at Guantanamo Bay, none of which are specifically identified in the standards. If approved, these standards will be in place for the next ten years. As most schools replace textbooks every six years at a minimum, students from across the country could be limited by this version of the past for quite some time.

It has always been difficult to write history as it is still evolving. In the case of the 9/11 attacks and subsequent conflicts in Afghanistan and Iraq, it has been especially difficult, not only because of the intense controversy that surrounds these events, but also because of the ever-shifting national rhetoric around the war on terror. How do we teach students about issues and events that many people do not agree upon? How do we teach about or present the history of events that are so recent and so unresolved? And how are textbook companies to respond?

9/11 and the War on Terror in Social Studies Texts

In the summer of 2005 we began to study exactly how textbook companies in the United States responded to the 9/11 attacks in their high school social studies textbooks published between 2004 and 2006 (Hess, Stoddard, and Murto 2008). We analyzed nine of the top-selling textbooks: three United States history texts; three world history texts; and three United States government and law texts (see Table 15.1). In particular we focused on how the attacks of 9/11 and the US response to these attacks were presented in the books, in terms of both the content and the rhetoric, and we examined the nature of the intellectual work students were asked to do with this content. We were particularly interested in whether or not anything controversial was raised in the text regarding either the attacks or the US response, and we examined whether or not the textbooks structured any tasks that would engage students in deliberation or analysis.

This chapter first highlights our findings from the initial study and then explores how textbooks' representations of these events have evolved over the past six years, especially in response to ongoing events in the war on terror (e.g., Guantanamo, Iraq, Afghanistan, and the Patriot Act). This new analysis focuses in particular on how the latest editions of social studies texts with 2009–2010 publication dates present the 9/11 attacks and the subsequent war on terror and how these representations reflect shifting national rhetoric and policies. Our

Table 15.1   Selected textbooks

2005 study	Publisher	2010 study
American history		
American Odyssey (2004)	Glencoe / McGraw Hill	
America: Pathways to the Present (2005)	Pearson / Prentice Hall	
The Americans (2005)	Houghton Mifflin / McDougall Littell	*The Americans* (2010)
World history		
World History: Connections to Today (2005)	Pearson / Prentice Hall	
World History: Patterns of Interaction (2005)	Houghton Mifflin / McDougall Littell	
World History (2005)	Glencoe / McGraw Hill	*World History* (2010)
US Government/Law		
U.S. Government: Democracy in Action (2006)	Glencoe / McGraw Hill	
MacGruder's American Government (2005)	Pearson / Prentice Hall	*MacGruder's American Government* (2009)
Street Law: A Practical Course in Law (2005)	Glencoe / McGraw Hill	

analysis includes a side-by-side comparison of the changes made to new editions of three textbooks that we analyzed in the original study, with one book selected from the high school US history category, one from the world history category, and one from the government category.

Five major themes emerged during our initial analysis of high school social studies textbooks drawn from both the representation and description of the 9/11 attacks and the war on terror, and from how the textbooks asked students to engage intellectually with this content in any included tasks (Hess, Stoddard and Murto 2008).

Lack of Detail

Overall, the 2005 textbooks provide very little factual detail of the 9/11 attacks. Five of the nine books do not even identify who the attackers were, and one provides simply a generic 'terrorists opposed to US policies.' This seems odd, given the frequency and prominence of the events in the texts. More than half of the texts do not specifically explain what happened on 9/11, who was involved, or why it happened. This is especially true in the government and law texts, which contain virtually no description of the events despite including them frequently as examples.

9/11 as an Unprecedented Attack

Even though they lack detailed descriptions of what happened, what was clear in the 2005 texts is that 9/11 was a significant and critical event, an 'unprecedented attack,' not only for the US but also for the world. We found that the textbooks included the events of 9/11 and the war on terror prominently in their texts, with US history texts often adding special sections on these topics and government texts using examples of the 9/11 attacks and, in particular, examples from issues that arose from the response to the attacks (e.g., the Patriot Act, Guantanamo Bay, civil liberties). The central message in these texts is also that the events of 9/11 united the world against terrorists in spirit and, in the case of Afghanistan literally, as allies in the war on terror.

Nationalistic Rhetoric

The images and rhetoric used in texts, and in the US history texts in particular, emphasize heroism and tragedy related to 9/11 as well as depict the US as the victim of an unprecedented attack. The evidence used in structuring the largely nationalistic narratives in these texts is often limited in perspective. The person quoted most often was then President George W. Bush. Glencoe's *World History* (2005) includes portions of his address to the nation after 9/11, in which he states, 'Freedom and fear are at war. The advance of human freedom, the great achievement of our time and the great hope of every time, now depends on us ...' (2005: 968). Although four of the nine texts included the war in Iraq, only one text, *The Americans* (2005), identified the fallibility of the evidence used to justify the invasion of that country by the US and its allies (e.g., weapons of mass destruction).

Conceptual Confusion

We found many disparities in how concepts such as terrorism are defined and utilized across the books, with different books providing different definitions and examples of other terrorist attacks that even contradicted the conceptual material. For example, several of the texts' (*American Odyssey, Democracy in Action, Glencoe World History*) definitions of terrorism state that terrorist acts are those waged against civilian populations but then proceed to include the bombing of the US naval warship, the USS Cole, and the attacks on US Marine barracks in Beirut in the 1980s as examples of terrorist attacks.

Little or No Controversy

Finally, we found that despite the many controversial and debatable issues surrounding the 9/11 attacks and the war on terror, including the wars in Afghanistan and Iraq, and domestic policies such as the Patriot Act, the textbooks present few as being at all controversial. Additionally, students are not asked to do much critical higher order thinking with this material, nor are they invited to engage with the material through open questions or deliberations. We found that the government and law textbooks, as a group, included more issues presented as open, meaning that the issues have multiple and competing legitimate answers or perspectives; however, most assessment items and tasks in the texts present issues as closed and engage students in lower order tasks such as defining terms contained in the textbook or questions for which students could copy answers directly from the text to sufficiently answer the question.

Rewriting the 9/11 Attacks and the War on Terror

In order to compare the representations of 9/11 and the war on terror with new editions of popular texts (those with publication dates of 2009 and 2010), we selected a subset of texts from the earlier sample that have produced new editions and conducted the same analysis.[1] We scanned the index and narrative of each text for particular key words used in the first study (e.g., September 11th, Afghanistan, Osama bin Laden) and also looked directly in the same sections that we had coded for the first study. In all three of these new editions, the locations of the information related to 9/11 and the war on terror were relatively similar. The substance of and content within these sections, however, have evolved to present a very different history of the 9/11 attacks, their impact on the US and the world, and the response of the US domestically and in the war on terror. These comparisons and the major themes that emerged from the comparative analysis are presented below.

Table 15.2   Comparison of descriptions of the 9/11 attacks in *The Americans*

The Americans (2005, p. 1100)	*The Americans (2010, p. 1100)*
Explosions and raging fire severely weakened the twin towers. Within two hours after the attacks, both skyscrapers had crumbled to the ground. One wing of the Pentagon was extensively damaged. About 3,000 people were killed in the attacks. **They included all the passengers on the four planes, workers and visitors in the World Trade Center and the Pentagon, and about 300 firefighters and 40 police officers who rushed into the twin towers to rescue people.** The attacks of September 11 were the most destructive acts of terrorism in modern history.	Explosions and raging fire severely weakened the twin towers. Within two hours after the attacks, both skyscrapers had crumbled to the ground. One wing of the Pentagon was extensively damaged. About 3,000 people were killed in the attacks—the most destructive acts of terrorism in modern history.

Still Little Description of What Happened

Despite many additions and updates in content related to the 9/11 attacks and the war on terror, there is still little description of the actual 9/11 attacks. In fact, *The Americans* (2010) removed descriptions of the specific groups who were victims of the attack (see Table 15.2).

Much of the description of the 9/11 attacks, the war on terror, and the war in Iraq is still relegated to special sections in the back of *The Americans*, and while the events are referenced throughout the government text, it is often with little detail or context.

World History did the greatest reorganization by moving a large section about the war on terror from its 'Contemporary Western World' chapter to its 'Africa and the Middle East' chapter. In this way, the center of the war on terror is physically removed from America and symbolically placed in the Middle East. It is also, however, the only text of the three that did add a small amount of detail about the 9/11 attacks (although the details are more clarifications than expansions). For example, the section now frames Osama bin Laden more prominently and as directly responsible for the attacks, changes the numbers killed in the attack to 'almost 3000' from 'thousands,' and correctly identifies the location of the Pentagon as being in Arlington, Virginia rather than Washington, DC (2010: 945). Although a few details were added, the overall lack of detail is striking and problematic. The context for the response to the attacks is not fundamentally set for students to make connections between the events because there is not enough detail or because of where the sections are placed within the book.

No More Heroes

One striking change is the shift in rhetoric; the tone of the textbooks in the 2005 study generally frames the United States as grand victim, simultaneously emphasizing the heroism surrounding 9/11, while more recent textbook narratives around 9/11 have struck the bland tone that marks many traditional textbooks. In *The Americans* (2010), references to Father Mychal Judge, the New York City Fire Department chaplain who was killed during the attack, were removed, as was reference to specific groups who helped on the scene such as the ironworkers who helped with the recovery (2005: 1101). The revised edition also removed much of the emotional rhetoric that immediately followed the attacks. For example, a sentence in the 2005 textbook reads, 'People felt that everything had changed—life would never be the same. Before the attacks, many Americans felt secure that terrorism happened only in other countries' (2005: 1102). The removal of this sentence is significant in that it indexes a shift in the way that national shock was described.

In addition to the narrative rhetoric, 9/11-related images were also less prominent in the new additions. For example in *MacGruder's*, the image of the giant US flag and flag-waving crowd at a 2001 football game that was used as the cover image for the 'Foreign Policy and National Defense' chapter (2005: 466) was replaced by an image of former President Ronald Reagan and former Prime Minister of the United Kingdom Margaret Thatcher walking past a military honor guard (2009: 480–481). Several other 9/11-related photos were also removed, thereby reducing the iconic nature of 9/11 that existed in the earlier text. Similarly, a preview section in the final chapter entitled 'A Time for Heroes,' in the 2005 *World History* that included a picture of firefighters and rescue workers in rubble along with personal stories of heroics (2005: 968) and a picture of a New York fireman (2005: 890) located in another chapter were removed from the new edition.

Justification for War and the WMDs?

At the time of the original analysis, only one of the texts in the study, *The Americans* (2005), asserted that weapons of mass destruction (WMDs) had not been found in Iraq, stating 'by mid-2003, chemical or biological weaponry had not been found' in Iraq, despite the fact that 'Much of the case for going to war against Iraq was based on the belief that Saddam Hussein had weapons of mass destruction' (2005: 1105). The texts in the first study not only avoid any criticism of the war in Iraq, as it was in its infancy, but they also fail to recognize the various groups who were opposed to the war or who questioned the justification provided for it. These new editions go much further in raising criticisms of the actions of the Bush administration, including the administration's justifications for and execution of the wars in Iraq and Afghanistan, as well as domestic policies.

The updated 2010 edition of *The Americans* describes the fallout that resulted from a lack of WMDs in Iraq, recognizes the discontent over the war and those who were against it, and includes the collusion of the British as well by referencing the 'Downing Street memo.'

> In May 2005, a top secret memo known as the Downing Street memo became public. It suggested that the Bush administration had planned to invade Iraq as early as July 2002 … In June, as U.S. casualties continued to rise, a majority of polled Americans supported withdrawal from Iraq.
>
> (2010: 1105)

The updated edition of *Glencoe World History* (2010) also raises the issue of the missing WMDs, stating 'No weapons of mass destruction were found' (2010: 766). However, the textbook also shortened the section describing how the war began, shifting the burden from the UN, which was prominently featured as the failed mediator with Saddam Hussein's regime, to then President George W. Bush as a form of personal mission. Along with the reorganization of information on the wars in Afghanistan and Iraq, new sub-headings are also used in both of these chapters and illustrate the more critical stance on the events: 'Bush and 9/11' (2010: 944) and 'Post-9/11: The War on Iraq' (2010: 1001).

Unlike the two history texts, *MacGruder's* does not raise the issue of the missing WMDs, although it does acknowledge in a photo caption that 'President George W. Bush plans preemptive combat operations against Iraq in reaction to reports of the stockpiling of weapons of mass destruction' (2009: 415). However, no specific reason is given in the narrative of the text, unlike the earlier text that includes the threat of WMDs as justification for invading Iraq (see the side-by-side comparison of these paragraphs with the major changes in bold in Table 15.3). In the new edition, the justification of war based on WMDs in Iraq is removed, along with several other examples of historic congressional resolutions to send the US Military to fight without officially declaring war that were previously in the same section, including the invasion of Afghanistan in 2001.

The invasion of Iraq is again referred to later in *MacGruder's*, but the reason given is solely democracy building, not as a response to a threat of weapons of mass destruction or terrorism: 'In 2003, the United States led an invasion that toppled Saddam Hussein's brutal dictatorship in Iraq. The United States … is committed to building a democracy amid the strife and sectarian violence there'

Table 15.3   Comparison of the descriptions of reasons for invading Iraq in *MacGruder's*

MacGruder's (2005, p. 402)	*MacGruder's (2009, p. 416)*
In 2002, Congress agreed that President Bush should take whatever measures were "necessary and appropriate" to eliminate the threat posed by Saddam Hussein and his Iraqi dictatorship. **It was widely believed that that regime had amassed huge stores of chemical and biological weapons and was seeking to become a nuclear power – all in direct violation of the Gulf War's cease-fire agreement.** In March 2003 **a new (but smaller)** international coalition, led by the United States, launched Operation Iraqi Freedom – a **well-executed** military campaign that ousted Saddam Hussein and his government from power. Some 140,000 American troops remain in Iraq today, engaged in the difficult and often dangerous tasks of stabilizing and rebuilding that country.	Most recently, in 2002, Congress agreed that President George W. Bush should take whatever measures were "necessary and appropriate" to eliminate the threat posed by Saddam Hussein and his Iraqi dictatorship. In March 2003, an international coalition, led by the United States, launched Operation Iraqi Freedom – a military campaign that ousted Saddam Hussein and his government from power. Some 140,000 American troops remain in Iraq today, engaged in the difficult and often dangerous tasks of stabilizing and rebuilding that country. **President Obama has declared that "our combat mission in Iraq will end by August 31, 2010" and that "all U.S. troops [will leave] Iraq by the end of 2011".**

(2009: 664). Here again there is a decided focus on the current events in Iraq rather than the history of the events, thereby reflecting current hopes and realities – not the historical record.

More Controversy and Perspectives

Although some controversial aspects of the war on terror were removed in the revisions, such as the WMD justification in *MacGruder's*, the texts overall raise more issues about domestic and foreign policies and the response to the 9/11 attacks and part of the war on terror. The rhetoric in the texts also shifts from one of nationalism and heroism to a more traditional textbook tone, albeit with a somewhat critical perspective on the war in Iraq and the Bush administration domestic policies in particular.

At the beginning of several chapters, *MacGruder's* (2009) adds a number of point–counterpoint quotes from differing perspectives that raise important issues explored in the corresponding chapters. For example, at the beginning of its section on 'Expanding Presidential Powers' a sub-heading of 'Perspectives' is followed by a description of the issue of the warrant-less wiretap program by the NSA (National Security Agency) that was directed by President Bush. It states that 'acting in secret' President Bush directed the NSA to 'monitor communications between people in the United States and suspected terrorists. Under current law, the NSA must obtain a warrant from a federal court in order to conduct spying activities within the United States. The President defended his actions as necessary to protect the American people from harm' (2009: 404). This description is then followed by quotes on the program from pro–con perspectives of then Attorney General Alberto Gonzales and Federal District Court Judge Anna Diggs Taylor, respectively. Although it is not completely clear that students would have enough information in the text to fully deliberate the issue, students are asked in the assessment tasks at the bottom of the page to identify the nature of the issue and the perspectives on that issue. Students are also asked, 'Which of the positions do you think most appropriate? Why?' *MacGruder's* (2009) also adds student tasks into the text that require them to examine multiple documents and perspectives in order to analyze and evaluate the issue.

Both *The Americans* and *World History* also raise controversial elements of the Iraq war in their updated editions, especially the justification for it described above, as well as historic connections to the conflict. *World History* includes a section on unrest in the Middle East in the 20th and 21st centuries and the connections to the West. It also includes tasks that ask students to weigh evidence and answer higher order and critical evaluation questions such as 'How is the unrest in the Middle East connected to terrorist attacks against the United States?' (2010: 1002). These new versions do not directly add much detail about the 9/11 attacks, but they do provide much more context and detail about the wars in Iraq and Afghanistan and the connections to US domestic and foreign policies presented in response to the 9/11 attacks.

To summarize, what the newer versions of the three textbooks include about terrorism, 9/11, and its aftermath are notably different than what was in their previous editions. Of course, some changes should be expected in newer editions of textbooks (in fact, they are demanded by US copyright laws), but it would have been possible to write the narrative differently without demonstrably changing the tone and central message. This was not the case. The newer textbooks are less nationalistic, do not focus attention on instances of heroism, broaden the perspectives of how the topics are portrayed, and include controversial issues related to how to respond to terrorism.

Discussion and Implications

Virtually all of the changes identified above strike us as laudable in comparison to what was in the earlier texts. In fact, in our previous writings about the earlier texts, we offered strong critiques of the narratives in many of the texts because they were blatantly nationalistic, factually misleading or outright wrong, avoided authentic political controversies, and were generally banal (Hess, Stoddard and Murto 2008; Hess 2009; Hess and Stoddard 2007). It is certainly not the case that all of the problems we noted with the older editions of the textbooks have been corrected, and it is also important to recognize that the analysis we have just presented of the new editions is based on three books, while the earlier analysis was based on nine. It may be that if newer editions of the other six books that are available were analyzed we would learn that the changes in these three do not mark a trend.

It is also important to point out that there are some parts of the new books that should have been changed and were not – creating even more opportunities for misunderstanding for students than with the earlier editions. In particular, given that the young people reading these new editions will have been too young to remember 9/11 well (if at all), the lack of detail about what happened on 9/11 that we first noted in the earlier textbooks is arguably a more significant problem now than in the past. We frequently hear from teachers that 9/11 is really 'ancient history' to the high schools students who will be reading these textbooks. They remind us that their students were likely in preschool when it occurred. Consequently, as one teacher recently remarked, 'teaching about 9/11 is not all that different than teaching about Pearl Harbor.' This illustrates that as an event recedes in the past, it becomes more important for textbooks to include specific information about relatively basic (although, by no means, simple) questions, such as what happened, to whom, for what reasons, and with what effects.

There are a number of possible explanations for why the 9/11 content in the textbooks is lacking in detail. One is that the authors are just not paying attention to the reality that their readers were so young when 9/11 occurred. Another is that providing detail about an attack on the US would convey a sense of the nation's vulnerability to the readers. Yet another is that textbooks are simply limited in the space they are allotted and therefore have to make decisions about what is more significant. Regardless of the actual explanation, the effect is extremely problematic.

While journalists are often deemed the writers of the 'first draft' of history, we think what is written about recently occurring events in textbooks falls into this same category. Because competition in the US textbook market is fierce and for school districts, hugely expensive, one way publishers advertise their history books is to emphasize how 'up to date' they are – after all, such books will not have to be so readily replaced if they stretch the meaning of 'history' to include contemporary events. Moreover, even though evidence suggests that most history teachers rarely get to the 1960s, much less to 2001, there are some teachers who really do try to reach contemporary events in survey history classes. Texts with such events will appeal to them and their students. This inclusion of important recent historic events such as the 9/11 attacks will also surely expand as they are included in updated state social studies standards and standardized tests. These factors combine to exert pressure on publishers to include narrative about events that are as up to date as possible. Of course, this is even more important for textbooks that are used in government or civics courses, where the expectation to deal with contemporary events is fairly standard. On its face, including contemporary events in textbooks seems like a good idea, but the findings from this study raise concerns about whether the costs of such an approach outweigh the benefits.

The problem, of course, is that 'first draft history' is often incomplete, and sometimes proves to be outright false. This is true for what is produced by journalists, but even more likely to be the case for the kind of 'first draft history' that appears in textbooks. Journalists are clearly also pressured by market forces, which explains why there was such a distinct difference between how the mainstream media in the United States covered 9/11 and its aftermath compared with media in many other nations. But the pressure on journalists pales in comparison to those facing textbook companies, which may be simultaneously being pushed in different directions by various stakeholders including company shareholders, special interest groups, state departments of education, and political think-tanks (Cornbleth and Waugh 1995). This pressure from multiple and competing interest groups, along with the fact that American society in general could not agree on what happened and why, explains why the narrative of 9/11 in textbooks was so bereft of the controversies that were actually on the public's platter within just a few years after 2001. This absence could simply be a matter of curriculum lag, the oft-noted tendency of 'official' school curriculum to be 'behind' representations that occur in other places (such as in the academy). It may just take curriculum a bit of time to catch up – especially textbooks that are only revised every five years or so (Issitt 2004).

But, of course, the ability for textbooks to 'catch up' assumes there is only one true narrative to chase. This is a very different representation of history than presenting it as contested terrain. Others have documented that one of the problems with many history textbooks is that they are literally 'ahistorical' in their portrayal of what constitutes history (Paxton 1999). Historians know that the field is ripe with debate, the questions that appear settled can become unsettled as new evidence emerges, or as the sensibilities of contemporary times warrant different interpretations than were done in the past. But in most history textbooks history is presented as 'what happened.' Teachers generally support this view of a textbook as an objective account through the ways they are used in classrooms (Stoddard 2010). This is problematic generally, but especially so for contemporary events when there is such potential for misinformation – after all, if you are presenting a narrative as 'true' then it is dangerous if it turns out to be wrong. Given that concern, perhaps it is better to not include contemporary events in history textbooks. Or, when contemporary events are included, they could be presented as still evolving and open to interpretation instead of reflecting unwarranted or value-laden claims that reflect contemporary politics more than the emerging historical record.

Although some dismiss the importance of textbooks in shaping students' knowledge of the past, in many schools districts and for many teachers, textbooks continue to be the coin of the curricular realm (Issitt 2004). Even though there is a wealth of curriculum materials available about terrorism, 9/11 and its aftermath (Hess and Stoddard 2007), it is likely that the role of textbooks as major curriculum resources and organizers will remain. Our findings here suggest, however, that perhaps history textbooks in particular should not attempt to include events still evolving or ongoing. Given the nature of the historical narratives in textbooks (authorless and static), the issues of writing first draft history are exacerbated as they do not allow for ongoing developments or new and differing interpretations. Perhaps textbook publishers should provide a window of time for historians to have a better sense of events before including them in texts. They could provide online materials that can be more easily updated – or teachers could rely more heavily on supplemental curriculums that are often available for free and are better able to adapt to new developments. This solution may also provide multiple and competing perspectives to be integrated into the curriculum from various sources instead of relying on the apolitical and seemingly neutral textbook accounts.

Conclusion

The challenge of writing about contemporary and ongoing events in textbooks, however, goes beyond even the issue of working with ever-changing information and circumstances. It is also apparent in these texts and the striking changes in rhetoric of *how* the events are presented in the five or six years between editions, that textbooks are heavily influenced by the dominant social and political views of the period in which they are written. This is not surprising. Textbooks both reflect the views of the time and cement them. This explains why there are often such heated battles about what should be in textbooks – there is a strong sense that their content matters, both symbolically and concretely. With respect to how textbook content about 9/11 and its aftermath has changed in the past five years, it is apparent that the dominant narrative has changed to reflect views in the world outside of school.

Of course, another solution to the problems with 'first draft history' that we have identified is for textbook authors to include more content about the controversies related to contemporary events. If the narrative focuses on different views about the issues embedded in contemporary events and less on describing what happened as if there were no controversies, then it is less likely that students will be misled. Moreover, such a focus could provide an excellent opportunity for students to engage in the kind of analysis and evaluation of competing perspectives on contemporary issues that has long been advocated as a powerful form of democratic education. The changes in the second round of the history books illustrate vividly that one of the problems with the earlier editions was the absence of the recognition of issues or enough information about the issues for students to thoughtfully deliberate on them. However, this scenario is unlikely as textbooks still remain one of the most official forms of the curriculum and as such are prisoner to the often politicized and problematic nature of the history and social studies standards that guide their development (Van Hover, Hicks, Stoddard and Lisanti 2010). Until a solution to the textbook dilemma is found, the best suggestion may be for teachers to select their curriculum and content from a variety of sources, including the available textbooks, to expose students to multiple perspectives on the past and recent past and ask them to begin to interrogate and reflect upon the multiple versions that they encounter.

Note

1 This study represents an initial exploration into how 9/11 and the war on terror have evolved in social studies textbooks. Therefore, we selected a sample from the available new editions that included one text from each content area (e.g., US history, government) that also represented each major publisher used in the initial study (e.g., Glencoe).

References

Cornbleth, C. and Waugh, D. (1995) *The Great Speckled Bird: Multicultural politics and education policymaking*, New York: St. Martin's Press.

French, H. (2004) 'China's textbooks twist and omit history', *The New York Times*, 6 December 2004. Online. Available HTTP: <http://query.nytimes.com/gst/fullpage.html?res=9A00E5DD1431F935A35751C1A9629C8B63&pagewanted=all> (accessed 2 April 2010).

Finn, P. (2007) 'New manuals push a Putin's-eye view in Russian schools', *The Washington Post*, 20 July 2007. Online. Available HTTP: <http://www.washingtonpost.com/wp-dyn/content/article/2007/07/19/AR2007071902707.html> (accessed 2 April 2010).

Hess, D. (2009) *Controversy in the Classroom: The democratic power of discussion*, New York: Routledge.

Hess, D. and Stoddard, J. (2007) '9/11 and terrorism: "The ultimate teachable moment" in textbooks and supplemental curricula'. *Social Education,* 71, 5: 231–236.

Hess, D., Stoddard, J. and Murto, S. (2008) 'Examining the treatment of 9/11 and terrorism in high school textbooks', in J. Bixby and J. Pace (eds.), *Educating Democratic Citizens in Troubled Times: Qualitative studies of current efforts*, Albany, NY: SUNY Press.

Issitt, J. (2004) 'Reflections on the study of textbooks', *History of Education*, 33, 6: 683–697.

McKinley, J. (2010a) 'Texas conservatives seek deeper stamp on texts', *The New York Times*, 11 March 2010: A18.

McKinley, J. (2010b) 'Conservatives on Texas panel carry the day on curriculum change', *The New York Times*, 13 March 2010: A12.

Onishi, N. (2007) 'Japan's textbooks reflect revised history', *The New York Times*, 1 April 2010. Online. Available HTTP: <http://www.nytimes.com/2007/04/01/world/asia/01japan.html> (accessed 2 April 2010).

Paxton, R. (1999) 'A deafening silence: History textbooks and the students who read them', *Review of Educational Research,* 69, 3: 315–339.

Stoddard, J. (2010) 'The competing roles of epistemology and ideology in teachers' pedagogy with historical media', *Teachers and Teaching: Theory and Practice,* 16, 1: 133–151.

Suh, Y. and Yurita, M. (2010) 'International debates on history textbooks: A comparative study of Japanese and South Korean history textbooks', in I. Nakou and I. Barca (eds) *International Review of History Education: Trends in contemporary 'public' debates on history education,* Charlotte, NC: Information Age Publishing.

TEA (Texas Education Agency) (2010) *Proposed revisions to 19 TAC chapter 113, Texas Essential Knowledge and Skills for Social Studies,* subchapter c, high school. Online. Available HTTP: <http://www.tea.state.tx.us/index2.aspx?id=3643> (accessed 18 March 2010).

Van Hover, S., Hicks, D., Stoddard, J., and Lisanti, M. (2010) 'From a roar to a murmur: Virginia's history and social science standards, 1995 to the present', *Theory and Research in Social Education,* 38, 1: 82–115.

Zajda, J. (2003) 'The politics of rewriting history', *International Review of Education,* 49, 3, 4: 363–382.

Afterword

16 The World in Today's Curriculum

Madeleine Grumet and Lyn Yates

When we initiated the proposal for this volume of essays, we were concerned that the growing emphasis on school achievement, and relatedly high stakes testing, was turning schools away from the worlds that surround them, preoccupying them with the machinations of student and teacher evaluation and competitive comparisons. Achievement and audit focus on emptied out measures of what curriculum does. Well described in Peter Taubman's essay as the 'audit culture', this obsession with achievement and its politics and semiotics distracts communities from attention to school experiences of youth, and diminishes public education's contribution to a student's capacity to develop a full and productive life, participating in the culture and development of his or her community. The audit culture simultaneously turns away from yet strongly influences the task that is a distinctive function of curriculum: the deliberate shaping towards personhood of young people. Admittedly, young people are receiving messages about their society's vision for them all the time; but it is the deliberate and explicit shaping of this project through the legislative and formal processes of curriculum that discriminates schooling's contribution to personhood from the multiple messages provided from family, community, popular culture, economy, law, advertising, etc.

While we still maintain that the purpose of schooling should not be about schooling, but about participation in the world, many of the essays in this collection reveal the ambiguity of this aim. The identification of this object of interest and focus, this 'world' is itself hard to fix. Now the world is never still. Its horizons and compartments and categories are in constant flux. Only an ahistorical and myopic consciousness could be convinced that our time was the only moment to see itself surrounded by flux. So instead of claiming exceptionalism, let us entertain the possibility that part of what curriculum does is fix, even if for a brief time, the sense of what matters. And let us also acknowledge that this process of deciding what matters, what is important for the next generation to know, to be able to do, to sense about themselves and their possibilities, will always be hotly contested. What the essays in this collection show us is that the curricula of nations around the world are formed in the struggle to make these determinations. This effort to name and construct and cohere the world that matters does not take place on some idealized plane, but is constantly informed by and reacting to events. This world that emerges from curriculum is always in conversation with the world outside schooling, a world where oil rigs spring leaks, where the Hubble telescope glimpses universe's earliest galaxies, where family reunions across the two Koreas are permitted, where mass murder continues in Darfur.

And so the world that is named and fixed *for* the young, is first named and fixed *by* their parents and grandparents, and expresses their joy and confidence, or their anxiety and fear. Arranged and ordered, specified, and evaluated by government directives, and by education bureaucrats, curriculum may appear clear and consistent; nevertheless, as many of the essays in this volume attest, within its documents, syllabi and practices flourish the contradictions and tensions of our history, our institutions and our politics. One theme that is apparent in a number of essays in this volume is that, in curriculum visions and practices, economic, social and cultural vulnerabilities generate demands that often thwart each other, or mute one in order to address another.

The One-World Fantasy

Confronted by global economics, and instantaneous communication, some see opportunities to embrace world peace by diminishing the antagonisms among nations competing for resources, power and recognition. Whether unity is encouraged by economic opportunism, and mutual dependency as argued by Tom Friedman (2005) in *The World is Flat* or by awareness of mutual risk and interdependence (Beck 2008), or by the flow of information that crosses boundaries, oceans and continents (Carnoy and Castells 2002), it is proffered as a necessary counter to the plurality of national self-interests. Nevertheless, as nations work to forge these international connections, they also struggle to retain national identity; for just as they desire students to develop the skills that will permit them to participate in an economic culture that spans the globe, they also desire students to develop a sense of loyalty and membership in the national community. As we write, news reports of the economic crisis in Greece attribute it, in part, to its citizens', from the very rich to the very poor, evasion of taxes: a way of life in which citizens repudiate responsibility for the common good. In his *New York Times* essay, 'Is Italy Too Italian?' (1 August 2010) David Segal describes the dilemma facing Italian manufacturers who want to retain the validity of the 'Made in Italy' label, sacrificing economic growth to tradition and family identity. And so we find nations struggling to compose curricula that prepare students to compete in a neoliberal arena of competitive individualism, while, at the same time developing a commitment to each other and to the common good.

Jason Tan's analysis of this struggle in Singapore portrays the tension between the country's economic ambitions that encourage stratification and ethnic divisions and the country's desire to create social cohesion and responsibility, identified in Singapore's plan for National Education, which was officially launched in 1997. He cite's Prime Minister Goh Chok Tong's 1995 claim:

> [g]iving them [students] academic knowledge alone is not enough to make them understand what makes or breaks Singapore ... Japanese children are taught to cope with earthquakes, while Dutch youngsters learn about the vulnerability of their polders, or low-lying areas. In the same way, Singapore

children must be taught to live with a small land area, limited territorial sea and air space, the high cost of owning a car and dependence on imported water and oil. Otherwise, years of continuous growth may lull them into believing that the good life is their divine right ... [students] must be taught survival skills and be imbued with the confidence that however formidable the challenges and competition, we have the will, skill and solutions to vanquish them.

(*Straits Times* 1995: 1)

He cites too the former Prime Minister Lee Kuan Yew's comment:

thirty years of continuous growth and increasing stability and prosperity have produced a different generation in an English-educated middle class. They are very different from their parents. The present generation below 35 has grown up used to high economic growth year after year, and take their security and success for granted. And because they believe all is well, they are less willing to make sacrifices for the benefit of the others in society. They are more concerned about their individual and family's welfare and success, not their community or society's well being.

(Lee 1996: 30)

The Struggle of Economic and Civic Interests

One problem, argued by Tan and also by Bathmaker, is that competitive individualism is implicitly encouraged, and empathy for difference discouraged, by the way work outcomes are being represented in the arrangements of schooling. Curriculum policy statements may proclaim the importance of citizenship and of developing values that bind the future community together, but from the priority that mechanisms of selection and differentiation receive, young people and their families grasp another message of what schooling is about. The story told about changes in the curriculum of schools in China by Miantao Sun and Jiang Yu is an interesting one here, showing a change in the priorities of the curriculum of China. At the beginning of the changes they trace, primacy is given to curriculum's role in instilling a common set of beliefs among its young people, at the expense of the potential contribution of schooling to economic productivity. As China is 'opened up' to the world, an interest in globally competitive economic productivity drives a more individualized directive to curriculum, to take up what is most powerful about contemporary science, and constructivist approaches to learning. What does this signal for the future? What kinds of developing personhood and relationships to each other will emerge in this large and prosperous economy?

Ursula Hoadley's discussion of South African curriculum reforms after the collapse of apartheid provides another account of the difficulty of melding social and economic agendas. Here the initial prioritized emphasis was on the social good, on building, through schooling, a new inclusiveness in which students from different kinds of backgrounds were not streamed and demeaned and tracked to different futures: a curricular celebration of the equality of all. But Hoadley's argument is that curriculum is more than simply a set of agreed agendas about the story of the nation and its citizens. It is, too, a set of practices aimed to develop the abilities and knowledge and skills of young people over time, to establish the means by which they will be able to effectively participate and flourish as workers and as citizens. As she puts it, 'While the political project of the new curriculum was very clear, its pedagogical shortcomings soon became evident'. Hoadley argues that because this curriculum project conflated curriculum with pedagogy it ignored the skills and powerful knowledge necessary to the economic strength of the country as it privileged open and inclusive pedagogies.

The aspirations of the initial South African curriculum project, dedicated to reforming human relations, addresses the role curriculum plays in building and rebuilding attachments and discriminations locally, nationally and internationally. This is clearly an important issue for nations and curriculum scholars today, as it has been from the beginnings of school systems. In the nineteenth century, as industry developed, the task was to move attachments beyond the family and to build nations and national allegiances. In this volume we see some of the complexity and diversity of this curriculum agenda in the early twenty-first century. The complexity of how identities and allegiances are being framed in curriculum policies and practices today is also mirrored in the perspectives curriculum scholars bring to bear to understand and evaluate what is happening.

The Double Face of Nationalism: Us and Them

One familiar interest of curriculum scholars has been in how the processes of identity-building rely on the presence of the 'other': how curriculum inducts the younger generation into who is the 'we' and who is 'other'; who is important and who is inferior; who are friends, who are sources of one's cultural heritage, and who are alien. This theme has been one of the pre-occupations of sociological, feminist and critical race curriculum scholarship since the mid-twentieth century (Yates 2009; Young 2008). This production of identifications and national imaginaries is seen particularly in history and civics subjects, through selections of textbooks, and the incidents given attention in them, and through language policies and choices. Tariq Rahman tracks in detail the way camps of friends and enemies are being constructed in history, social studies and religious textbooks used in Pakistan. He argues that 'because the "Other" is often defined in both nationalistic and religious terms, such image construction creates grounds for further Islamic radicalization among the youth'. Rahman describes the building of a sentiment directed against India, but also, in the case of the *madrassa* schools, an 'anti-West [perspective] at both the deep, theoretical level as well as the emotive level'. Writing about history textbooks used in Israel, Eyal Naveh argues that these construct a history in which both Europe and Islam appear as flawed 'Others'. The textbooks are designed to 'construct both a humanistic and national identity' which 'will strengthen their ties with Zionism and the state of Israel as a Jewish national homeland and sovereign unique state'. But both Rahman and Naveh also draw attention to the way in which such analyses of intentions for curriculum via the selections made in approved textbooks is only part of the story. In the case of Pakistan, Rahman argues, 'the *madrassas* will lose their appeal only if the state invests massively in welfare and education': for the poor they offer a means of education not otherwise available. In the case of Israel, Naveh reminds us that 'an enormous difference exists between the official goals of the curriculum, the message of the approved textbooks, and the final outcome of the learning process'. He argues, as do Hoadley and Bathmaker in other parts of this volume, that the pressures of the school environment, the concerns and skills of teachers, and the very diversity of students and their families, makes the outcome of this formally approved curriculum story of the nation some distance from the intention.

Nevertheless, national concerns and fears and intentions which curriculum changes are intended to address are evident in many of the contributions to the volume. Anatoli Rapoport's depiction of Russian reforms traces an initial move after the dissolution of the Soviet Union in the direction of opening up the sense of being part of a more extensive world; then, more recently, reasserting or attempting to rebuild a renewed patriotism. He points out that nation-building, drawn from history and ideology and mythology, is an endless and elusive project and then contrasts the liberal agenda with the more traditional curricular vision that has emerged to shape nationalism. The liberal agenda, developed in the 1990s was directed to instill 'common human values'. It was a time of close cooperation with civic educators from Europe and the United States. The priorities of civic education then were to educate a democratic, knowledgeable citizen who would be concerned with the well-being of the country and the world and who would work to continue the democratic development of Russia. Stoddard, Hess and Hammer's account of the response to 9/11 in social studies textbooks, reverse the direction of the militarism described in Rapoport's piece. They show how initial accounts promoting the Bush administration's interpretations and rationale for the Iraq invasion were modified in later iterations to include more information and broader, somewhat less partial analysis.

In part, the backdrop of these and other developments is the issue glossed as 'globalization', the movement of people and the forms of communication and inter-changed economy, that confront curriculum with the dilemma of how the story of the local is to be placed in a story of the global. As Kenway, Kraack and Hickey-Moody (2006) show in their study of masculinity in rural communities in Australia, the issue of recognizing the global in schooling is not just about what information is to be conveyed about those parts of the world that are separate and different from us. This distinction between distant and close diminishes as the connections and effects of technology and economic exchange and production, are being experienced by communities locally as part of their daily lives. Industrial employment opportunities move elsewhere, and tourism and service industries replace them. The boundaries that formerly enclosed information in national networks dissolve. Culture and popular culture are not simply derived from or circulating within local or national spaces. Nevertheless, the story of this world that curriculum tells does not congeal into one generalized discourse. In a recent discussion of globalizing and education policy, Rizvi and Lingard comment:

while the pressures on curriculum reform might be similar throughout the globe, the reforms which result always have a vernacular character as they build incrementally on what has gone before within specific educational systems.

(Rizvi and Lingard 2010: 97)

Examples from Pakistan or Russia or the USA immediately after 9/11 show how the sense of national vulnerability skews curricular portrayals both of relationships to the larger world and to different groups within their nations. Karseth and Sivesind take up the question of national and international depictions in a more optimistically framed reflection on how Norwegian history and a more permeable and connected world are to be put together. They argue that local cultural heritage should not be seen in opposition to a curriculum being opened to a wider world, but rather that local cultural specifics are necessary, not just tolerable, components of appreciating a wider world that is inherently diverse.

Nevertheless the task of identity-making in this world today is one with which curriculum struggles. As Tsolidis explains, in countries such as Australia, where nation building has relied on immigration, curriculum policy is burdened with multiple responsibilities: assimilating minorities; providing them with opportunities to maintain distinct cultural identities; and promoting understanding of cultural difference within the general population. She discusses the issue of what imaginaries are being built in curriculum for such a nation, and the changing forms they assume as particular new fears of difference are evident. One recent curriculum response is an attempt to contain diversity and rebuild an old established story of who Australians are, in contrast to a previous, more optimistic attempt in the 1970s and 1980s to build a new multiculturalism. However Elizabeth Macedo, writing about Brazil, questions whether multiculturalism can provide a curriculum resolution or a national imaginary which embraces diverse identities. Drawing on Derrida, she argues that in principle an imaginary of such a type can only be built if it is empty or emptied of the concreteness that would allow difference to be seen, that would allow marginality (of different kinds of young people and what they bring to curriculum) to be recognized for what it is. Ironically, she notes, in this formulation, citizenship becomes elusive and must be earned through academic achievement. William Pinar also addresses how curriculum can distract us from the reality of national challenges and problems as he interprets Canadian curriculum as preoccupied with its differentiation from the United States: a fixation which distracts it from a critical analysis of its own culture and civics.

Curriculum is an important conduit of national and global imaginaries, and there are both deliberate and also unconscious and tacit themes being drawn on as nations confront the contemporary world. In some cases – Russia, Australia, the USA after 9/11 – there is an evident explicit attempt to regroup and re-establish some earlier forms of national themes about what it means to be Russian or Australian or American in the face of new times and new anxieties. In a number of countries the wearing of the hijab by young women has become a visible lynch-pin for anxieties about what is changing, and for newly prescribed curriculum definitions about how the 'we' of the nation is to be identified. In times of evident political vulnerability, and in countries at war, the theme of building loyalties to a particular sense of the nation (and enmities to those configured as hostile to the nation's interests) becomes more explicit.

Global Imaginaries

But the imaginary of a more expansive set of global relationships is also now being built in a number of ways for young people. The northern European tradition of *didaktik* frames schooling and curriculum within concerns about how young people are to be formed (Hamilton 1999) and that has to be re-imagined as former national entities confront new economic and cultural relationships. Working from that history, Karseth and Sivesind confront the challenging question inherent in much glib talk about the twenty-first century: into what kind of personhood (other than economic) is the task of curriculum to now be directed?

The OECD DeSeCo project named the education agenda for the twenty-first century in terms of developing three sets of competencies:

> First, individuals need to be able to use a wide range of tools for interacting effectively with the environment: both physical ones such as information technology and socio-cultural ones such as the use of language. They need to understand such tools well enough to adapt them for their own purposes – to use tools interactively. Second, in an increasingly interdependent world, individuals need to be able to engage with others, and since they will encounter people from a range of backgrounds, it is important that they are able to interact in heterogeneous groups. Third, individuals need to be able to take responsibility for managing their own lives, situate their lives in the broader social context and act autonomously.
>
> (OECD 2005)

Many school systems, in their overview statements of purpose, now take up a similar rhetoric: 'skills for the twenty-first century', a 'global world', 'the knowledge society', 'ability to communicate and work in teams with others', 'learn to become a flexible lifelong learner' and the like. Some of the phrases are empty (what *does* it mean to act autonomously in a network of social relationships?) and many are glib. Nevertheless, the commissioning of the DeSeCo project, and the clichés that now circulate in many countries about curriculum, do express the sense that the world for the generation of students now at school will be constituted in new and interdependent forms of communication, and interaction. They remind us that curriculum is a projection towards a future as well as a drawing from the past.

What the essays in this volume reveal is the incessant curriculum problematic: that curriculum is a field that brings together rhetorical hopes and enacted practices. Many of the essays address what is being set in train by different systems as the curriculum formulation through which young people will indeed be 'able to engage with others' or to 'interact in heterogeneous groups' or to 'situate their lives in the broader social context'. Beyond those phrases, we see the questions with which curriculum actors and scholars are grappling: What sense (or what version) of their history and heritage is relevant to such a purpose (see Karseth and Sivesind; Rahman; Tsolidis; Tan; Stoddard, Hess and Hammer; Macedo)? What knowledge and teaching is powerful and what is empty as foundations for work and skills for these world citizens of the future (see Young; Hoadley; Bathmaker)? Can curriculum accomplish any of these hopes while emptying it of emotional engagement (see Taubman)?

Much of this discussion speaks as well to a further issue about curriculum formulation today, the focus on its forms of realization as well as its aspirations. The need to address the dynamic and relation between knower and known, learner and learning, student and teacher has engaged curriculum studies over the last half-century. The analyses produced by curriculum scholars have both cognitive and sociological dimensions concerned with difference, equity, inclusion and marginalization. In Sun and Yu's account, a move towards greater recognition of the first of each of these pairs (the learners and their activities rather than the teacher and the message) is seen as the very marker of China's modernization of its curriculum, at least in the sense of thinking about the need to generate motivation and active engagement, to focus on learning activities rather than texts and messages to be conveyed. In South Africa a new attention to the knowledge and orientations the mass of students bring to school drove some radical changes to its traditional curriculum. But the imbrecations to focus on learners are ambiguous, not just in the extent of the slippage between policy rhetoric and enacted practice (especially practices governed by constant testing and benchmarking), but also in obscuring what it is that learners are intended to be drawn into via curriculum. As Michael Young argues concerning the emphasis in this era on extending the period of formal education for everyone:

> these policies neglect what this access is *to*, and what it is assumed students are encouraged to participate *in*. It is as if an *organisational* criterion – are students attending school or college or are they gaining certain certificates, is replacing an *educational* criterion which refers to the intellectual development of students and the conditions for it, and whether they acquire that knowledge – powerful knowledge – that enables them to generalise from their experience and move beyond it.
>
> (Young 2008)

Eyal Naveh, as he concludes his essay on the presentation of history in Israeli textbooks, addresses the inevitable slippage between curriculum policies and textbooks and what actually transpires among teachers and students in the classroom. He points out that lack of time, inadequate materials, testing pressures, and other distractions make it difficult to determine what, if any, form of curriculum is present in students' experiences. This very complexity and unpredictability inspires efforts to order and control, recently expressed in high-stakes testing, scripted instruction, constant comparisons of scores and threats to fire teachers and close schools whose students are not reaching satisfactory scores of achievement.

What is too often overlooked in these accounts is the ways that teachers experience and understand the issues of their times. They, too, live in the world where local jobs are lost to outsourced production, and where security is threatened by international terrorism. Employees of the state, teachers are expected to carry the message of the curriculum as it reaches them in edicts, documents, and laws. Nevertheless, the resistance of the teachers of Norway to Quisling's directives to comply with the Nazi occupation and the curriculum it imposed on Norwegian schools to propagate the Nazi program, reminds us that even in the most vulnerable times, teachers have recognized the power of curriculum and have risked their work and lives to stand for freedom. When we compare our time with theirs, it is tempting to assume that their solidarity and clarity were possible because they faced a single, identifiable threat: Nazi occupation and propaganda. There is a perverse kind of nostalgia that envies the era of World War II as a time when tyranny and freedom, good and bad, and national interests were clear and compelling. The essays in this book show us a world that appears more complicated yet caution us not to seek the simplicity offered by an over-generalization or by the denials and distractions of testing and evaluation. They challenge us to construct curricula that acknowledge tension and ambiguity and encourage young people to see themselves and each other as persons capable of thinking and acting in this complicated place and time.

References

Beck, U. (2008) *World at Risk*, Cambridge: Polity Press.

Carnoy, M. and Castells, M. (2002) 'Globalization, the knowledge society, and the Network State: Poulantzas at the millennium', *Global Networks*, 1, 1: 1–18.

Friedman, T. (2005) *The World is Flat*, New York: Farrar, Straus and Giroux.

Hamilton, D. (1999) 'The pedagogical paradox (or why no didactics in England?)', *Pedagogy, Culture & Society*, 7, 1: 135–152.

Kenway, J., Kraack, A. and Hickey-Moody, A. (2006) *Masculinity Beyond the Metropolis*, Basingstoke: Palgrave Macmillan.

Lee, K.Y. (1996) 'Picking up the gauntlet: will Singapore survive Lee Kuan Yew?', *Speeches*, 20, 3: 23–33.

OECD (2005) *The Definition and Selection of Key Competencies. Executive Summary*. Online. Available: HTTP: http://www.oecd.org/dataoecd/47/61/35070367.pdf (accessed 11 August 2010).

Rizvi, F. and Lingard, B. (2010) *Globalizing Education Policy*, London: Routledge.

Straits Times (1995) 'Teach students to live with S'pore's constraints: PM', 5 March: 1.

Yates, L. (2009) 'From curriculum to pedagogy and back again: knowledge, the person and the changing world', *Pedagogy, Culture and Society*, 17, 1: 17–28.

Young, M.F.D. (2008) *Bringing Knowledge Back In: from social constructivism to social realism in the sociology of education*, London: Routledge.

Index